Act Your Age

Act Your Age

A Coming of (Middle) Age Memoir

PRISCILLA LINDSEY BIDDLE

RESOURCE *Publications* • Eugene, Oregon

ACT YOUR AGE
A Coming of (Middle) Age Memoir

Copyright © 2025 Priscilla Lindsey Biddle. All rights reserved. Except for brief quotations in critical publications or reviews, no part of this book may be reproduced in any manner without prior written permission from the publisher. Write: Permissions, Wipf and Stock Publishers, 199 W. 8th Ave., Suite 3, Eugene, OR 97401.

Resource Publications
An Imprint of Wipf and Stock Publishers
199 W. 8th Ave., Suite 3
Eugene, OR 97401

www.wipfandstock.com

PAPERBACK ISBN: 979-8-3852-5942-7
HARDCOVER ISBN: 979-8-3852-5943-4
EBOOK ISBN: 979-8-3852-5944-1

To my parents, Bill and Linda, whose voices sing in my heart, argue in my head, and shout in my achievements. To my children, Colin, Alec, Ellen and Graeme, and my granddaughters, Grace and Moxie, whose voices are the future. To my husband Mark, without whom I would never have found my voice.

Contents

Preface ix

Introduction: *Act Your Age* 1

Love's Labor Lasts 8

Come 'Round Right 24

Victory 42

Ties That Bind 59

Auld Lang Syne 77

School Days 92

Snake Charming 108

Harvest Home 124

People Can Surprise You 139

Reunion 156

Homemaking 175

Preface

THE FOLLOWING COLLECTION OF narratives is drawn from my imagination inspired by memory—mine and those of others. Seemingly unrelated, each tale combines to recount a chronicle of living. Although their inspiration is from my life and other's lives, the characters and the events are fiction. No real person or event is depicted. Although they may bear a semblance of truth, they are true to life only in fragments, and those fragments are embellished. They are not meant to be an accurate likeness of anyone, but rather a collection of impressions as one might get when passing a town or a person in an automobile, given shape and action only later in imagination.

Just as the characters are a fiction, the narrator is as well. Although she bears some of my traits and shares similar experiences, she is not me. Through her, I hope to communicate that strange and awkward vantage point middle age brings, as we empathize with the inept liveliness of our teenagers while feeling our parents' aching joints, on the extraordinary experience of an ordinary life.

The narratives themselves, although memoir-like in nature, are also not arranged chronologically. Rather, they are independent reflections on the thousands of daily anecdotes we all live each day in the course of growing up and growing older. They are accounts of small every-life episodes of births and deaths, weddings and funerals, which in turn evoke memories of still other stories. In their totality, the reader will gain a broad sense of the recurring characters, but that totality is not required for each story to mean something.

In some ways, it may be like going through a shoebox of old photographs, not arranged in any logical order, and reminiscing when, where, and of whom the photo was taken. I hope that the stories evoke for the reader the same feeling I used to get during a good long visit on Momma's screened-in porch over a pitcher of iced tea. Our conversation would wander and take random tangents, but it usually came back where it started, and we got life and ourselves straightened out for a time. Life was lived and relived, mulled over, digested and philosophized through on those long, lazy afternoons, when the biggest task seemed to be refilling the ice trays and remembering what year we last saw this person or last went that place.

By weaving story into story, I hope to emulate how one weaves the fabric of a life. By taking time to recount the narratives, either fact-based or fabulous, I am playing with time, making it stand still as it does in a photo album, and, in so doing, hoping to see an overall picture and therefore maybe the material of meaning in my life. The telling of these stories became as didactic for me as listening and reading once were; the patterns in my tapestry are made clearer by giving my narrator her voice.

I must invoke the memory of my grandparents and thank my parents, siblings, my friend Jennifer, and my children, Colin, Alec, Ellen and Graeme, for their love and support. The richness of our family experience is the bounty from which I drew courage.

Most importantly, I want to thank my husband Mark who has lived, read, labored, laughed and cried over every word with me. As my best critic and biggest fan, he gave me the courage to even attempt this project. Finally, I could not have accomplished this work as a whole without the patient and thoughtful mentorship of Dr. Irby Brown, under whose guidance the seed of this project was first planted. The example of his life and literary experience provided motivation, while his wit and sensibility mediated between my creative turmoil and my love affair with prepositional phrases.

Introduction

"ACT YOUR AGE!" MY mother would admonish me throughout my childhood. After all, I was the oldest, the big sister, and was supposed to set the example. I've never really figured out exactly what one does to *act one's age*. What age would that be exactly?

When I was a child, I thought it meant to act more grown up. But, since I was usually just acting childish when Momma would say that, it didn't make sense that the statement was supposed to elicit in me a knowledge how I was supposed to act older than I was. Once I became an adult with chronological and life-event measures of maturity, I remained confused as to the question of what acting one's age meant.

Part of the problem was living in the same town until I was forty. Anywhere I went, I would see someone I knew, but knowing when I knew them became harder and harder to place. He could be someone who knew Granny and Papa or Momma and Daddy, or someone I went to school with, or someone who taught me or whom I taught. All those identities, all with lives of their own, coexist, layers of time continuing simultaneously, sometimes independently, sometimes integrated. Living in the same little yellow house in which my mother was born and in which my parents lived when I was born, I could, in any given minute, be a grand-daughter and a mother, a student and a teacher, a child and a grown-up.

I can still see my Papa—aged and ailing, his old man's skin pale, his formerly blue-sky eyes cloudy, his white hair yellowed and tired, his once broad shoulders stooped—holding my baby Edward, a dimpled cherub, his large dark eyes and ruddy cheeks radiant, creating a contrast of youth and age at their extremes.

They were in love with each other, those two. Papa loved to recount just exactly how and when they had fallen for each other. It was at a big family holiday get-together shortly after Edward's birth. As usual, I arrived with too many things to carry—baby, diaper bag, casseroles for the festivities. Without thinking, I plopped my newborn down in Papa's lap, since he was the first person I stopped to greet. Quickly on my way to the kitchen, I left Edward in his great-grandfather's care.

Papa later would confide to us all that he wondered what in the world he was supposed to do with an infant. Babies were Granny's domain, but, with no one nearby to hand Edward off to, he was stuck. He shifted the squirming baby in his arms, bringing him up to face him, supporting Edward's back and head with his long forearms and big hands in front of him in a posture as though he were tossing a bale of hay or, given the circumstances, imploring the Almighty.

Not knowing what else to do, he started talking to Edward. According to the legend, at the sound of Papa's voice, Edward's eyes, fuzzy and unfocused in that newborn's way, suddenly cleared and his gaze sharpened, focusing on Papa, looking him right in the eye. The next thing Papa knew, he and Edward were having a "conversation" that only they understood.

I think each one instinctively saw a missing part of himself in the other—Papa, a young man hostage in an old body, and Edward, an old soul renewed in an infant. Papa was always full of mischief. Every morning, he would take a walk, touring the yard and garden. He would stop and talk baby talk to the morning glory blossoms that grew up the downspouts and kiss each blossom good morning. Anyone else and you would have thought he was out of his mind—like poor Mrs. Devine, the once proud and commanding voice of the third grade at Pinewood Memorial Elementary School, who ran around her neighborhood in her slip and stole people's newspapers from their driveways until her family had to put her in a home. Since it was Papa, no one thought anything at all.

Then there was the time Papa cut his hand on the tin roof of the garage. He was in the garden, admiring the straight and bountiful rows of vegetables in his prolific garden when he was seized by a sudden urge to play Tarzan. He grabbed the nearby wild grape vine, thick as a man's arm, which hung from the live oak tree adjacent to the garden and took a running jump down the incline of the back yard. After all, people had always told him he looked like Johnny Weissmuller.

So, off he swung, but this vine, unlike the green and supple tropical vines in the old Tarzan movies, was old and gnarled with age. It held Papa's weight and transported him through the air a good distance, but instead of swinging true, its trajectory took a sudden twist, taking him dangerously close to the tin garage roof. He must have put his hand out to prevent himself from crashing like some cartoon character into the side of the building. That was when he cut his hand.

The injury required stitches, but Papa's stitches were not just the medical kind. He delighted in telling the busy and imperious triage nurse exactly how he had been injured, breaking into hearty laughter. She looked over her half glasses with incredulity and disapproval. What was a man on Medicare doing swinging on vines in the back yard?

Edward was the opposite. From the time his blueberry-blue eyes focused on the world, it was not with that surprised expression most babies have. His demeanor was more like he was seeing an old friend again, rather than experiencing it all anew. He didn't startle and fret in new surroundings or around new people as most babies do. Instead, he looked out at the world with a steady and even gaze, a beatific Buddha.

My first days of motherhood were in the age of the astral plane. Shirley MacLaine's channeling was all the rage. Bridey Murphy was rediscovered by a public who wanted a new answer to old and nagging doubts. I had read that if you ask children what they remember about being born when they have enough vocabulary to communicate but not so much to be able to embellish with imagination, you can actually get an authentic response to the question. According to the experts, these memories fade when the synapses are assigned new tasks and the old memory pathways are paved over with new experiences.

Edward's responses were eerily accurate. In his two-year-old's lisp, with his characteristic seriousness, he described a bright light, a long tunnel, and his Daddy, a pretty exact reporting of what his initial experiences would have been. At that age, he surely did not possess the knowledge of childbirth or hospital child delivery practices, nor had we ever recounted to him the saga of his birth at that point. We surmised that his response could not have been formulated out of anything but his own memory.

That is why it wasn't terribly surprising when Edward, a year later, began talking about when he had lived before. He would begin these conversations by saying, "Remember before I died, when I was an old man?" He would go on to describe himself as a soldier, as balding, and as wearing a blue uniform. At that tender age, Edward had had no contact with war or soldiers—especially Union soldiers or US sailors as his description might indicate—much less the concept of the transmigration of souls. I attributed it to Granny's recent death, his strong identification with Papa, and a very fertile imagination making sense of his first profound loss.

But I always wondered. Although as a matter of faith I don't believe in reincarnation, I don't find it implausible as a concept. Since all matter is recycled—Momma used to make us squeal as she poured us a glass of water by telling us it could be Alexander the Great's bath water—why not spiritual essence? If it were so, it would add another dimension to the concept of age entirely.

After Granny died, we took Papa to our family mountain retreat to distract him, to enjoy him, to stuff ourselves with memories while we still had him. I made a photo album of the pictures we took on that trip and gave it to Papa for Father's Day. He kept it beside his chair so he could go there when being here got too hard. Eventually, it was all too hard, and I received the album back again along with several other trinkets of his. The last picture is a precious photo of Edward sitting on Papa's knee with both of them wearing rubber animal snout masks. Their faces and poses are solemn, but their eyes are full of mischief. What sort of example for acting my age did I have?

And my parents were really no better. When I was five, I encountered tumbling in first grade physical education. Forward rolls were no problem, but cartwheels seemed completely beyond my abilities. How could I let go and trust my own strength and the laws of physics to fling my legs into space over my head, and turning upside down, return to land aright with precision? I went to my Daddy as I did with most everything else.

The next Saturday, we found a flat, grassy spot in the yard and commenced our lesson. I don't remember how long it took or anything he said. I just remember him showing me how to do it, doing a series of cartwheels the length of the yard. I was astounded that my big ole Daddy—he must have been thirty at the time—could propel himself through space without breaking the bonds of earth's gravity or collapsing into a broken heap. Inspired, I reckoned that if he could do it, maybe I could too.

I can still see him in my mind's eye, wheeling across the yard, his blue-black curls bouncing, his face red with exertion and laughter. After his performance we fell into a pile on the grass and laughed and laughed. I had no trouble learning to do cartwheels after that.

My mother's model also didn't help at all to act my age. Our house sat on a hill. Momma delighted in teaching us how to roll like a log down that long hill. What was better on a crisp fall day than to feel the utter abandon of free-fall rolling, the crunching of leaves under us? The smell of the dirt mixing with our dizziness intoxicated us. It was better than a roller coaster. Despite the dignity of grandmotherhood, she even taught my children the joy of rolling like a log. She always loved to frolic in the grass.

Once, when fund-raising high schoolers arrived early one Saturday morning to deliver fresh Krispy Kreme doughnuts, Momma exploded out the front door, trumpeting, "The doughnuts are here! The doughnuts are here!"

She vaulted down the porch steps, and started skipping across the front lawn. All was fine, if ridiculous, until she forgot to account for her Daniel Greene bedroom slippers' leather soles' lack of traction on the wet and slippery morning grass.

Out her feet went from under her, and down she went, down her rolling hill, this time bouncing on her backside in the morning dew. The teenagers' eyes went wide and then rolled with their affected ennui. It seemed perfectly natural to me to have a Momma who frolicked in the morning's wet grass.

Cavorting wasn't the only way my parents didn't act their age. Momma's childhood hero was Wonder Woman. She even looked like her—tall, with long dark hair and a confident manner. For her birthday one year, Daddy commissioned a comic book artist to paint a portrait of Momma as Wonder Woman. There she was—Momma in Wonder Woman's costume with the bracelets and magic lasso as well. Mother, not to be outdone, commissioned the same artist to paint Daddy as Tarzan in honor of Edgar Rice Burroughs' series we read as a family and the movies they had loved as children. The portraits hang in their bedroom in my house now, paired with the traditional portraits—Daddy's gubernatorial pose and Momma's glamorous black and white profile.

Daddy is an old-fashioned, macho kind of Southern male, but, after he read *Watership Down*, he became fascinated with rabbits. What had once been a boy's prey on a late autumn afternoon became a grown man's secret obsession. After his confession, we started getting him bunnies for special occasions like birthdays and Christmas—expensive bone china bunnies, exotic stone carved bunnies, playful plastic or soulfully painted bunnies. I don't know anyone else who has a Daddy with a bunny collection.

I also don't know anyone else who has a Daddy who went out in public with pink magic-marker radiation targets drawn on his face. Daddy had a brain tumor when I was a teenager, and the follow-up treatment to prevent its recurrence was radiation. We were relieved and elated that he didn't die—the anniversary of the day he survived the surgery is forever known as Not Dying Day—but then the reality of radiation set in. Food didn't taste right. He was tired most of the time. My sixteenth birthday rolled around about three quarters of the way through his treatment.

Now, in the South I grew up in, a girl's sixteenth birthday was a special event. But, with him so weary and with those pink boxes drawn on his face, it looked like any celebration might be a casualty of his illness. But he decided we needed to do something, so it was resolved we would go out to eat. I was to invite four of my closest friends, and we would all dress up in formals. Daddy, tired and pale, which accentuated the pink boxes even more, donned his tuxedo, and squired us gowned girls down to the coast to dine on shrimp wrapped in bacon, hushpuppies and grits.

It must have been quite a spectacle since heads turned when we entered. We amused ourselves by making up wild and imaginative explanations for why a dignified man in a tuxedo with wife and children and five gowned girls would have pink boxes on his forehead and temples. His silliness saved the evening.

Having now matriculated and maneuvered my way to my fifties, what am I supposed to act like to act my age? How am I supposed to feel about it? If adolescence was awkward, what then is middle age? A woman ought not to have to deal with more than one beauty crisis at a time; it might be pimples or wrinkles, but not both at once. Previous generations demarcated the lines between youth and age with dress and music. Not today. Today, you can still be an over-forty hot mom centerfold or be a geriatric rock star. Sandwiched and stretched, our age finds itself in constant contradiction.

If age is determined by context, I am sandwiched between aging parents and growing children. But, unlike previous generations who did it all under one roof or at least in the same town, for a while, I did it spread out over 1600 miles of interstate highways. Then, once we were united in the same house again, it didn't really get any better. Momma always said you become a grownup when your parents die. I might add that having to parent your parents might also qualify.

All authorities agree that good parenting requires time, energy and attention, but try being a stay-home parent. Well-meaning people ask what you do all day, questioning you like some sort of mental defective or political subversive. That is, if you can afford for one of you to stay home.

Caught between the wild dreams of our youth of going to the moon and making a difference and the constant clamoring call of the dishwasher, the washing machine, and the mortgage, all of whom must be fed like pagan gods, we have become like the Silly Putty cartoon images we transferred in our childhood, stretched and distorted in comic proportions, sometimes beyond recognition, into caricatures of ourselves.

In old photos, most people can always tell it's me because of my big, dark eyes. Those same eyes stare back at me in the mirror. Just now, however, they are framed by tiny lines and wrinkles that television advertising pledges to rid me of. I am Warrior Princess strong and have greater stamina than I did in my twenties, but when I stop moving, my back aches, my hands hurt, and my mind won't be quiet enough to let me rest. I have my own personal heat waves, but I get cold as a corpse at bedtime. My husband, Jeremiah, challenged our teenage boys to an impromptu foot race in a restaurant parking lot after being teased that he was old and slow. He won, but he couldn't walk the next day.

Jeremiah and I have theorized that parents age differently than regular people, aging more years in a single year, as dogs do. With four children, we estimate that we have really lived more two hundred parent years in the last sixteen. We had a door jamb in the house where we have tracked the growth of the children, the children gradually overtaking and surpassing us both. Maybe growing up for grown-ups isn't a factor of height or the calendar. It isn't measured by months and years or inches and feet, but by the experiences lived and the spiritual inches grown. But the events that mold us at this age are not always on a grand scale. Instead, they are small, daily, and mundane but utterly profound. My story is a coming-of-age story, a coming of middle age story, archetypal in theory, but awkwardly average in actuality.

Love's Labor Lasts

IN MY FAMILY, ON your birthday, someone is supposed to tell the story of your birth. Granny and Papa would recount to Momma every March that Aunts Norma and Ginger were quite disappointed that she had not been a bunny rabbit since they had been told that a surprise was coming and Easter was around the corner. My aunts would turn that story of childish discontent around on Papa and remind him how he had fallen to the floor in disappointment when Momma, his third child, turned out to be a girl.

At my birthday, Daddy would always describe how I didn't look like a newborn at all—all red and wrinkled—but instead more like a three-month-old, round and pink. Aunt Norma added her part to my brother Dawson's story as she described how the nurse had held him up above his layette cubicle and opened his diaper to offer proof that our family had finally been blessed with a male after two generations had rendered only females.

I have continued the tradition with my children, recounting the days that ran up to their births as well as the ordeal of their arrivals. I have encouraged Jeremiah to tell the stories of my stepsons Wilson's and James's births, even though I was not a participant in the events, as their special days arrive. Somehow, to me, it seems an important way to remind children of who they are, and serves as a reminder to parents of who these large, hairy and sometimes sullen teenagers were—our precious babies.

The telling of the story also puts the limelight back on the Momma, where it belongs. After all, if it weren't for us, there would be no birthdays. Jeremiah, as a representative of the male contributor to reproduction, finds a flaw with this point of view, but I just smile at him.

I don't think this type of story-telling is peculiar to my family. If you get a group of women together for a long enough period of time, the conversation will eventually drift toward children and child-bearing. Men have their hunting and fishing sagas or their college prank tales, in all of which the point is to try to one-up each other over who was the most daring, the most imaginative, or the bravest. Most women, regardless of what level of education they have attained or kind of profession they have pursued, cannot resist their own version of this—the childbirth story.

As a result, you can get to know unusually intimate details about ladies whom you otherwise don't know that well—or may not want to know that well. Women don't hesitate to inflict these gory details on any man who may be in listening distance either. It is popular to talk about testosterone toxicity, but an elevation of estrogen can account for similarly extreme behavior, if you ask me. The more horrible your story is, the greater its badge of honor, not only to outdo your fellow females but to gross any nearby men out of the room. Jeremiah claims that this male display of squeamishness is either a sign that the man is not a father or is merely being chivalrous and discreet around the ladies. I think that he just doesn't want to be outdone. Regardless, I have heard stories of having babies in elevators or of labors that lasted for 48 hours or of breech births from women I barely know—and have guiltily shared my own feats in turn.

July is the big birthday month in our family, with all three of the boys celebrating their nativities that month. Wilson and Edward are now closing in on 30 while James will finish his Masters', and it seems unbelievable to me that I am the mother of men. You would think that their towering size or Edward's beard or their living away from home should have been clue enough, but those birthday landmarks were still a bit of a shock.

It seems like only yesterday that I was an expectant mother, anticipating Edward's arrival with impatience. Now, he calls home once a week—maybe—and comes home occasionally. It seems I am still waiting for him to get here, in some ways. Pregnancy was an object lesson in control for me—or how to live without it. Being a typical type-A, high-achieving, upwardly mobile, modern woman, I was used to calling the shots. My classroom, my home, my body, my finances—all were in my control. I was good at managing myself and managing others.

The trial of having my body possessed by another creature changed that. I noted each little transformation in my condition as my belly hardened and then protruded and as my bosoms blossomed. Just how big would they get? How much would I weigh when I stepped on the doctor's scales each week, even if I could eat only peach yogurt and Cheerios?

Other alterations gave me an enhanced sense of vigor, but still had little to do with anything over which I was in control. My hair darkened and thickened; my fingernails were like iron; my complexion was radiant and clear. The growing life within me already had a mind of its own, so to speak. The baby's first movements were unintelligible initially, although after you have experienced them, you are forever looking for them, even if they *are* gas pains now.

The shockingly loud sound of the heartbeat, that first time you hear it, is like the cannon bursts in *The 1812 Overture*, with its fast, insistent, POW-POW-POW over the amplifier. The heartbeat and the first ultrasound confirm that there is indeed a little alien, floating like an astronaut in his inner space, growing inside you, providing the relief of evidence that you are not simply getting fat.

A confirming sign of pregnancy is also an irrepressible and overwhelming sleepiness in those first months. Momma describes it as feeling like an old momma cat that can sleep all day and, in any location, or position. I was known to fall asleep sitting up and in the middle of a conversation when I was with child.

For all the sense of being inhabited by a Martian, I loved being pregnant. I felt beautiful and alive and powerful—the center of the universe. I had life growing inside me. Heck, I *was* the universe. Yet, there still were those moments when being the universe was pretty comical. When I was carrying Edward, I was still teaching. My enlarged belly provided no end of amazement for my students. Edward was a kicker who seemed to have his own regular *in utero* schedule of exercise regimens. As he kicked within, my dress would jump without, and the kids would lose track of whatever I was saying.

"It's moving," someone shrieked in horror.

I would remind the student that it was not a beach ball up my dress and that babies move in the womb. The most curious was a class of ninth graders—sixteen girls. Astounded, one would ask if I could feel it. Shyly, someone would then inquire if she could feel it. Not necessarily knowing how appropriate touching teacher's stomach was for high school students but knowing that they saw me in the most motherly way and were genuinely and lovingly aware of the miracle in front of them, I carefully let one place her hand on my distended abdomen to feel the baby's hearty kicks.

She would quickly draw her hand away, like she had been stung or like she had put her hand in a bucket of slimy worms or something.

"Ewwwww! It's moving," she would exhale.

Laughing, I would try to shift the attention away from the wonder of childbearing back to the lesson.

As shy and reticent students had been about it, however, there were people at the other end of the spectrum who felt like my protruding stomach was public property. I had men whom I knew only casually or professionally—who would never grope my stomach under different circumstances—grab my belly with both hands and rub, like a gypsy prognosticating with a crystal ball, and offer their opinions if it were a boy or a girl. I had to stifle the urge to slap them in indignation, since somehow when you are pregnant, you are everyone's friend. Old ladies stop you in the grocery store to talk when you are pregnant. I guess it is a good thing, but again, it was all pretty out of control.

You have to have a sense of humor about being pregnant. Even though from behind I still had a waistline, from the front I looked like an egg with legs. Being pregnant in the hot weather, I took on the appearance of a Cabbage Patch doll with my hands and feet so swollen I had dimples instead of knuckles.

Then there were the underwear problems. I was young and refused to wear the old-lady-looking maternity underwear available at the time. For a long time, I kept wearing my usual bikini underwear that fit conveniently below my extended tummy—that is, until that fatal day in class. As I was teaching a lesson on subject-verb agreement, I felt the elastic in my panties give like a tire blow-out on the highway, and I sensed my drawers starting to sag.

As I kept on talking calmly to my students, my interior dialog was screaming hysterically. All I needed was for my panties to drop around my ankles, and I would be finished as a teacher. I didn't panic, however, but instead clinched my buttocks as tightly as I could and slowly backed up so that I was leaning casually against my desk. That thankfully stopped the progress of my errant underwear.

The bell finally rang, and I all but ran—such as I could in my rotund state—holding on to my panties surreptitiously through my dress, to the restroom where I could safety pin them back into an appropriate semblance of setting.

Fitting a brassiere—which, according to those who had born children before me was *de rigueur* to prevent sagging—was no less awkward.

Instead of subjecting myself to the horrors of the department store fitting room in which an old lady with cold hands would intrude upon my privacy with the latest and largest model to try on, I decided to order several styles from a catalog to try on in the privacy of my own bedroom. I did invite my sister to participate with me because, even though she is younger, she is my sister after all, and sisters share that sort of thing.

Finally, the anticipated garments arrived, and Samantha came over as quickly as she could. We tore open the package with excitement. What emerged from the innocuous brown wrapping, however, was more than I had anticipated, literally. Although I had ordered the size that the instructions indicated would be appropriate, the article I removed from the packing could only be described as monumental.

First, its length seemed to exceed my extended arms. If that weren't horrible enough, the cups looked big enough and rigid enough to function as giant serving bowls. Samantha's eyes widened, and she erupted in laughter. I held the offending piece of lingerie out at arm's length in amazement. Then, I held a cup up over my head and put it on like a cap. The enormity of it pretty much swallowed my very large head, falling down over my eyebrows.

At that point, Sam and I were laughing so hard that I almost wet myself—a pretty likely danger when pregnant. It was then and there that I made up a rule that I live by to this day: no matter how big my boobs may get, I will never wear a bra bigger than my head. My dignity just could not stand for it.

If I had only known at that point the depths at which my dignity would be tested. Bra fitting was nothing to the delivery room. First, both of my children were late. Next, they were both summer babies. I don't know what I was thinking—or maybe that wasn't the problem—in planning to have babies born in the hottest, stickiest, most unpleasant part of the year in the Gulf Coast South. I was beyond miserable in both cases, with complaining and chewing ice as the only joys left in my wretched life.

After those long days lapsed past my due dates, both of which had been preceded by some weeks of false labor, making me even grumpier, I would have just about given birth in the football stadium to get it done with. With Anna-Aileene, I nearly approximated it.

The first time around, however, little did I know that labor and delivery nurses have their own special cynicism. They are trained to be skeptical of anything a new mother might say, since obviously none of us know what we are talking about, especially about our own bodies.

I had been having regular labor pains all day, and had called the doctor to find out if or when he wanted me to go to the hospital. Since I lived pretty close to the hospital and since it was my first baby, he said I could probably wait until the pains were about two minutes apart, implying it could still take a long time even then.

Momma and I had whiled away the time that day, trying to think of anything but the pains and trying to keep from checking my suitcase for the hundredth time. Mostly we baked all day. A friend had harvested a bumper crop of blueberries, so we made jam, pie, muffins—anything you could think of we cooked with blueberries that day.

Eventually, at about dinner time, we decided to head to the hospital. I went through the necessary check-in procedure of forms and checklists and insurance cards. I was hooked up to the contraction monitor and examined. As my pains got stronger and stronger and the nurses remained nonchalant, I chanced a look at my chart for a reason for their indifference.

It read, "Patient *says* she is in labor." I was beyond indignant and called for the nurse.

Thankfully, the doctor came in just at that moment, and he discovered two important things: the contraction monitor was not working, and I was indeed in labor. I was vindicated but unfortunately, given the strength of my pains and the length of time I had had them, I was disturbingly not very far along. Again, I felt a flush of annoyance. Nothing was cooperating with me, and it turns out that Edward was cooperating least of all.

At that stage of labor, babies are supposed to be head down—which he was—and face down—which he wasn't. This problem was slowing down the labor. Looking back on it and knowing Edward, the dreamer, it seems entirely appropriate that he was looking off somewhere else and not paying attention to the task at hand.

They were afraid to give me the longed-for epidural for fear it would slow things down even more and end in an emergency C-section. So, I was given Demerol and told to do the best I could. I didn't know I was allergic to Demerol, never having had it before, so that best was pretty dismal. If I thought that the force of unproductive labor pains was dreadful, then throwing up all over myself and everything else in the throes of those pains was appalling.

At some point, feeling fuzzy with the drugs and pain and nausea—and not wearing my glasses because I had gotten vomit on them—I asked the nurse who that man was sitting across the room. It was Daddy. If I could have thrown myself out the window I would have. None of the books I had read so thoroughly and conscientiously said it would be like this!

After six frightful hours of hospital labor with dear Edward, I was finally rescued with the blessing of an epidural. When they lure you with promise of no more pain, they don't tell you what you have to do before you get this miracle drug. In my awkward, vomit-stained mess, I had to sit on the edge of the delivery bed, and, even when gripped by a labor pain, I had to sit absolutely still so I wouldn't be paralyzed for life with the needle they were sticking into my spine.

The stalwart labor nurse stood in front of me while the anesthesiologist did her magic behind me. When a pain came, I was instructed to grasp the nurse round the waist and rest my head between her copious bosoms. I remember thinking that this was darned weird, but I was thankful for her amplitude in both areas. The relief of the drugs was instantaneous, and I drifted off to sleep, exhausted from a long day of blueberry baking and hard labor.

I awoke with that inescapable feeling that the books described as the need to push, beginning the next phase of the adventure: delivery. Since my condition had been difficult and there loomed the possibility of C-section, the doctor and nurses decided I should be taken to a surgical delivery room, just in case. I was hefted like a sack of potatoes off the delivery bed and on to a gurney. The hospital gown offered little protection for my modesty, but at least I finally got a clean one after having been ill all over myself.

We wheeled down the hall out of the home-like atmosphere of the regular labor-delivery room and into the clinical, antiseptic, turquoise-tiled, surgical suite. All the machines and tubes were a bit daunting, but the nurses were reassuring and my pains were coming so fast that I didn't have much time to be afraid. The epidural had taken most of the pain away, but the pressure of the contractions left me feeling like a toothpaste tube clutched in the hands of a small child.

Despite the vigor of my pushing, my Edward still didn't seem to want to come. The medical professionals, after some quiet conferring, decided to try out some of those fancy gadgets that adorned the room. First was the vacuum extractor, which made this dreadful gloppa-gloppa noise. Apparently, the baby's head was too big because the sucker part wouldn't adhere, so out came the salad tongs—or at least that's what they looked like.

At this point, the doctor gave me a fatherly but serious look and said that if this didn't do it, we would have to do a C-section. They were getting worried about me and about the baby, he said, as both of our heart rates were becoming dangerously erratic.

That was enough for me. With a yell and a strain that left my arms and throat sore for days, I all but sat up off the flat gurney to push. Following this terrible exertion was that amazing feeling that no book can describe. Even with the anesthetic still partially in effect, I felt like a balloon in which all the air was coming out followed by this astounding wiggling feeling. The most remarkable aspect of it all was the sound: that deep, loud gasp for air of the baby taking his first breath. It was almost thunderous—and most welcome. The doctor held my boy up for me to see and commented on how big he was.

"I told you that I was having a big-ass baby," I told him triumphantly.

I was exultant for two reasons. Because of my temper and my love of the English language in all its forms, especially words of Anglo-Saxon origin (the f-bomb, in particular), many people were afraid that the rigors of childbirth would loose in me a stream of profanity our hometown hospital had never known. My descriptive intensifier-inflectional ending concerning my first-born's size was the first and only bad word I had used in the entire twelve-hour ordeal.

My triumph was more than just my pride in having survived and produced a substantial male child. The doctor and I had also had an ongoing debate about the size of the baby. I knew where my baby's head and legs were *in utero* and periodically got out my seamstress' measuring tape to estimate how big he was going to be. I also knew that, of the twenty-three pounds I gained, most of it was baby.

My proud ten-pounder had trumped the doctor's placating description that most babies weigh around six and half pounds. But, between the gloppa-gloppa machine and the salad tongs, my poor Edward was pretty beat up, looking more like a Winston Churchill impersonator who had gone toe-to-toe with George Foreman than like a newborn.

Swaddled, he lay on my belly and looked about in that blind baby way, sniffing. I held him closer and talked to him and, in the stereotypical act of new motherhood, counted his fingers and toes. At the sound of my voice, he stopped crying, his dusky blue eyes cleared and we studied each other. Bumps and bruises or no, he was blueberry beautiful.

Three years later, Anna-Aileene was on her way. In some ways, you wonder why, if childbirth is so awful, women do it again and again. I read that, in the process of labor, the body releases hormones that stimulate a type of amnesia. It is nature's way of propagating the species in spite of our good sense.

Unlike with Edward whose sex I didn't know, I knew Anna-Aileene was a she, due to a late term ultrasound to determine her size. Since Edward had been so big and I was another three years older, the doctor wanted to make sure she wasn't so big I couldn't deliver her.

I had heard horror stories of Momma's friend Estelle who gave birth to a twelve-pound boy whom they didn't realize was too big until his head was delivered. They had to break the baby's collarbone to free him. They didn't tell Estelle they had to do this until after the fact, adding that her baby could have irreversible nerve damage. Estelle, undaunted, worked and worked with little Howard, and he grew up to become a classical guitarist.

I didn't want to find myself in that situation, despite its fortunate outcome, and the miracle of ultrasound gave us the luxury of knowing.

I thought about how much Aunt Ginger could have used ultrasound when she was pregnant with the twins, two years my senior. The only indicator of something out of the ordinary was her size, which Papa called the worst case of pregnancy he had ever seen.

Just after the delivery of the first baby, Leeanne, the doctor turned to the nurses and exclaimed, "Oh my God! There's another baby in there."

Everyone was terribly surprised, and the family had scrambled to purchase another of everything in the layette to prepare for the second baby, Louanne. I was happy not to have to live with such surprises, although I didn't really care if I knew the baby's sex or not. As long as I had a baby and not a Billy goat, it didn't matter if it were a girl or a boy.

Now, having had a boy, I secretly harbored a desire for a daughter, but I was not about to put myself in the position of being disappointed with a healthy baby. During the ultrasound, I burst into tears, seeing her squished little face in the dark depths of my insides. According to the measurements of the test, she would be between eight and ten pounds—and that would be just fine.

Not so fine, however, was the fact that Anna-Aileene was two weeks late, and the doctor was getting anxious. They don't like you going much beyond that point because of its dangers. Papa had been a post-term baby, born blue on a cold, January morning. The midwife, thinking quickly, dunked the baby, who didn't seem to rouse with all the traditional ways of stirring signs of life, into a big tub of ice-cold water. That must have shocked his little system into animation because he breathed loudly and spit up, and everything seemed to be fine from then on. Papa always said that he thought he did pretty well for someone who had been born dead.

My doctor decided that they would try to jump-start my labor with a day at the hospital hooked up to a Pitocin drip. I was told not to eat anything after midnight and to report to the hospital at six the next morning. I couldn't eat anything any way; it was too hot, and there was no room for anything left in my body because the baby took up so much room. Again, I had only gained twenty-three pounds, but it felt like 123. I had repeatedly asked my doctor to his probable annoyance just where my liver was supposed to be.

Full of hope and expectation, I reported to the hospital that morning. I was attached to the IV and sat and waited—and waited and waited and waited. As the hours dragged on and as I started and finished the book I had brought, nothing seemed to be happening. Nurses came in and out, the shifts changed, and nothing happened. Finally, it was getting to be suppertime, and not only had nothing happened, but it looked like nothing was going to happen.

So, I was unhooked from the apparatus and sent home in disgrace, and I expected a gloomy greeting by my expectant family. Our extended family had suffered several serious setbacks since Granny's death the year before. Papa had developed pancreatic cancer, and Aunt Norma had been diagnosed with breast cancer. Everyone wanted me to get my baby-having out of the way so that they could concentrate on the life and death struggles of the aged. Like I had any control over it.

I had already tried everything I knew before the fruitless induction of labor process. I walked vigorously and even tried some jumping rope. My mother-in-law, who was eager to set out for Oregon to be with her other son who had his firstborn due in a month, had taken me on bumpy roads, hoping to jog something loose. I warned her that if something else let loose and I wet her car, I was not paying to have her upholstery cleaned.

When the doctor sent me home, I tearfully told him that my ability to be a good sport was waning severely. Kindly, he put his hand on my shoulder and told me that these things take their course, and that we may have gotten things going and not known it. He gave me a sleeping pill to take later, and admonished me to go home, eat something, and go to bed. Nature would take its course. I told him to tell that to my impatient family.

Forewarned that I was not in a good humor about my failure to deliver despite all the benefits of modern medicine, Momma welcomed me home with tenderness and a plate full of scrambled eggs. I was starving, having not eaten for two days.

My mother-in-law asked if there was anything in the world I wanted, probably feeling guilty for our wild ride, and, in a moment of madness, I asked for a coconut cream pie. She produced not one, but two beautiful creations, topped with toasted coconut on the perfectly golden meringue. I ate half a pie.

Hugged by one and all, I was sent to bed with my sleeping pill—and I slept like I had not slept since losing the ability to sleep on my stomach or go more than two hours without getting up to pee.

At about four in the morning, I awoke, still a little blurry from the medicine, and thought to myself, "Darn, I'm having cramps. I must be starting my period."

Then the fog cleared, and I remembered that I was having a baby. The next cramp came quick and strong, causing my legs to draw up with the discomfort—at last! I woke up my husband, but we waited until daybreak to call Momma to come get Edward. Things were happening.

I checked in to the hospital by mid-morning in time for my water to break. There was no surly and cynical nurse this time. I had left proof that I was in labor all over the floor. That experience hadn't been so dramatic with Edward, so it was a pretty surprising event.

Suddenly the room was filled with a strong animal smell, and I was gripped by pains stronger than ever. It seems that the Pitocin had a delayed effect for me, something it does in some women. No one had told me that. Also, unlike Edward's arrival, this labor was moving along quickly; this would be no twelve-hour ordeal. Having learned from the first time, I also had decided that there would be no Demerol. I would go natural until time for my epidural, having what I hoped was the best of both worlds.

The labor was short but comical. Sam had arrived first thing, beating Momma there, with a big box of Dunkin Donuts in hand. Since my first labor had taken so long, she came prepared for a siege.

Sam was in between jobs and had been trying to set up an interview with a public relations mogul who was chronically out of town. In those days before cell phones, she left the hospital number with the man's office, never dreaming the hospital would transfer a call up to my labor room. The call came, and I answered it, since I was the closest to the phone. As I handed her the phone, a contraction set in, and I encouraged her in the strongest terms to make it quick.

Yet, the phone rang again in a few minutes; this time it was my mother-in-law, checking on my progress. My husband's cheerful voice recounting my progress suddenly was getting on my nerves, as yet another pain came unexpectedly quickly. Sam later described the voice I used to tell him to get off the phone as sounding like something from the *Amityville Horror*.

Shortly after that, the phone rang yet again, and I snatched at the phone, speaking in my authoritative teacher voice and through gritted teeth to the person on the other end of the line, seeking my sister," Thank you for calling her, but this is a labor and delivery room and I am in the middle of having a baby. You will just have to talk to her later, "at which I hung up the phone on the surprised caller, and gave over to yet another contraction.

During all of this phone calling, I was trying to use my Lamaze method breathing. This was part of the reason the interruption of the telephone was so annoying; it deprived me of my concentration. With this baby, I was not going to lie on my back and suffer like I had before. I sat up, breathed in the rhythm I had practiced, and rode the waves of the pains. It was exhilarating, once the telephone interruptions ceased.

The only drawback was my tendency to hyperventilate. To remedy that, we were supposed to have included in our labor equipment kit a paper bag into which to breathe. Not having a tidy small bag, our bag was a full-sized grocery sack. Rather than breathe into the enormity of it, which would do no good since I was supposed to be breathing in my own carbon dioxide, the nurse just put the whole bag on my head after each contraction. So, there I sat, looking like a pregnant Charlie Brown with a paper bag on my head trying to keep the roof of my mouth and my cheeks from going to sleep. Thank goodness I had the foresight to forbid any cameras in the labor room.

As the contractions arrived about a minute apart and I had been checked that I was sufficiently far along, I put in my request for my pre-approved epidural. The nurse assured me that the anesthesiologist was in the room next door, and I was already on the slate to be next.

Minutes went by, each with its contraction, and turned into an hour. I phased into the labor stage called transition, where the contractions are the strongest and come the quickest. Mine came two at a time. On the contraction monitor, you could see it coming, the inked needle scratching on the chart like it was measuring an enormous earthquake. Apparently, things weren't working too well with the woman in the next room since I could still hear her screaming.

"Why is she still screaming?" I asked the nurse in a low and uncharitable moment. "Why can't someone just put her out of all our misery and send that doctor in here to me?"

For those who have never been with a woman in the transitional phase of labor, this is the time when many expectant mothers turn nasty and curse their husbands and all their predecessors back to Adam. Jeremiah knows someone whose wife bit him and he spent the birth in the ER getting stitches. I thought I was being rather well behaved, considering.

Finally, Dr. Gray came in, white-coated and calm. "Thank goodness you are here, Dr. Gray. I could kiss you on the lips," I said.

The stiff and apparently humorless doctor coughed uncomfortably. Seeing his discomfort, I joked, in those rare seconds when I could summon humor, "I guess you don't get propositioned from too many women from the delivery room, eh, Doctor?"

I heard a "hmmph" from behind me as I positioned myself on the bed to receive the needle and its relief. I wondered where he had left his sense of humor. After all, if I could have one under those circumstances, I thought anyone should.

The rest following the relief was short-lived. The nurse said, in passing, to let her know if I felt like pushing. Enjoying a moment of much deserved rest, I was not paying attention to my body, but at her words, its clamor became insistent. Suddenly awake, I told the nurse that I thought I did need to push.

Some of her labor nurse cynicism flashed across her face, but she checked me anyway, and it was a good thing she did. Not only was I complete, but the baby was crowning, pushing her way into the world quickly now after such a lingering delay.

The nurses flew into action, called the doctor from his office in the building next door, and shooed my wide-eyed family out of the delivery room. I sat up, ready for action, excited that I was finally going to meet my baby. The nurses cautioned me not to push yet since the doctor was not yet there—as if I really had any control over it, I laughed to myself.

The doctor, having been caught on his lunch break, sprinted into the room, sandwich still in hand. Curiously, the room kept filling up with people. I had okayed the presence of student nurses and their supervisor who had been with me the day before in my failed attempt to get things started, and since I had an epidural, I had to have a nurse anesthetist as well. There were still several people unaccounted for in the growing throng, and I asked my labor nurse who they were, especially the one who looked about fourteen in his surgical scrubs.

"Oh," she said, "they are just the neonatologist, the neonatal resident, and the neonatal nurse," as if that explanation was sufficient.

Busy at the moment, I didn't ask more questions, but it didn't make much sense. What they had not told me is that they had signs that there could be complications. Blessedly lucky, Anna-Aileene was born to that on-looking multitude. The doctor confided to me, after the fact, that there had been some concern, but she was perfect in every way.

That is, as perfect as any baby who looks like a cross between E.T. and my Daddy can be. But, to me, she was beautiful, and she cried with a loud and husky voice that is her trademark as a mezzo soprano. I laughed thinking that, at this point when Sam was born, Momma, under the influence of drugs, had asked her doctor if he did any other sort of sewing as he stitched up her episiotomy. I was happy finally to get one of those donuts Sam had brought.

Having joined the ranks of those who had given birth, I didn't realize in how many ways that nothing would ever be the same. In theory, I understood this. I knew about babies and their never-ending needs, and even looked forward to my altered life. Yet, if I thought any sense of control would return once the alien had arrived, I was sorely deluded.

If you nurse your baby, your body is still not your own. The breasts that had grown like watermelons now had a mind of their own with their seemingly endless supply of milk. Granny had been so proud when

Edward was born, likening me to a Jersey cow. Now, from anyone else, my feminist sensibilities would have been riled, but I knew what she meant. My baby was thriving, and it was all from me.

Yet, nursing had its drawbacks. If you think about your baby at the wrong time, your milk will come in, and there you are, ready to feed a starving third world nation, whether your baby is there or not. With the mortifications of childbirth behind me, I thought I was ready for anything. That was before I had to tell the dry cleaner that the stains on my leather vest were breast milk.

Then there are the things that happen to your body after the children come. After you have lived through spit-up on your clothes and survived years without sleeping more than two consecutive hours, the bountiful bosom you sported so proudly either dries up to the size of mosquito bites or sags like expended window shades. Sam said that, when she was nursing, she felt like a *Penthouse* pinup, but after Emily was weaned, she felt more one of those photographs of naked, native women in *National Geographic*.

Then there is the ignominy of having the daughter you had prayed for. No matter how you have strived to maintain health and vigor, no matter how well-preserved you are, there is your daughter, looking you over for every flaw. You could resort to plastic surgery as some of my friends have. Sam says most women she knows will try either bangs or Botox for a youthful brow. Or, you can put on a few pounds to alleviate the sagging and the wrinkles. Then, having assuaged the seven signs of aging that moisturizer commercials warn against, you may have also added to your girth. It is a cruel choice: to make a woman choose between her face and her fanny.

Cruelest of all, however, is that teenage daughter who sneers at you in the way only an adolescent can. Momma says that daughters are a mother's revenge. Sam, when she was about six, once asked Momma, who had donned shorts in warm weather, why her legs were so fluffy. Sam's daughter Emily was her grandmother's avenger when she asked Sam when she got to get long boobies like her Mommy had.

For all the trials of childbirth and babies, I have really never gotten over wanting to have more, regardless of the chaos it unleashed in my life. When Jeremiah and I married, I was forty, and plenty of women have babies at that age these days. But, with four children between us, we decided we would concentrate on doing a good job raising the ones we had. We grieved a bit in those early days for the baby we wouldn't have together.

Now, I harbor a residual nostalgia that never goes away for the animal simplicity of mothering babies. Despite the grinding fatigue brought by lack of sleep, that time in your life lends a psychological and emotional restfulness. Your aims are simpler—feed the baby, change the baby, rock the baby—and are easier to accomplish. Keeping them alive is simpler.

Soothing a crying baby seems effortless when face to tear-stained face with a raging, disappointed adolescent. No matter how old we get, when we are in pain, emotional or physical, we turn to Mother, unable or unwilling to share what trouble we are in, and expect her to know what is wrong with us like she did in our first days. This power comes from the one time in life that you, as the Momma, have the capability to meet every need your baby might have, to be the center of her universe. Nursing a baby, you are her sustenance, her safety, her social awareness.

It doesn't last long, and when past, it leaves an emptiness that is never filled again. It is also very easy to overlook this ultimate satisfaction in the flood of fears of new motherhood, the responsibility of keeping a baby alive in a world of germs and crazy people.

Little do you know that the fears only get worse—boyfriends, automobiles, drugs, college—and you have less and less control over what happens to your baby. You can only hope that they have listened to the stories you have told them over and over again.

Mary Antin, late nineteenth century Russian Jewish immigrant and famous writer, said, "We are not born all at once, but by bits. The body first, and the spirit later; and the birth and growth of the spirit, in those who are attentive to their own inner life, are slow and exceedingly painful. Our mothers are racked with the pains of our physical birth; we ourselves suffer the longer pains of our spiritual growth."

Once you are a parent, giving birth never really stops, making those horror stories of childbirth seem like child's play. You must trust in your children's raising and their emerging judgment, and pray that circumstances don't find them in the wrong place at the wrong time. They will make their decisions—what road to take, whom to marry—and you can only sit back and watch. Compared to that, breast milk and spit-up stains on your clothes—or wrinkles or stretch marks on your body—are an insignificant inconvenience.

Come 'Round Right

As the car careened around a sharp curve in the back country road, I could tell that Jeremiah was lapsing back into his boyhood driving mode learned in the mountains of east Tennessee. It always makes me a little bit nervous when he drives like that, but the roads were all but deserted, and he was having fun. The tensions of work, the checkbook, and child-rearing were visibly easing in Jeremiah as we got farther and farther from town.

He turned the radio up to hear a song better, singing along. We loved these adventures in the countryside. Our escapades into the neighboring rural counties ranged from exploring junk yards for parts for Henry, Jeremiah's vintage Ford truck, to investigating a vineyard we had read about in the newspaper, to attending the rich and various musical festivals that flourish in the bucolic backwoods.

For a Christmas present the first year we were married, I gave Jeremiah a five-string banjo. It was one of the few instruments he didn't know how to play, and he had made a passing comment about wishing he could learn. That was enough for me, since it was hard enough to think of gifts for Jeremiah much less surprise him. He had been astonished that Christmas, to my glee, and had promptly arranged for lessons. Through his teacher, we gained access into the abundant bluegrass music scene in our area of which we had been totally oblivious. The city was rich with concerts from pop artists to symphony orchestras, but the bluegrass circuit has a bountiful culture all its own.

So, as we nearly broke contact with the road as we sped too fast up over a hill, we were seeking to lose ourselves for a time, forgetting the crisis of the moment, in this other world. I can tell some people don't quite know what to think about our interest in bluegrass music. I guess they associate it with *Deliverance* and those menacing stereotypes of shotgun-toting, still-hiding, overall-wearing hillbillies. Yet, for us, it simply added a new range of hues to our musical palette.

Both Jeremiah and I confess a love of just about any sort of music if it is done well. We both come from musical backgrounds. When I was growing up, every little girl took piano lessons. Despite the fact I took lessons for eight years, I was never really very good, but the exposure colored my world from then on. As a child, it took a long time for me to realize that other people didn't hear the music I heard in my head, the snippets of tunes that conversation or scenery inspired, like an underlying score to a 1940's blockbuster musical.

I took up other instruments throughout my childhood: the recorder, the flute, the guitar. With each new spark of interest, Daddy would bring an instrument home for me—and always the best. In the fourth grade, when all the students bought the plastic flutophones the school offered, I had a real recorder, beautifully crafted in pear wood. The same would happen the next year when I wanted to play flute in the band; Daddy came home with a Gemeinhardt, a much nicer brand than my inexperience merited. I can still remember opening the brown leather case with its shiny brass locks, and seeing the cool, silver parts of the instrument nestled in its blue velvet cushions like crown jewels. Unlike with the piano, I had a knack for wind instruments, and play them to this day.

Daddy's nurturing of my musical interests probably stemmed from the fact that he was a frustrated musician himself. He loved music, and we always had music playing at home, from Cesar Franck to Rogers and Hammerstein to Spike Jones to Simon and Garfunkel. He even tried to learn the guitar several times over the years. For his first foray, he bought a Gibson classical guitar and signed up for lessons with a Cuban Bay of Pigs escapee who fostered Daddy's dream to be Andres Segovia. Somehow, despite the lessons and the desire, Daddy never got very far. He never could seem to practice.

I think part of it was that he wanted it all to make sense. Music is as logical in some ways as mathematics, as any music theory teacher will tell you. Yet, there is another level in which you just feel it, knowing it intuitively, letting your fingers just do the music. He could never let himself get to that point, and when I picked up his guitar and emulated the piece he had been working on with frustration for weeks, he declared he would never touch the guitar again. That evening, he gathered up all his guitar lesson books and put his instrument in its case and brought them into my room.

I objected, not wanting him to give up his dream.

"No," he said, shaking his head, "you have it and I don't. Enjoy it for me."

I was thrilled but humbled by the gift of both his guitar and his confidence. That guitar would be my sanctuary throughout my teen years, as I would retreat into my room behind the closed door and find refuge in its strings.

Jeremiah too had found music early in life. He had started piano lessons young, but, unlike me, he was both gifted and dedicated. He was one of those children whom you had to make stop practicing, as opposed to most of us whom our parents had to blackmail and threaten. His first piano was an aged upright grand in its last days. When his family moved after his dad's job change, it would have cost too much money to bring the piano along much less bring it back to proper condition, so they left it. Jeremiah cried.

But, when his family settled back in the family lands of northern Alabama, Jeremiah bought his next piano—the one that sits in our music room—with money raised by blackberry picking. His teachers were pedigreed back to Liszt, and he played Chopin, dreaming of being the next Glenn Gould, sans the mental instability. His piano playing and his brains did not endear him to the rustic youth of Owenby's Crossroads. Jeremiah learned to trade knives as well as fight with one at Crossroads' School, where grades one through eight were taught by five teachers.

By the time he got to college, much to the chagrin of his conservatory trained piano teacher, he was also an accomplished gospel pianist who had played in churches all over the Southeast. Later, this talent would surprise people—a man with a European doctorate in theology who was a classically trained pianist who could also fit right in on the *Porter Wagner Hour* of old. Learning the banjo reconnected Jeremiah to those Old-Time roots of his grandparents as well as provided an often much needed distraction from the worries of raising four teenagers.

So, it was that banjo that brought us that early Saturday summer evening to our current outing to The Good News Chicken House. Large corporate chicken farmers had run most small, family farms out of business. The family of this particular chicken house had then used the building for music practice. More and more people came over the years to listen and to play. Then at some point, the owners felt led to transform their former chicken house into a house of worship. So, for the last thirty years, every Saturday night, unless that Saturday is Christmas, they have opened up their tabernacle to any and everyone who would come, providing a venue for traveling and developing bluegrass, gospel and Old-Time musical talent and offering a community of music and prayer.

Not only could your soul be filled but your stomach too. You could buy your dinner there; grilled hamburgers and hotdogs, French fries, and some of the best homemade coconut cream pie you ever tasted were on the menu. I had never heard of anything like this in my life. In another time in my life, I would have been horrified at the very idea of it. This type of music evoked a species of Christianity that made me queasy—a sort like my grandparents who loved their neighbors as long as they weren't black. The hypocrisy behind the hominess was all I could see in those days.

Entering the long, low building behind its bank of mimosa and fig trees, we had to duck our heads at the entrance to avoid being clobbered by the lintel. The interior was dark, but our eyes quickly adjusted. The former abode for fowls had been finished off to some extent inside. Its cinder block walls were covered in prefabricated paneling of varying colors and qualities, creating a patchwork effect; it was air-conditioned and the silver ducts snaked through the exposed rafters overhead.

The walls were decorated with various religious hangings—the Last Supper in black velvet and a white empty Easter cross wreathed in flowers, for example—and photos of the soloists and groups who had played at The Good News Chicken House over the last thirty years. The age of the photos could be determined by how badly the color had shifted or faded over time as well as the variety of dime store frame in vogue in that year in the intervening decades. Yet, in each photo, the performers smiled the same bright, hopeful, determined smile.

A stage was at one end of the building, with piano, organ and large speakers, and the kitchen was at the other, complete with a table from which you could order CDs from groups who had or were playing there. This arrangement allowed visitors to satisfy their appetites without disturbing the viewers. Between the stage and the kitchen were rows and rows and rows of seating. Many seats were salvaged from old movie theaters or high school auditoriums, with ages of layers of different colors of paint covering the former wood inlay and decorative iron work. Other rows were church pews. The remaining ranks of seats were filled out with odd straight chairs or even lawn chairs. The room's ironic effect, as with the walls, was of a coat of many colors, seemingly haphazard but carefully and even lovingly constructed.

Just as varied as the chairs they sat in were the people assembling at this meeting place. Young and old arrived, individually, as couples like us, or by the busload. They were from all walks of life, too. Old men in overalls and work boots and blue-haired ladies in cotton print blouses over double knit slacks with elastic waists and Keds tennis shoes were one social stratum taking their places in line for food or selecting their seats in the audience. These folks had arrived in trucks or by buses from backwoods churches. Then there were those old folks or even those of late middle age, arriving in their Cadillacs or Buicks, in fashionable sports clothes, corduroy blazers and cowboy boots on the men, and sequin-spangled, silk pants suits and high heels on the women.

Young people turned up, too, but not in the same numbers as the adults. Some were young children, coming with parents or grandparents. Teenagers came with their church groups. Their t-shirts and jeans created another gradation of apparel in this growing multitude. Most of the faces were white, but all received a warm smile of greeting as they crossed the threshold into the cool depths of this odd hall of worship.

At some point that must have been a part of the Chicken House tradition—because it wasn't about the time or the fullness of the hall—the program got started with a dimming of the lights over the rows of seating. The emcee—or preacher, if you wanted to call her that—was introduced, with a spotlight and organ flourish, as Miss Jenna. She had one of those husky voices right for Old Time Gospel or country music, lowered by a fourth with age. Yet, it was hard to pin her age down. Her short, brunette hair was smartly styled, and with loving care, no grays were apparent. She was tanned, slim and well-dressed, in a colorful silk running suit. Adorned with bling, she glittered under the spotlights that now focused on her.

Microphone in hand, and with a nod to the piano player, she opened with the old favorite, "The Old Rugged Cross." At the start of the music, the audience quieted, and those in line for food lowered their voices. After a verse or two, in which the audience, with no prompt or cue, joined in singing the refrain, Miss Jenna crooned to an end, at which applause erupted from the spectators. Then, she began what we deduced was her welcome ritual. First, she introduced all the fixtures of the tableau—the owners, the pianist/organ player, and the house band, as well as those that acted as ushers and plate passers—and the three groups who would perform that night.

Then, Miss Jenna began the outreach segment of the program and the part that must have most famously bound the Chicken House community together. She inquired of the gathered faithful who came from the farthest, at which hands shot up from the crowd. The honors went to both an older couple from Ontario and a young Native American from Arizona as the best of those who came from afar. Blessings were showered on all those who came from someplace else, and the host clapped in approbation. Next, Miss Jenna marked all the birthdays and anniversaries. Everyone who had celebrated over the previous week stood, as their turn came, and spoke into the mobile microphones that were circulated down the rows of the congregation, sharing their ages or how long they had been married. Some made jokes about their longevity; some were proud to have survived that long. Some men acquiesced to let their wives announce their anniversary; other men teased about finally getting their first chance to get a word in edgewise in many long years. After all the celebrations were shared, the assemblage offered their approval once again.

At this point, Miss Jenna sang another song to set the mood for the next phase of this part of the program, "What a Friend We Have in Jesus." After a shared chorus, she opened up for prayer requests. Again, the mobile microphones circulated along the rows to those who required them. One lady stood to testify to the healing power of prayer as her sister's cancer was now in remission. Miss Jenna offered thanksgiving for the lady and for her sister. A young man rose and requested prayer for his best friend who had a drug problem. Miss Jenna tendered appeals for mercy and assistance for the young man, his friend, and all who suffered from chemical dependence. Supplications and thanks continued in similar fashion for the next twenty minutes or so. To bring it to a close, Miss Jenna offered another song, "He Lives," while those who stood as ushers passed Kentucky Fried Chicken buckets to take up a collection for a child who was fighting leukemia. As Miss Jenna came to a poignant end of the song, amen's punctuated the applause.

The program was then turned over to the in-house band, an odd assemblage of men and instrumentation. There was an older man of extensive girth who played an orchestral tuba. Joining him were a younger bearded man playing a trumpet and a man in a leg cast playing trombone. A skinny, red-haired clarinetist and the omnipresent piano/organist filled out the ensemble. They played a variety of hymns in a style that could only be described as eclectic—a cross of Dixieland, oompah band, and street corner musician. What they lacked in skill, they made up for in enthusiasm, and they reminded me of all the concerts Jeremiah and I had attended for our children.

Given Jeremiah's and my musical bent, it is no wonder that our children were musical. Music provided a glue that held our blended family together as well as a field of battle on which to enact many a parent-child drama. Before we married, our older boys had already started down their musical paths, Wilson on the trumpet and Edward on the bassoon. When the younger two approached middle school age, it was not a matter of *if* they would play in the band but *what* they would play in the band. Anna-Aileene chose the flute and James chose the clarinet, and both joined the band in their turn.

Despite our delight in our children's approbation of music, that too was not without cost. To a musician, there is no greater test of parental love than a middle school band concert. The young musicians are just beginners, so the clarinets squeak, the flutes are sharp, the trumpets are flat, and the bassoons squawk. We were treated to plenty of that in at-home practice, at which we were patient because that is what it takes to get from novice to expert.

Performing is the next step of development for a young player, and was therefore essential. Yet, to listen to the yearly renderings of "Tequila" or "Rock Around the Clock" or "Stars and Stripes Forever"—or the novice string ensemble attack Pachelbel's "Canon"—was enough to try even the most doting parent's musical patience. If one child has intonation problems, you can only imagine what fifty of them sound like together. Then, there is the whole counting problem; some kid invariably gets lost, or miscounts, and comes in early in the dramatic silences or rests. The effect, usually rendered in the gym in which the acoustics are suitable only for shouting, is cacophonous and migraine-inducing. Add to that a band director who had aspirations to be an Elvis impersonator, and the experience entered the realm of the bizarre.

But we were always there, always proud. Nothing does your heart good like seeing a bunch of surly and awkward pre-adolescents, scrubbed and in their pressed, white shirts and dark pants, making real music. Both Jeremiah and I saw it, in agreement with Kurt Vonnegut, as all the evidence anyone needed for the existence of God.

Yet, it always seems that the very characteristic that is your greatest strength is also the source of your greatest weakness. Our very pride and support became a weapon our children could employ at various times in their crusade for independence. Jeremiah was thrilled that Wilson chose to play the trumpet, envisioning later father-son brass ensembles. Yet, Wilson got braces on his teeth in middle school which seemed for a time to derail his progress on the instrument. We tried wax and Anbesol, but his playing suffered. Wilson was ready to quit, but Jeremiah wouldn't let him. This began a struggle between father and son that would go on for years, flashing hot or icing up, depending on the circumstance.

As parents, you see your child's talents and strive to encourage him so that he grows as an individual, finding that passion and that sustenance that feeds him for a life time, but, if you seem to care about it too much, then the child becomes coy, or even worse, defensive. Wilson would get a music scholarship to college and even make first chair in the all-state collegiate honor band, but he gave it up, telling his father that music just wasn't that important to him. Jeremiah fought with himself, whether to be heartbroken or furious, wondering where he had failed. He raged at Wilson's hubris of giving up money for college over what seemed to be a passive-aggressive stab at his father. After all, plenty of people trade military service for a college degree. Was it too much to ask?

It was almost like Wilson wanted to say that since music was important to Jeremiah, he wanted nothing to do with it—a new twist on an old story for fathers and sons. At what point do you make your child do what you know he loves, even when he tells you he hates it? It was a riddle with unanswerable, mythological overtones.

Edward's bassoon was also to serve as a bludgeon to his parents' nerves. When we relocated and I remarried, Edward did not own a bassoon. My son *would* have to pick one of the two wind instruments which cost more than my car. The schools we had attended in Alabama had always had one which we were able to rent. Not so in our new home. That meant we would have to buy one, and at a time when money was tight.

Trying to emulate my Daddy, I set out to find an affordable bassoon, which I soon learned was an oxymoron. On the internet, I finally found a horn, albeit old and a student model, we could afford, and bought it. Edward's experience with his first bassoon was exactly the opposite of mine with my flute, I am sorry to say, despite the fact that it cost me ten times more than my flute had cost Daddy back in those days. The case was beat up and the interior velvet threadbare. The horn, instead of warm wood, was plastic composite, but it was the best we could do. I combated my own enemies of alternating shame and resentment in presenting my son with such an instrument. Yet, to his credit, Edward was grateful at that moment, although I could see in his eyes his disappointment.

Since he was an adolescent, that disappointment would flash mean at his Momma. Edward, chided because he wasn't practicing commensurate with the financial investment we were making with lessons every week, lashed out by saying he hated the horn and music and probably me. I resisted the temptation to club him with the horn. Later, when tempers had cooled, we talked about the horn and about reality. We made a deal with him that, if he stuck with it and was really good, we would buy him a *real* instrument in high school. Indeed, the day came when we did spend more money on a bassoon than I had on my new van, but the enchantment in Edward's eyes when he beheld Roxanne, his true love in mountain maple, made it worth every cent. We sold the old horn, and Edward shed tears over it. Funny how that works.

In our early days, our family had its own version of the band Jeremiah and I watched on the strange stage in front of us. Our ensemble's instrumentation was imbalanced with a trumpet, a trombone, two flutes, a clarinet and a bassoon. But we bought easy renditions of Christmas carols and classical chestnuts for our various voices and regularly played together. The children, especially the older boys, were often embarrassed by these little concerts, but even their shared misery bound our family together in the cooperative experience. Providing opportunities for embarrassment seems to be part of the parental job description, and we were more than happy to oblige, since, in doing so, it served a higher purpose.

Wilson and Edward got their revenge, however, and joined the high school marching band. We proudly joined the ranks of band parents in the stadium as our boys donned their uniforms and took to the field—the football field—and marched in their first shows. The feel of the crisp autumn air, the smell of grilled burgers, and the sounds of colliding football pads transported Jeremiah and me back to our youths. Both of us had been ardent band members, and we were pleased to see our boys become a part of something larger than themselves and make music in the process.

The first year of marching band was full of pitfalls for the boys and for us. Wilson and Edward had to learn to march and play at the same time—a pretty complex thing to do, especially when you seem to have to watch your feet as you march so you don't fall down. It was always easy to spot the freshmen in the band; they were the ones whose instruments were held even with their hats as their heads bowed in prayer that their feet hit the mark without stumbling.

For us, it was hard to learn to walk the thin line between praise and constructive criticism, as we watched our awkward boys find their way. For Jeremiah and me as parents, it was also the first time we were confronted with nostalgia in conflict with current practice. At one point, we even heard the words "back in our day" come out of our mouths. We had done it; we had turned into old farts. Talk about embarrassing.

While the players on the Chicken House stage started yet another verse of "Nearer My God to Thee," Jeremiah and I answered the call of our stomachs and the aroma of the grilling hamburgers and hot dogs. Standing in line, we raised eyebrows at each other, communicating without words the fact that we had also both had enough of the gusto of the homely group playing on stage. We were there for the bluegrass, but homemade pie and a couple of grilled hotdogs would help our patience.

Our endurance was rewarded upon our return to our seats as the band had cleared the stage and the sound crew was setting up for the first ensemble, a bluegrass band called the Piney Creek Players. As they were setting up, Jeremiah offered commentary on the musicians as was offered to him by his banjo teacher, a member of the group. The mainstays of the group were the five-string banjo and the guitar. The stand-up bass provided the foundation for tuning and for keeping the beat. This group also boasted both a mandolin and a fiddle, sometimes a hazardous combination if egos were inflated, since both instruments often vied for the solo breaks. This particular group seemed to get along pretty well, according to Jeremiah, and had been together long enough to gain a good enough reputation to travel the circuit and cut a couple of CDs.

As the ensemble began to play, the atmosphere in the Chicken House changed. Toes tapped and hands clapped soundlessly in time with the music as if they had minds of their own. At the tight and playful harmonies of the singers, smiles flashed among the listeners and between Jeremiah and me. I don't know if it is some atavistic response, but all I know is that you pretty much can't help it. Bluegrass lyrics are usually about a limited range of subjects—lost love, found love, and the love of Jesus—and employ equally limited images—trains, roads, tears, Jesus, and Mommas. Yet, even though many of the songs sound pretty much the same and are about the same things, there is something fresh about them. Maybe it's the high tenor part, sung above the melody line, in a plaintive drone descant, that pulls at my heart. Maybe it's the whine of the harmonies as they slide into place, finding the sweet spot and as quickly leaving it. Maybe it's the driving tempo that quickens like my pulse. Whatever it was, it was definitely something visceral for me, taking me back to times and places I knew only through my grandparents and never realized were important to me.

Granny's daddy had played the fiddle, but he had put it away when he got religion. I—reluctantly at the time, admittedly—watched *Hee Haw* with my grandparents on many an evening. Although I didn't necessarily enjoy the music at the time, being a teenager who thought that guitars should be electric and amplified, I did value the time with Granny and Papa. Looking at the backs of white-haired ladies in the audience, I could easily envision one of them being my Granny.

They say that smell is the sense that evokes the strongest memories, but music must hold a close second. The next group was a men's gospel quartet. Although they weren't bad, they didn't hold my interest like the instrumentalists had. Some of their movements were wooden, and the bass was weak. It made me think of other times where music made me or those around me a bit uncomfortable. Jeremiah and I took the kids to hear various groups from our youth, trying to let them hear and connect to the sounds of our past. My brother Dawson says that one of the best things about being a parent is being able to inflict your musical taste on the next generation.

We went to hear the Doobie Brothers one summer. Most of the crowd, seated on blankets or in lawn chairs in the meadow around the pavilion, was over forty, our young ones noticed. They wrinkled their noses in anticipatory disdain. As the music began, we old folks rose from our places and began to move to the music. Anna-Aileene's eyes rolled. I looked around us, trying to see with her eyes.

There was a balding and bespectacled guy standing next to us in a blue oxford, button-down shirt and a pair of gray slacks, looking for all the world like a CPA and someone's dad. Yet, as "China Road" cranked up, the stiffness that his clothes communicated was eased, and he started dancing to the music. In the half-light of the fading day, he was no longer a forty-something but the kid who listened to the radio, bought the albums, went to the concerts back in the day. Although the kids started to really enjoy the music, they still kept shooting Jeremiah and me that skeptical look that maybe we weren't their parents after all but something that had been replaced by alien beings.

The big boys had taken up electric guitars at our encouragement, Wilson on lead and Edward on bass. They turned up their noses at it at first, but gradually, they began to be convinced of the possibility of coolness that amplification could bring. They corralled a few of their friends and formed a garage band, practicing on Saturday or Sunday afternoons. Thank goodness we had kindly neighbors because I thought that if they played Lynyrd Skynyrd's "Gimme Three Steps" one more time, I would scream.

So, when that band—or a reconstituted version of it since its vital members had died long ago in a plane crash—came to town, we had to go. Although plenty of rides in the car were punctuated with "Sweet Home, Alabama" and I had danced at many a high school dance to "Free Bird," I was unprepared for the adult fan base that followed the still-popular band.

Just like the Doobie Brothers' concert, the crowd was mostly our age, but they were garbed in clothing that people I know don't wear, at least in public. Never in my life had I seen so much overweight, suntanned flesh stuffed into overly-tight apparel. Bosoms spilled out of leather vests, and fanny cheeks peeped out from under Daisy Duke shorts on women who should have given up wearing that type of clothing decades—and pounds—ago. There were tattoos on both sexes in places I wondered how modesty allowed them to be implemented on the wearer much less displayed to the world.

At that concert, it wasn't so much the music that made me feel odd, but the apparent fact that the music could unite people like me with Hell's Angels in training. Sitting in the Chicken House that night, I guess Jeremiah and I may have stuck out a bit there too—a bit too tweedy and academic looking—but somehow the music brought us all together.

Music has the power to do that. When I was in high school, our band went on tour to an international music festival in Austria. Part of the value of the experience was its introduction of European culture to a bunch of small-town Alabamians. As we traveled and played in the Tyrol, there was a lot of comment—as is typical in the young and inexperienced—about how people dressed, how they didn't put ice in their drinks, and how they smelled. Yet, we were suitably awed as we saw castles and churches that far outdated our nation's history.

One event allowed most of my peers to make the shift from their parochial pretensions to a genuine appreciation of the land and the people we visited. One evening, we bused through the snow-covered, storybook mountains to a small, rural village where we were scheduled for a concert. Once there, the venue was a bit small for us, and not as grand as many of us expected, so we were all ready to turn up our noses at the experience. We came to the end of our repertoire of Broadway hits, Disney favorites and Sousa marches for the concert, but the director asked us to pull out one last number.

As we started playing that piece, Mozart's *Ave Verum Corpus*, the event transformed—and changed us. While we played, the audience started singing. Many band members' eyes went wide as we noted that although most of the audience were working people, people whose hands were rough and whose faces were leathered with labor, they knew the Latin lyrics and could sing all the parts. Mozart was their native son, and we silly children wouldn't realize until later that many Europeans, even those of lesser education than we had at that point in our lives, spoke much better English—not to mention other languages other than their own—than any of us spoke German.

In the dim light of the hall, we could see tears streaming down the faces of many of the folks in the audience. It wasn't long before we too, including our director, shared tears of appreciation. This moment was a beautiful and unexpected episode, and one that taught many of our number about making judgments about others, but more importantly about the universality of the language of music.

Our boys had a similar experience, but instead of a multi-cultural experience, it allowed them to see their peers in a kinder light. Every few years, the music department of their high school would put on a musical extravaganza which would include all music students—choral, wind, and orchestral. Anyone who has been to high school and had kids in high school knows that one of the banes of high school existence is the cliques. As students strive to find themselves and their place, they often vie against each other, not in friendly academic or athletic competition, but in those vicious ways we all remember—snide comments, ostracization, and mean pranks.

Music students are not exactly the coolest kids in a comprehensive high school, so our boys were pretty accustomed to the moniker *band geek*. But, even among the musicians, there was a pecking order with the band kids looking down on the choral students, and everyone looking down on the string players. For their senior year, the choral director decided to undertake Carl Orff's *Carmina Burana*, a phenomenal work of titanic proportion. Rehearsals were grueling and subject to many of the prejudices and cliquishness that pervaded the different ensembles. The boys despaired that they would be able to pull it off.

But performance night came and with it, the magical conversion that music offers. First, miraculously, there were nearly five hundred students on the stage. Singers stood on risers and the band and strings had merged into a symphony orchestra. If anyone would ever lose heart about the future in the hands of today's youth, he need only go to a concert such as this. That so many students, all of whom may not speak to each other off stage in that vicious way teenagers—or any of us—can treat one another, could come together and cooperate to bring beauty to life is a testament to hope.

Then they started playing and singing. The high school auditorium was almost inadequate to contain the volume of the performance. The shimmering orchestral element contrasted with the magnitude of the vocal harmonies, all in an offering to the quirks of fortune. It was magnificent. As the final chord sounded and its echo sparkled in the auditorium, many cheeks in the audience glistened with tears. When we reunited with the boys after the concert, they were elated. There were the odd complaints about this missed note or that problem, but they were held in the euphoria of the experience, and that was all that mattered.

The last group at the Chicken House was a family of six, ranging from the father on bass fiddle, to mother on vocals, to the nine-year-old boy on mandolin. They hailed from the hills of east Tennessee, Jeremiah's home, but they toured all over the country. One of their members, a sixteen-year-old fiddle player, had recently won an important national competition and held the title of best young fiddler in America. As they started playing, their enthusiasm and wholesomeness recharged our audience. Toes tapped again.

Watching the children play, it made me think about my own children and their music. For a parent, music offers some of the most important life lessons that can be taught. I know, most folks think those lessons are best learned on the athletic field, but not everyone wants to carry, hit or throw a ball—and a musician's career is a lot longer than an athlete's. Playing an instrument or singing, the musician must find balance within himself. First, there is the relationship between talent and hard work. Talent can take you pretty far, but hard work actually gets the job done.

Once the tendency to depend only on talent is conquered, then you have to realize that, no matter how hard you work, you won't ever be perfect. Each performance has its peaks and valleys, missed opportunities or even outright disasters; then, it is over. A musician's equilibrium is gained when she can let those glitches go, and be in the moment with the music.

To be a performer, you must stifle that grimace when your C sharp isn't in tune, but acknowledge later that you will work on C sharps for the next time. What better lesson could any of us learn than to give our best in the present but to learn from our mistakes for the future?

Although these lessons sound so noble, they are, like most things, a lot messier enacted in real life. Wilson's love of the lead guitar was somewhat dampened by his father's enthusiasm. We had helped him buy his first electric model, thinking that it would mean more to him if he had something invested in it. It was blue and white, the standard axe model so many youthful rock-artists-in-training start on. Yet, he outgrew that one, and bought another, fancier model, cherry red, and replete with knobs and a whammy bar. Jeremiah was pleased at his son's initiative.

The old one stayed in the closet until one awful night, in the midst of Jeremiah's and Wilson's ongoing war over Wilson's music scholarship in college. We heard an odd noise out in the backyard, and looked to see what was going on. There we saw Wilson, holding the guitar by the neck like an axe and crashing it into a tree. He got in about three good whacks before Jeremiah was out in the yard and all over him. Jeremiah grabbed the mangled guitar from Wilson and pushed him to the ground.

Yelling and crying, he raged, "What in the hell are you doing?"

Both of them, breathing hard, wrath spitting from them at each other, just looked at each other, in a moment of love, hatred and mutual resentment. The flash of fury passed, and Jeremiah extended his hand to his son who still sat sullenly on the ground. Wilson wouldn't take his hand, but got up on his own. Maybe that was what it was all about, wanting to do it on his own, but afraid.

Fear that you won't measure up is a big dread to overcome in music and in life, and the battles children and parents wage with one another is the result. Edward and I had our own skirmishes. It wasn't long after that pivotal moment of despair over the plastic bassoon that Edward knew he wanted his life to be about music. When he applied to colleges, it was with that in mind. Our first tiff was over whether he should go to a liberal arts school with a good music department and save conservatory for graduate school or to start at the conservatory. Edward wanted to be conservatory bound from the start, but I had my doubts.

Yet, knowing that young people will ultimately do what they want, if it is really what they want to do, I encouraged him to apply to several conservatories as well as universities. For one prestigious conservatory, the application process was complicated and the forms were numerous.

After I had nagged him yet again about getting his essay written and forms completed, he spat out, "Why don't you just leave me alone. I will do it when I get ready to." I flashed hot, then cold. Alright then, you just do it, I thought to myself.

The deadline day came and went, and I left him alone. The next day, I asked, with mock innocence, if he had gotten his application mailed okay yesterday. A look of abject horror flashed across his face, followed by adolescent defensiveness.

"No, I didn't," he snarled, "and it's all your fault since you didn't remind me."

Rather than throttle the life out of him right there in the kitchen and spend the rest of my days in the penitentiary, I ran out into the yard, wishing I had something to bash up against the trees. Instead, I pounded my fist against the side of the house in thundering frenzy. Jeremiah, hearing the banging and the screaming out in the yard, came flying out the front door. So angry I could barely combine words into sentences, I blasted out a recital of what Edward had said. Jeremiah's eyes went wide and then narrowed. Edward had done it this time.

As I hit the side of the house, the pain caused my ire to cool. I remembered my Daddy whose temper caused him to try to put his fist through a solid oak door, only to realize its unyielding nature when his hand felt as if it were crumpling into pieces. Jeremiah called my name to get me to stop as my hand hit the house for the last time, and the vinyl siding split under my blow. I didn't suffer a broken hand like Daddy did, but it took us nearly two years to find a replacement for that one panel of siding. It greeted me there, every time I went in and out of the house, a shaming testament to my temper.

Jeremiah, happy to play peacemaker instead of enforcer for once, made a flurry of phone calls after I had calmed down, and received permission to fax the belated application to the conservatory. He was also the one who took Edward to his audition. As they got to the appointed building and signed in, the place was thronging with young musicians, all very serious and stern. Edward was assigned a practice room in which to warm up. Passing the other cubicles to get to his assigned space, Edward was treated to the sounds of his competition. Jeremiah later described the look on his face as cold terror.

Many of these musicians had been playing since they could walk, and had been playing for hours and hours a day. Now, most of the other musicians were string players, and so not Edward's direct competition, but if this was an indicator of the level of the overall competition, Edward, swallowing hard, might be out of his league. He played brilliantly in that audition, and was even accepted into the conservatory, but, perhaps as a reprimand for the tardy application, he was not offered any scholarship money.

Edward walked away from the experience with several lessons learned. For one, he had what it took to compete at that next level; he had been accepted. As important, however, he learned the price of procrastination, and that it may mean you lose out on something you dearly want. Although we joke about it now, I think he also learned that there are some things you don't say to your momma, or risk her turning into a whirling demon of death.

Jeremiah and I left the noise of the Chicken House to return to the night, now punctuated with the songs of summer bugs. We were both pensive on the ride home. It was a strange experience and took some digesting, I guess. There was the oddly nostalgic connection to the religious practices of our youth, some of which we loved and some of which we despised. Somehow, maybe I had finally grown up enough to really hear the music, and lose all the other stuff I had come to associate with it.

Regardless of how many false-eyelash-wearing, embezzling, or skirt-chasing televangelists called on Jesus like he was their next-door neighbor, there was sweetness and sincerity in the Chicken House that night that burned pure in the voices of the singers. Despite my grandparents' apparent flaws and mistakes, they had loved me and I loved them. In the crucible of the grave, maybe love was stronger than human failing.

Maybe that was really all it was about, to learn to be able to get to that place—where the love is ultimately all that matters. In that realization was also the unspoken hope that our own children would eventually see us with these same forgiving eyes, eyes that overlooked the mistakes and the defects and saw only the loving intentions.

When I was in high school, we played selections from Aaron Copland's *Appalachian Spring*. I got to meet Copland the next year when he came to the university to direct a rehearsal of his opera *The Tender Land* which the school's opera company was preparing and in which my college roommate was a member of the chorus. There was something very special about getting to meet someone who had created such beauty in the world. I would later learn that he was a real tyrant in the rehearsal hall, but, at this point, he was at an advanced age and seemed to have mellowed.

Students got to ask him questions, and many of them focused on what had inspired his work. He talked about taking simple and familiar things and converting them into something that seemed new and complex. Later I would l would look up the lyrics to the hymn, "Simple Gifts," on which Copland based a movement of his *Appalachian Spring*:

> 'Tis the gift to be simple, 'tis the gift to be free,
> 'Tis the gift to come down where we ought to be,
> And when we find ourselves in the place just right,
> 'Twill be in the valley of love and delight.
> When true simplicity is gain'd,
> To bow and to bend we shan't be asham'd,
> To turn, turn will be our delight,
> Till by turning, turning we come round right.

Those words came back to me in the car that night, and it dawned on me that those words and music specifically—and even music in general—held the answers to so many of my nagging questions about life. That is, how we can love and be loved, in spite of our flaws? Like why I could love and even admire my grandparents even when there were things I hated about what they believed. Like why Jeremiah and I had found happiness in each other in flawed middle age. Like why I could love my children and want to strangle them at the same time. Like why I could finally see Jesus in faces like Miss Jenna's in places like The Good News Chicken House.

Love, like music, doesn't have to be perfect; it just has to be the best we can give in the moment. It's just that simple, and apparently, as it seemed to have taken me so long to understand it, that complex. As we got home that night, the house was full of music, coming from all corners of the house. The younger pair was getting ready for the next day at band camp and another marching season. It is always funny as a parent when you finally get to live your own lectures. I had gone to the Chicken House that late summer evening with a smug superiority and left the grateful beneficiary of an unexpected gift.

Victory

THE WEEKEND PROMISED TO be hectic in a way that could take a special moment and crush it under the weight of logistical details if we weren't careful. To me, the most special moments in life are those unscripted occasions that just happen. That's why I never have bought all that talk about quality time.

You cannot manufacture a real Kodak moment, or it ends up being posed, artificial and perfunctory. How many pictures are pasted in Momma's photo albums of holiday gatherings that depict varying degrees of disgruntlement among the people pictured? Granny looks tired. Papa looks like a movie star from another era. Momma or one of her sisters is caught mid-sentence, fussing at one of us nine children to be still. The men-folk have plastic smiles—except Uncle Ewell who is in the kitchen because he refuses to be in any picture any way. At least one of the children doesn't want her picture taken and is hiding behind her momma's leg.

Our special weekend was going to be one of those hell-for-leather weekends typical of today's busy families with teenagers: difficult to organize, orchestrate, or enjoy if we didn't look out.

It didn't start out that way. The younger two children, Anna-Aileene and James—we call them the little ones although neither was *little* at fourteen and sixteen—had made the decision to join the church. Several months before, after a month or so of visiting, my husband and I decided to join this new church. We asked the little ones what they wanted to do and invited them to think about joining with us.

As older folks, having been baptized, communicated, confirmed, ordained, and sanctified in just about every way one can be committed in a church, Jeremiah and I would simply declare our desire for membership and be welcomed. Our letter would follow us from our previous church and that would be that. I always have wondered what my letter said exactly. Was it like a chain letter or even a resume with all the different memberships of my lifetime reflected in it? For the children, it would be more demanding. Their commitment would involve making an adult confession of faith—and in a Baptist church, that means getting baptized, totally immersed, or as they say fondly, dunked.

It was really even more complicated than that, but it always is. Jeremiah's and my marriage is a second one for us both. He has been a life-long Baptist—and a minister and theology professor to boot. My religious past was checkered. My parents' strife with Granny over Church was the stuff of childhood lore, and that struggle was passed down to me. When I entered the story, I was sprinkled, as were my siblings, at the First Presbyterian Church, but I remember neither the church nor the event.

Momma has a photograph in an album of us both on that day. She calls it her Madonna Portrait. In the black and white photo, with its now old-fashioned ric-rac edges, a 23-year-old Momma, her short dark hair curled in soft petals around her face, soft round and high cheeks, and smiling dark eyes, holds a two-year-old me. Our faces are cheek to cheek, our expressions the same—pure and expectant.

Daddy and Dawson were the reason the Presbyterians didn't work out for us. Daddy fell out with God's Frozen Chosen pretty early over the sending of foreign benevolences when God's children were hungry only a few blocks away. He claimed he would start his own religion, a reformed sect of Druids—who worship small shrubs, don't you know—and he would be its prophet, Botanus. We children rolled our eyes and giggled about it, but things got difficult when Aunt Norma would try to save Daddy's soul since he never went to church.

The last time I saw Aunt Norma a few months before she died, she pulled me aside to ask me if I thought Daddy was saved. At one point in my life, this behavior would have irritated and embarrassed me. Then, realizing how very sincere she was in her loving concern for Daddy and, on another level, realizing she was dying and wanted all her loved ones left taken care of, I assured her all was well.

But, for us, it was like father like son: Dawson rebelled at the idea of church membership when he was twelve. We should have known he would be trouble. At four, he accompanied his Sunday school class into the sanctuary. The children were told they were going to God's house and to be quiet and well-behaved. Dawson confessed to Momma after church, most indignant and disappointed, that God had not been home.

At twelve, Dawson wanted to know why anyone would want to join something as boring as church? Mother didn't have a good answer, so we visited the Episcopalians at St. Luke's. Our family's sojourn in the Episcopal Church was more satisfying and long-lived, with most of my immediate family but me—and Daddy—Episcopalians still.

Perhaps still under the influence of Daddy's aspirations to cult figurehead, I thought maybe it was because the church building itself appealed to my inner pagan. It was an old building, the second on its site, of the brick Gothic style, with half timbers and stained glass inside. It smelled of candle wax and lemon oil. The kneeling cushions at the altar bore pomegranates as well as other symbols to reinforce for us worshippers the idea of everlasting life.

Now, pomegranates are biblical fruits after all, but I never saw any apples or figs or dates on any of those cushions. Some mothers read their children nursery rhymes; ours read Greek myths to her babes in arms. Dawson was so enamored of the stories that he even prayed to Zeus as a little boy. When Momma found out, we started going to Sunday school more often. I guess my conflict was a matter of whose voice whispered in my ear when it came to religion—Daddy's or Momma's.

For whatever reason, St. Luke's captured our imagination and our hearts. The priest had been an anti-war protester who had mellowed into a local, loveable curmudgeon. His sermons usually raised more questions than they answered, and he always sang the hymns two beats ahead of the choir and congregation to keep the organist from dragging the hymns out into a small eternity. But he lived his Christianity in a way that appealed to even Daddy.

Shortly after our family, my brother included, found God with the Episcopalians, Daddy's brain tumor was diagnosed. Suddenly, a strong and vital man striding through his prime was reduced to crouching in the fetal position in a corner of the couch. We were afraid. As fearful as the illness was, the surgery would be a brand new and frightfully experimental procedure, and even then, the removal of the tumor might not mean he was cured. He could be blind as well. Complications with this type of tumor are more the norm than an exception.

The hospital chaplain as well as many well-meaning folks of the cloth came to pray over Daddy. One left an "inspirational" paperback book—*I Heard the Owl Call my Name*—about a young priest who fights a losing battle with brain cancer. Surrounded by thoughtfulness like that, it became one of Momma's jobs in her vigil at Daddy's hospital sickbed to run interference and keep the ministers at bay—except Father Stewart. For some reason, Daddy let Father Stewart come in and pray all he felt like praying.

Maybe it had been the way Father Stewart had faced our friend Earlene's house fire. Battling the smoke until the fire department got there, he rescued her dead mother's oriental rugs and precious antiques, bringing them gently out into the yard and to safety.

So, I came to my middle-aged marriage with four hooded rats, two kids, two cats, a dog and a goldfish—and as an Episcopalian. In an effort to bring our two families together gently, Jeremiah and I decided we had to approach the whole church thing slowly and carefully. Since Jeremiah and I were good Southern "church people," we wanted our family to have a church home and the support of a community of faith, but which community? I did not want my children to feel like we had abandoned the religious heritage of their childhood with my remarriage and our move.

We visited many different churches as well as followed Jeremiah around to his different preaching engagements, part of the life of a divinity school professor. We went to Episcopal churches, but the first was too hip and charismatic, singing pop spirituals with inanely simple lyrics like "Gee, God, You're great" which offended all the children. They had always attended churches that approached worship with a larger dose of formality.

But, when we went to a more traditional church, it was so dignified that they were benumbed with boredom. The building's beauty, in this second case, couldn't save the sermon whose text was "There's no place like home." Edward, at the sardonic and sarcastic age of thirteen, asked Jeremiah, his eyes gleaming, what book of the Bible that text came from. Jeremiah snorted. We didn't go back.

After trying all varieties of Baptist, Episcopal, and other assorted flavors of Protestant Christianity, we settled at a large and very dignified church in an older part of town, Baptist in heritage but ecumenical in practice, according to their literature. When Momma asked me what kind of church it was the only way I could describe it to her was as a "Baptipalian." The neo-classical interior echoed its structured liturgy and choreographed processions. It didn't feel very Baptist, but we always sang "Bless'd be the Tie that Binds" after the Lord's Supper.

The preacher was good, of the same cloth as Father Stewart had been, challenging his flock with more discomforting questions in his sermons than providing the comfort of sure answers. The music was good, too, and the building had a balcony where we could slip in and out unnoticed. Anonymity is not exactly the way one should approach being a member of a church family, but many of Jeremiah's colleagues, including the divinity school's dean and his eagle-eyed wife, were members there. Jeremiah did not want our presence there—or not there—to be of note. St. James'—although even the name didn't feel very Baptist—was fine enough until the old and beloved pastor retired and a new one came.

Admittedly, following in the footsteps of a beloved anything is hard. The new preacher would have to be his own man if he were to survive in a congregation as large and opinionated as St. James'. For all its elaborate Anglican liturgy, they were Baptists after all. Well, Mr. Higginbotham had ideas of his own alright.

There were the Easter and Christmas sermons in which he preached about the serendipity of the events. I thought Jeremiah would come right out of the pew. As an Old Testament professor, he has that wild, Moses-saw-God look any way, but at church, after running his hands through his hair in an effort to be quiet and still, he looked more like John Brown or some other wild-eyed abolitionist in photographs of old. Even the children's eyes flashed large. Serendipity, indeed.

Then there was the placing of the American flag on the altar. Jeremiah had lived through the fundamentalist's hijacking of the Southern Baptist Convention in the late seventies and its fallout. Now, that event isn't written into history books like the storming of the Bastille, but its effects blasted through people's lives just the same. A colleague of his, with a Doctor of Philosophy from Oxford, bagged groceries for two years at the Food Lion when his theology and his politics were branded heretical.

Many people think that the persecution of "heretics" went out in this country with witch hunts. They are wrong. Jeremiah's record as an alumnus of the American seminary from which he graduated has been mysteriously expunged. He simply does not exist.

With the Fundamentalist insurgence, being Baptist became synonymous with ignorance and bigotry in many people's minds. The very denomination whose early activists provided us with the safety of the separation of Church and State is now associated with intolerance, and a mixing of religious and nationalist zeal that makes folks like Jeremiah start getting jumpy and sniffing the air for the smell of smoke. He started emerging from Sunday worship with that wild look on his face, the veins on his neck standing out, his eyes bulging, and his blood pressure elevated.

I had just about decided that there really wasn't a church for us. Besides, even old Father Stewart's church had been torn asunder in the schism over homosexuality. I had always been a little uneasy about church, even though it offered familiarity and therefore comfort—a lot like kinfolk. It was probably Daddy's fault. He raised us to be skeptics. We three children had had opportunity to live our skepticism when we were enrolled in a Christian school, established by one of the local Baptist churches. Momma and Daddy weren't usually so reactionary, but after I had changed schools three times living in the same house due to perpetual rezoning, they decided enough was enough.

The school offered the promise of traditional reading program and conservative values in a world where "Burn Baby Burn" and "If it feels good, do it" were cultural mantras. The school provided me my first outside-the-family, real-life exposure to hypocrisy in action, where the science teacher required us to answer on a test that evolution and rock and roll music were responsible for the downfall of America, but he always found a way to be alone with Lorri, a girl who wore a D cup in the eighth grade.

One of my first real moral dilemmas was how to handle answering that test question, and I decided to follow a passive-resistance path by answering the question as he wanted it but by including a footnote at the bottom of my paper that although this was the answer the teacher wanted, it had no basis in fact.

Then there was Bible class where the teacher claimed that Louis Leakey had recanted his belief in evolution and found God. To myself I thought that was a pretty neat trick since, at that point, Leakey had been dead for several years. When I came home from school with stomach aches every day, my folks decided it was time to change.

As a child of the seventies and of a potential pagan prophet, I had also toyed with other religions. Most of my friends in high school were Jewish, and I went to services at the local synagogue often. I fantasized about converting, but the picture of Granny's face if I did leave the fold ultimately put an end to that idea. It had been hard enough to be an Episcopalian, but at least they believe in Jesus most of the time.

After I read *Siddhartha* by Hermann Hesse in the tenth grade, I was attracted to Buddhism. I read the teachings of Buddha and the *Bhaghavad*

Gita. Transmigration seemed to make a lot more sense than the Rapture. After all, even Emerson had found the answers of the East more satisfying than the epistles of Paul.

I didn't really think I even liked Jesus, to be truthful. The way most folks portrayed him was embarrassing and lacked humanity. That same year I also read *The Catcher in the Rye* and Holden's comment that "ole Jesus woulda puked" at the Radio City Music Hall's glamorous Nativity production. Maybe Jesus didn't like the way he was being portrayed either. Maybe what old Father Stewart said was right: Jesus has a lot of crummy friends.

Then Jeremiah and I found *Agape*. The name of the church was prophetic. For me, it was like coming home. You couldn't put your finger on the one or two things that made it right, but you just knew it was. Even Edward, having advanced at twenty beyond sarcastic and sardonic to ironic and wry, liked it. The church building, although clean and well-loved, was in a slight state of disrepair on the outside. He noted it as we entered on that first visit.

Very much like his grandfather to my mind in that moment, he said, "Looks like they don't spend all their money on buildings."

The minister at St. James' hadn't been able to answer Anna-Aileene's probing questions about Christianity in practice in the world—she was the step-daughter of a theologian, after all—in their pre-baptism classes, but she seemed to find some of the answers she was looking for at *Agape*. James, apt to follow Anna-Aileene in whatever she did at that point, liked the fact that the church was small and familial but had a mission spirit, helping people both near and far. Wilson, our oldest and most reserved who never likes much of anything, didn't hate it.

I remember thinking that Granny would be so pleased. Anna-Aileene got over her fear that getting baptized again—she was christened as a baby—comprised some sort of liturgical double jeopardy or spiritual overkill. Everyone was ready.

The baptism date was set for the third Sunday in May. Unfortunately, everything seems to always be scheduled in May, from high stakes tests that affect children's entire future happiness to end of year banquets to awards assemblies to concerts. For that reason, I hate May. It is not that I don't love basking in the reflected glory of my active and outstanding children; the problem is just that the recognition of their activities and excellence must be done all at once. The baptism would have to elbow its place in among band and chorus concerts, but that date was the soonest we could schedule to be sure that the older boys would be home from college. Life unscripted sometimes gets complicated.

The minute I announced the date to the children, Anna-Aileene wailed, "But that's prom weekend!!"

I took a deep breath, remembering all the times over the last two months I had asked her what weekend prom would be and her telling me that she didn't know and she would look it up later. What I *didn't* know at the time was that she and her boyfriend, a senior, were in heated debate about actually going to the prom *at all*. For him, that weekend was the opportunity for a Boy Scout camp retreat and the last time to get with the friends with whom he had camped since childhood before they all spread to the winds in college.

Anna-Aileene was understandably upset about this possible change in her plans since her dress was already purchased. My daughter, already a skilled litigator, was then able to turn their negotiations into a mandate on his support of her—of her religious feelings as well as of her expectations. As is often typical of life with teenagers, I knew none of this.

Although we approved in principle of Anna-Aileene's boyfriend, there were many things about him that had not grown on us with time. Maybe it was because he had never looked Jeremiah in the eye, nor had he ever shaken his hand in the two years the children had dated. Maybe it was because when he ate dinner with us, his face was nearly in his plate. Maybe it was because he was a spoiled child who had been over-indulged but who was resentful and mocking to his mother—and, he had never had a job. Maybe it was because he was a senior and Anna-Aileene was a sophomore, and we didn't want her growing up too fast.

Whatever it was, we secretly enjoyed it when there was trouble, hoping there would be a breaking up and moving on. This made Anna-Aileene defensive and resentful. Isn't that how the dance goes? This then would erupt into our own living stereotype of screaming mother and crying daughter.

Now, before I sound like an ogre, I must recount Momma's and Samantha's battles back and forth over her boyfriends, whom we laughingly called them her Alumni Association. Whenever one of the unfortunate boyfriends would become too irritating, Momma would offer Samantha a shopping spree, sapphires or some other delectable, just to encourage getting the inevitable over with.

But, despite the poor boy's flaws and whatever meager will he possessed in the overwhelming wake of Anna-Aileene's determination, both the prom and the baptism were agreed upon. I wondered what Granny would have said. Anna-Aileene and I engaged in our final negotiations over curfew, discussions that rivaled United Nations dialogues. Jeremiah stayed in the background during these debates. He knew himself well enough to know that engaging in ground level talks of this nature would send his blood pressure into the stratosphere.

Momma says that it was so much easier in her day and that *fun* has escalated beyond being manageable. In the Fifties, a girl needed a dress, a corsage and a date. Girls got together and did their hair. By the time I came along, prom meant a dinner date, then the dance, then maybe breakfast for several couples at one friend's house.

Today, everything is ever so much more orchestrated and so much more adult. Many students hire limousines to carry them to the prom. Schools release seniors mid-morning to attend hair and nail appointments. Dinner out is mandatory, usually prefaced by hors d'oeuvres at one of the friends' houses with a mass photo-op for all the parents. After dinner and the dance, the celebrants have an after-prom party at the local YMCA which, according to our older boys who chafed at tight dress shoes and cummerbunds, is more fun than the actual prom itself.

Then some teens' parents get together and rent hotel suites so that the kids have somewhere to crash after the after-prom. I may be old-fashioned, but putting teenage couples together in hotel rooms makes me wonder if we are living in the latter days of the Roman Empire.

I had not let Anna-Aileene go to "after prom" her freshman year because I didn't think she had any business staying out with a boy after midnight. But, trying to be reasonable, I was willing to let her go until two in the morning, but no further. After all, she had to get up for church the next morning and hopefully have some sense of what she was doing. Only some screaming occurred, and fewer tears fell; Anna-Aileene was not the only one with a will of iron.

The prom went off without incident. Anna-Aileene was beautiful, and she got home on time. All was well, so far. Looking back at the pictures, she *was* really beautiful. She has one of those Renaissance faces, like a Botticelli painting. Her delicate but definite features give her the aura that she has a secret of some sort.

Like most teenage girls, she doesn't know she is beautiful and thinks she is fat. She did go through a pudgy phase in elementary school, just as I did. But, as she grew up, she grew into herself, as Momma described it. Tall and willowy at sixteen, she carried residual fears of fatness.

Once we were shopping for an Easter dress with Jeremiah's Momma. Anna-Aileene was going through the agony of trying on every dress in the store in a tight confined space and in front of mirrors that most women swear are like funhouse mirrors, designed to exaggerate every physical flaw you have.

As I asked her through the door if one of the dresses was working out, she wailed, "But Momma, I'm faaaaat."

Jeremiah's Momma snorted—like mother, like son—and announced to anyone who would listen, "I'm sorry, but anyone who wears a size five does not qualify as fat." Anna-Aileene didn't complain any more after that and found a dress that made her look twenty-five.

The blessed morning dawned with an unseasonable coolness in the air, blackberry winter as Jeremiah's grandmother would say. All six of us got up, got dressed and got ready with an unusual amicability. Despite the size of our house, there never seem to be enough bathrooms, especially when college boys take their hour-long showers.

That Sunday, everything seemed to go more smoothly, and everyone was cheerful about it. We had reason to be a little tense, though. Not only was it the children's big day, but Jeremiah was also to play the piano during the service, introducing our new church family to his gospel pianist talents. With me reading scripture, we were all a little nervous. But the kids had their swimsuits to wear under their baptismal gowns, and we chattered with a controlled hilarity in the car on the way to church.

We got to church early. We always get everywhere early. To facilitate our various roles in the service, we had decided ahead of time to sit on a different side of the church than we normally do. All six of us are creatures of habit, I am afraid. Where we sat in church had been the subject of humor in our new congregation at first. The first time we visited, we sat on the very back row, but were invited to move closer to be able to hear and have access to hymnals. We acquiesced, but only a few rows.

With every succeeding visit, we moved a few rows closer to the front. The pastor noted our forward migration. We established ourselves on a pew about a third of the way from the front on the pulpit side as we settled in at the church. With the six of us, we pretty well dominated a whole pew, but the congregation made room for us lovingly.

On baptism day, however, we sat on the opposite side of the church, near the piano and the lectern so that neither Jeremiah nor I would have to make a production of going to the front. To set us all at ease, the pastor feigned mock surprise at our change in choice of seating. We laughed at our own compulsiveness, and relaxed comfortably in the foreign pew.

I have neglected to mention that there were more than six of us on the pew that day. Not only did Anna-Aileene's beau take his place with the family, but so did Jeremiah's first wife and her boyfriend. Anyone who tells you that divorce is really the end of a marriage is not telling you the truth. Once you have bred with someone, you are tied to him or her forever, for better or worse. A lot of the time, it is for worse or at least terribly awkward.

But, for the sake of the children, Jeremiah and I tried to act like grownups, which meant sitting with Juliana at football games, at band concerts, or at any other event featuring their boys. Parents' Night photos for the boys' senior year marching band show depict Jeremiah, Juliana and me with a grimacing Wilson. Juliana consulted me about everything from what size her boys would wear to how to treat their colds.

When she called to ask about the details about the baptism, I automatically shared that we would be going out to eat after church in celebration, and ask her if she would like to go with us. Jeremiah had nearly gone into apoplexy, but, upon reflection, he realized it was the only thing we could do. We shared the children, so we had to share their events, even though it always feels really weird.

So, there we were: the boyfriend, Anna-Aileene and James, Juliana and her boyfriend, Edward and Wilson, and then us. We were a pew full. But, instead of being anxious, with my stomach churning as it would normally do, I was blessed with an amazing calm. I attributed it to a minor miracle that occurred when we sat in the pew, heralded by none other than the spirit of Granny.

When I was little, Granny always had Juicy Fruit gum—in her purse, in a kitchen drawer, in her jewelry box. After giving us a stick of gum, she would take the foil wrapper and craft it into a cup, or rather a goblet. She would wind it around her finger, and then twist the tube of foil in the middle. Finally, she would flatten the bottom for a base of the stem and present the goblet to us delighted grandchildren. What should be in the pew but one of those little foil goblets, sitting where the discarded communion cuplets go. It was like a sign from heaven—or from home—that all would be right.

And it was right. The service was one of those special moments you find yourself in, and, if you are lucky, recognize the magic of the moment. The music ranged from transcendent to traditional.

A harp soloist began. Despite Mark Twain's negative opinions about harp music, the strings sang the familiar folk hymn, "Simple Gifts," through the quiet and stilled me. We "mortals joined the mighty chorus" with Beethoven's "Ode to Joy"; all six of us sang the parts in full voice.

Jeremiah looked at me and then at the children and then back at me with pride glowing in his eyes, as if to say, "Look at them. Remember when they were embarrassed by our loud singing?"

I could tell he was taking pleasure in this tangible manifestation of the harmony, literal and figurative, our family was capable of. As the organ sounded the grand and final chords of that sublime hymn, the children left the sanctuary to prepare for their baptism and mount the back stairs to the baptismal. I was then to ascend to the lectern to read the morning's scripture. I noted to myself how funny it was that, even though I am a veteran teacher who talks to crowds for a living, I had butterflies in my stomach.

As I walked to the front of the church, my heels clicked as I walked, making me even more self-conscious. Remembering it was not about me, I took a deep breath and found a friendly face in the congregation and began to read from I John: "Whosoever believeth that Jesus is the Christ is born of God."

As I read, I remembered Anna-Aileene's birth. I saw her at her christening from what seemed another life ago. I saw James as he was when I met him, with round, red cheeks, a skinny little preschooler with an appealing lisp. Now they were making adult decisions and commitments, asserting who they were and what they believed. The clicking of my heels on my return to the pew was drowned out by the rising chords from the piano, of Jeremiah playing "Victory in Jesus."

When he rejoined me in the pew, it was time for the children to receive their baptism. He and I were caught up in an old, old story not just of the Church, but of parenthood. Jeremiah and I wept as the liturgy was read, as our children's clear, young voices rang out from the cavern of the baptismal. We held each other's hands, my small cold ones in his large warm ones, in our shared and separate parenthood, and cried tears of nostalgia, of knowing what was ahead for our two children, and of the nearness of God in a moment.

After the service and the warm greetings of the congregation, we piled into the van to go to the restaurant. We normally went out for Sunday brunch after church. When Wilson and Edward had lived at home, we had our big Sunday dinner at home—crock-pot pot roast, or ham and sweet potatoes, fried chicken and mashed potatoes. With the older boys in college, going out seemed a nice way to change our routine but still mark the Sabbath. For this occasion, we decided not to go to our regular spot, but chose instead a new place, to mark the uniqueness of the event.

That was our first mistake. Upon entering the restaurant, we were greeted with the stale smell of Saturday night's cigarettes. Then, it took forever to get served. The conversation was a little nervous, with Juliana and her boyfriend Billy sitting at one end of the table and Jeremiah and I at the other. Billy kept asking polite questions of us and of the children. James started looking like he could be sick at any minute, and Wilson was starting to scratch, hives threatening to erupt momentarily if things got any more tense or if the food didn't come.

Eventually, to everyone's relief, the food did finally come, but to add insult to injury, it was terrible. The event started to take on an air of absurdity as we measured our relatively simple expectations against the actuality of what was—the bad service followed by worse food. Despite the hilarious horror of it all, it didn't seem to matter.

We were all together, even with the boyfriend and the ex-wife and her boyfriend. The bad food and our jokes about it served to distract us all from the awkwardness of the strange extended family group present. My brother used to say that you could have a good time or a good story. We did not share a good meal, but we did have a good time.

When we got home, we were all hungry and fell on the kitchen like a plague of locusts. Everyone managed to find something to eat and the frenzy subsided. Later, in the still and quiet of Sunday afternoon, I climbed up into the attic to dig through boxes of baby clothes to find Anna-Aileene's christening gown. There it was, folded in tissue paper, and it brought back surges of memory.

I had made this batiste gown by hand, with its delicate stitches, lacework and embroidery. She was supposed to have worn my former husband's family heirloom gown, the one Edward had already worn, but her cousin Zack was to be christened with her and, being a firstborn, he got to wear the family gown.

When I started the gown, I didn't know how to do fancy French sewing, but that had never stopped me from starting something before. I bought books, looked at pictures and just did it. I managed to figure out how to do entre-deux, shadow stitches, French seams, and pin tucks. I had worked obsessively on that gown, infant Anna-Aileene cradled in the crook of my leg, over many months. I clambered down the ladder from the attic and sat on the bed, fingering the seams and embroidery and remembering that day so long ago.

Baby Zack and his family were coming home from Oregon for Christmas, and my mother-in-law decided that the babies should be baptized together. Never mind that it was still Advent and, in the Episcopal Church, not a baptismal season. She managed to convince the priest to do a private ceremony on Christmas Eve morning because, to her mind, it was already Christmas somewhere. My inner Baptist, dormant at the time, didn't too much like the idea of a private service since baptism was supposed to be the first step to joining the family of God.

My theological scruples were insignificant to the will of my mother-in-law and her desire to have those babies safely baptized so they could go to heaven if they died. Her lapsed Catholic trumped my latent Baptist, and we christened the children that frigid morning.

To make it worse, someone had forgotten to turn the heat on in the church that morning, and it was cold enough to hang meat in the sanctuary. We could see our breath as we recited the liturgy. The babies, dressed in their gowns, new and old, were swathed in blankets so that only the crowns of their heads were visible to prevent them from catching pneumonia.

Anna-Aileene howled when the healing but cold waters doused her head. Edward giggled uncomfortably and tugged at my hand at what he believed to be her transgression against the dignity of the ceremony. He hadn't wanted to even come at first, bursting into tears when I had tried to explain that this was the way a person becomes a part of the family of God. In his three-year-old mind, this was a little bit too close to going to live with God, as we had described Granny's death to him, and he wailed that he didn't want the baby to die. Anna-Aileene did not go gently into piety, but she was not going to die, and Edward smiled.

The posed pictures from that long ago morning show a forced amiability. No one is looking at the camera in the same way. All are bundled up in their overcoats, forcing a sort of alienation on everyone, in layer upon layer of clothing. Insulated against the cold, we were also cut off from each other. The hugs look stiff—and they were since we couldn't move our arms in our winter coats. We new mothers look tired, the grandparents look anxious, Papa looks pale, and the aunts and uncles look eager to get it all over with and return home to warmth.

There was a brunch afterward at Momma's house. I remember feeling very tired and very sorry for myself that morning. I had been up to the wee hours for several nights, cooking for the brunch as well as our other annual holiday festivities. The beeping stove timer, the crying baby, the ringing phone of someone wanting to know one more thing—all demanded too much of me that holiday as I felt swallowed up by the mechanics and logistics of the events.

The meaning seemed secondary to getting through it all and putting on a good face. The brunch and the subsequent holiday parties and dinners went smoothly. The food was perfect, the table was lovely, and everyone seemed pleased. I remember just being glad it was over.

Sitting on my bed sixteen years later, the dress in my lap, I was submerged in that time for a moment, a time that was supposed to have been so sweet and so special but that turned out to be too crowded with irrelevancy, schedules and other's needs and expectations. Holding my work of art and labor of love that I had worked so hard on, I mourned over the years of misery that took me so long to acknowledge—but that thankfully had gotten me to where I was.

I grieved for my Granny and that she never got to see Anna-Aileene, then or now. I lamented my own inability to balance others' wishes with my own needs in those youthful years which placed me in that sad spot, chained to a stove, rather than finding a way to savor the moment. I missed my parents, eight hundred miles away.

But, for all that was lost, more had been found. Today with its terrible breakfast and its weird company was a day of triumph, of victory. The fussy baby had grown into a self-confident young woman, deeply spiritual, searching for meaning in her life and the world.

Her mother had done some growing up too. Instead of being a martyrish Martha of biblical fame, I had learned to let some of those "should's" and "supposed to's" go. Our restaurant meal certainly suffered in comparison to the sumptuous feast I had helped prepare for that cold Christmas christening, but I enjoyed the horrible food much more because it was shared in good humor, part of the setting, not the event itself.

Anna-Aileene had chafed a little bit about having wet hair in church and afterwards, after she had styled it so particularly that morning. I reminded her that her hair was a sign of what she and James had undergone, and that it was a special thing, not the same as having wet hair because you overslept and had to run out of the house, unprimped and uncoiffed.

The picture we took of the two of them after shows their wet hair, Anna-Aileene's blouse darkened in spots from her long damp locks and James's hair curling without benefit of taming gel. But they look so happy and so open to life, so innocently sure of the promise of life's goodness, wet hair or not.

When Jeremiah and I had first married, I too had chafed at things not being just as I was used to, but I came to realize that that was the cost of real happiness. Careless teenagers loading the dishwasher led to chips on my china. The dogs we added to our menagerie chewed on my needlepoint pillows and my antique oriental rug. A silver fork got a bit chewed up in the disposal.

Unhappy, I forced myself to remember Granny's underwear when she died. Although she had numerous packages of brand-new panties in her drawer, the panties she was wearing when she was taken to the hospital were held up by a rusty safety pin since the elastic in the waistband had long ago lost its stretch.

At her death, I had promised myself that whatever I had I would use and not save for some far-off special occasion that might never even arrive. We ate dinner together as a family every night—on Granny's table—with china and silver. I sewed up the pillows and repaired the rug. An imperfect perfect love is the best any one can expect, but you have to have the sense to appreciate it as it is and not mourn over what it isn't.

That night as was her habit, Anna-Aileene came into my room to kiss me good night. She noticed the christening dress hanging there and asked why I had gotten it out.

"I just wanted to think about it and you," I said.

She rolled her eyes in that mockingly tolerant way teen-agers have with parents and their sentimentality. "Oh," she said, kissed me and went to bed.

I looked once more at the dress and the slip with her initials and the date of her christening embroidered on it. Her initials were joined with those of her cousin Emily, Samantha's daughter, and her baptismal date. I thought about gently spot-cleaning the dress around the neck to remove stains left by long-ago baby drool, but I let the stains go. It had been worn and used. Those stains were precious mementoes of the lives that had touched the dress.

Later, when I am long gone, that dress will touch lives of babies I will never know, as Granny touches Anna-Aileene in ways she doesn't even realize. Even though the dress came out of a bad time, the fact that it was made with love allows it to transcend its circumstances. The beautiful children that grew out of two failed marriages saved the years that otherwise might seem irretrievably spoiled. The baptismal day with its warm love and cold food was a triumph.

Life with chipped china and a boisterous, rollicking family was a success. In that quiet moment as the house settled down for the night, I put my mourning away as I put the christening dress back into the attic. A snapshot of James and Anna-Aileene now sits, framed, on Granny's coffee table in our family room, a reminder of what a real victory is—love with wet hair.

Ties That Bind

My sudden trip home was more arduous than expected. A cold northern front collided with warm, moist, Gulf air to create storms over Atlanta. They used to say that you couldn't go to heaven unless you went through Atlanta. But the difficulties began even before Atlanta with the anxiety-filled taxi ride in the gypsy cab from the train station to Samantha's house—which I had noticed too late had no meter, no posted license and no rates.

With scenes in my head of far too many television crime dramas, I chattered to the back of my driver's head purposefully, dropping all sorts of hints about the significance of my life as mother, teacher, wife, sister, so that—if the faceless driver were indeed a maniacal murderer—he could form a human connection with me, saving me from becoming yet another big city murder statistic. Even as I elaborated on, I clutched my cell phone with 9-1-1 punched in and ready, should he seem to stray from an appropriate route.

I all but burst from the vehicle upon arriving at Samantha's, cool air and relief blowing over me as the familiar sight of my sister's house offered security against the unknown. The next morning did not start off much better. At the airport, either Samantha or I—neither would own up to it—misread our boarding passes, and we mistakenly decided we were at the wrong gate after we had already undergone the arduous security clearance procedures. We then wound our way through the bowels of the airport, through darkened corridors that had to be left-over sets from a *Dr. Who* episode, off to the farthest gate, only to realize, after once again taking off shoes, belts, coats and subjecting our belongings to X-ray at security, that the original gate had indeed been the correct gate.

Our hysterical laughter drew stares as we retraced our steps, less briskly this time. Samantha and I have always been a public menace.

There was that time we tried to run over the man who stole our parking place in the mall parking lot and then stalked him through the mall, trying to frighten him into some trace of regret for having behaved so rudely. Filled with indignation at his transgression, it took us a while to finally visualize what we must look like to him.

Thinking back on it, I would think our sudden and loud laughter might have been equally disconcerting to him as we went on our way to buy shoes or whatever it was we were there to do. Now was not much different; the comic idiocy and incongruities of life, along with a constant stream of one-liners, triggered old memories and new laughter, much louder than was appropriate for the circumstances. We drew more glances as we returned to our rightful gate, Samantha's long strides syncopated by my short, fast ones. Those Southern storms had forced an hour delay on our departing flight, which then turned into another hour for reasons not apparent even to the pilots until after we had boarded and were preparing to depart from the gate. It was already getting to be lunch time, and the idea of another hour's delay plus the hour and a half flight spelled a headache—if not starvation—for us both.

The flight attendant had already started intoning her speech about staying put, but Sam and I looked at each other. Six more hours with no food was definitely an emergency. Like bad children or escaping inmates, we made a break for it. Luckily there was an overpriced but suitably bland airport deli nearby which met all of our dietary restrictions. I had visions in my mind's eye of the two of us—not at 44 and 37 but at 84 and 77—the way we were carrying on about getting fed at the appropriate intervals.

Although Samantha and I talked on the telephone nearly daily, we had not seen each other face to face in a year. We were as hungry for each other as we were for those sandwiches, and our laughing exchange was silenced only by the temporary necessity of chewing our food. We inhaled the sandwiches, drinks and fruit, as we breathed each other in, comforted by the companionship that only sisters can give. Sisters. That was the reason we were on a plane heading south and home. Our mother's oldest sister had died the day before yesterday, and we were going home to comfort and be comforted. Samantha's voice on the telephone late on Sunday night brought the not unexpected news.

It was Sam who had also been home only two months before when Aunt Norma was diagnosed with ovarian cancer, a mutation of the breast cancer she had faced fifteen years earlier. Norma had exhibited strange and troublesome symptoms all that summer, and Sam and I had prophesied, after a little Internet research and over several long-distance telephone conversations, that troubling conclusion. It was not at all rewarding to be right. In the subsequent months, I had followed long-distance Norma's struggles through chemo-therapy until an email from Mother that Sunday afternoon heralded that things were not at all good and that Norma was hallucinating. That hallucination turned out to be the first of many small miracles that week. I cannot remember who told me the story first; it was told and retold so many times. Sam and I recounted it together on the plane. Norma had reached the nadir of her second treatment, the poison reaching maximum toxicity to kill the disease within her, but she was not bouncing back as she had done with the previous treatment.

She had felt poorly all day. As Sunday afternoon waned, she sat in her recliner with her eyes closed as her daughter Della read to her from the Bible. As Della had paused, Norma opened her eyes and fluttered her hand in front of her, saying something about a figure.

Distractedly and probably a little dismayed at her mother's incoherence, Della asked, "What, Momma?" "There and there, figures . . . angels . . ." Norma had responded in a quiet, breathless voice, tired, closing her eyes again, relaxing against the cushioned headrest. And then, in a stronger, surer voice, but with eyes still closed, "But I am not afraid." This exchange evolved from symptom to significance after Norma collapsed that night on her way to bed, never to recover consciousness. Even in the horror of that moment, Della said, there had been a kind of peaceful finality—as if her mother had stepped from out of that room into another one beyond.

Daddy, ever the Rationalist, said it was all due to the cancer in Norma's brain, creating the hallucination. Yet, as jaded as our collective psyches might be, reflected in Hollywood's portrayals of Gothic guidance of dwarfish mediums who beckon souls to "come into the light," Samantha, Momma and I later exchanged glances that affirmed, to us at least, that this event was something more than cancer cells in Norma's neurons. Sam and I finally arrived in Atlanta in the midst of the storm, steady rain accented with occasional thunder as we disembarked. We had already missed our connecting flight and now faced the task of getting another. Our Southern woman's heritage of Iron Magnolia-hood (which preceded the more commercially popular Steel version) provided us with strength and strategies to sweetly but relentlessly face airline bureaucracy. In a triumph of will, we achieved seats on the next flight out, leaving forty other passengers to wonder why we were so special.

Never underestimate the power of the determined, polite pseudo-docility of the Southern female. We had been prepared to exaggerate the immediacy of the funeral, shed tears or even faint, but such histrionics proved thankfully unnecessary. Finally arriving home, I wondered if all these near-catastrophes were prolog to some greater difficulty. Yet, what could be more difficult, I asked myself, than putting someone you love in the ground? Stepping off the plane, I stepped back in time, literally and figuratively. I had left Pennsylvania crisp and cool and full of autumn. I arrived home, oppressed under the Gulf Coast's extended summer's humid heat. The overgrown greenness, the air like dog's breath—I was home.

The humidity also triggered a spontaneous outbreak of pimples, plunging me back into the awkwardness of adolescence. The graying woman now only slightly taller than me turned into Momma, as she greeted us with her usual breathless kisses of welcome. Do we ever really see our parents? In my mind, mine are always 30 and 35.

Daddy was in the car, she said, circling the parking lot, awaiting our emergence from the airport. We hugged and kissed harder and longer than the short time since our summer visits would normally have warranted. Arm in arm, three conversations at once, making the obligatory restroom stop, we made our way to retrieve our luggage. As I watched and waited for our bags to be disgorged onto the conveyor, the cold front and moist air, the tears and laughter, the past and the present clashed in dissonance in my now pounding head.

Sam and I were grimy and hungry, both with migraines threatening, but the lateness of our arrival necessitated us going directly to Norma's house. Norma was dead, but it was still—and always would be—her house. Just as, even after Granny's death sixteen years ago, with Aunt Ginger living there and even redecorating, we still call it Granny's house. Sam and I regaled our parents with our airport adventures as we made our way from the airport into town.

In counterpoint, Momma and Daddy started arguing over how we should behave in a House of the Bereaved. I wondered again if I had gone back in time and I was a girl, not a grown up, as they disputed whether cheerful supportiveness—Daddy's choice—was preferable to sad supportiveness—Momma's option. It was ultimately decided that sad was alright as long as no one employed the Voice—that lower pitched, downward-inflected tone that certain sanctimonious adults get when they talk to people who are bereaved. I rubbed my head

and wished that I didn't have to be bereaved at just that moment.
It was under these tense and unlikely circumstances that the second miracle unfolded. We entered Norma's familiar house, tearfully embracing our kindred. The house was full of people yet empty at the same time. Norma's absence was palpable. The time warp I had experienced at the airport played tricks with me again; the little cousins whose births and first steps I had witnessed were grown men and women, husbands and wives and even expectant parents in their own right.

How could this be as I was myself a child again, in Norma's timeless living room, the scene of so many childhood dramas, the young face of Uncle Ewell smiling down from us from his portrait over the mantle? There were the faces of Norma's daughters—Diana and Della—teenagers with smooth, slim faces and long, silky hair. I caught a glimpse of my face in the mirror beside those portraits. Who was that tired, middle-aged woman looking back at me? Whether it was my own mental murkiness or that miracles are supposed to be shrouded in mystery, the next miracle's details began cloudily but, in the end, gained and gave a clarity that situations like this often afford. This one involved the heavenly agent of a lost dog. I don't know when the dog showed up at Norma's—whether the Friday before or the Monday after she died. I do know that Della's youngest son had been the first to see her, saying, "Momma, there's a little pink dog out in the yard."

Regardless of the actual timing of her arrival, Li'l Dog's entrance into our lives was significant. The small poodle-mix dog had once been fluffy and white, but through some agent, either accidental or intentional, she was now light pink. Her large, soulful eyes were accented with tear stains beneath, giving her a mournful expression, sympathetic, in our minds, to our situation. By the time I met Li'l Dog Tuesday night, Della had taken her to veterinarian and to the groomer's, evidenced by the pink collar which complemented her still pink fur.

The miracle became apparent, however, not just in the timing of her arrival or the color of her coat; when she entered the house the first time, she behaved like a familiar and long-lost friend. She had gone straight to Uncle Ewell and jumped right into his lap. Hearing this story for the first time, I had flashbacks of the previous fluffy little dogs that Uncle Ewell had tolerated to please his wife and daughters. There had been the notorious and neurotic Pepe Le Pew, who formed an inappropriate attachment to one of Diana's stuffed animals and was known to make obscene advances to people's legs in public—that is, when he wasn't urinating or flatulating indiscriminately all over everything. I don't remember exactly what became of him, but it was ignominious.

Much later there had been Drummer, a silver teacup poodle that Della had brought home from the mall in her coat pocket at Christmastime. Uncle Ewell, circuit court judge and rebuilder of classic cars, must have often felt a bit ridiculous, accompanied by such a poor excuse of canine-hood. Yet, in Li'l Dog, the name that stuck to the new arrival, he may have recognized another soul lost and alone, finding solace in her soft fur as she found safety in his warm lap. Also relevant to the validation of this miracle was the prophetic fact that Uncle Ewell had only recently watched a television movie about a white dog that brings healing to a grieving widower. Li'l Dog was proclaimed a ministering angel or even the spirit of Norma herself. I don't know which was the greater miracle—the animal's healing presence or our own willingness to accept such an event as divine intervention.

Even Daddy fell under the spell of Li'l Dog. He fell in love with her to the extent that he even, only half-jokingly, offered Della $500 for him. I remembered Daddy had hated Gus, Momma's latest foundling, who found a new home with me when Daddy was being treated for prostate cancer. I guess there are all kinds of miracles if grandfathers can find love in pink puppies. I reckoned it had been nearly 25 years since my brother, sister, and I had slept under our parents' roof together. So much had happened in the intervening quarter century—college educations and moves from home, marriages and a divorce, births of babies and deaths of grandparents, sickness and health, holidays and visits, misunderstandings and reunions. My last visit had been a brief one that summer to collect Granny's furniture, but even that had been the first in three years.

Our entire family had been all together at my house the previous fall for Daddy's 70th birthday, the first time all the grandchildren had been together under one roof. Our family had become like so many modern families, far-flung and busy. Yet, without question, we all returned to the scene of our past at the time of our mutual and present sorrow, all three of us children now gray-haired parents ourselves. It is funny how things were different but the same. Sam's childhood room had been converted into an office when I married, and she had moved into my room. The furniture was in the same place I had left it over 25 years before, and although the bedspread was new, the curtains were the same muslin Priscilla curtains I had ordered from the Penney's catalog.

Dawson's room downstairs was the same but for the pictures on the walls. Instead of his autographed pictures of astronauts and framed mission badges, there now hung pictures of ancestors, some in Confederate uniforms. Instead of Major Matt Mason's moon base was Granny's trunk. His old Lego set and a basket of Barbie dolls, waiting for visiting grandchildren and friends, were still there from of old, allowing the room to retain some of its previous character.

Now, Sam and I slept downstairs in Dawson's room. It made sense for us girls to share a room and have the twin beds rather than cram two adult women into the rather short antique double bed upstairs. I remembered the last time I had slept in the same bed with Sam, so many years previously. She had talked in her sleep with nightmares about schoolwork, declaring emphatically, "This is ridiculous!" Other things had the clumsy comfort of childhood. The next morning Samantha and I awoke at the same time to early morning dimness. With the gray half-light of morning peeking around the shades, we whispered like conspiratorial little girls. Now we talked of husbands and children, but our sleepy voices were low and childlike. We resurrected the giggles from the night before when we, over-tired and over-wrought, had removed the baby dolls that had found homes on Dawson's old beds.

What is it about some Southern women who never lose their fascination with dolls? I had boxes of them up in my attic, and Aunt Ginger's house was full of them. Della and I often fantasized about being old ladies in the nursing home, wearing bright red Lee Press-On Nails and carrying around our baby dolls. Sam's husband had drawn the line early in their marriage—no dolls on the bed. One of the dolls who inhabited this room was a Mammy doll.

The anachronism had tickled Sam, but it turned to hilarity when I, in my best Satchmo voice, sang with the doll in front of my face like a puppet, "Mammy's little baby love sho'tnin', sho'tnin'! Mammy's little baby love sho'tnin' bread." We wondered what our urbane and suburban friends would think about "Mammy"—or even what we ourselves thought about her in our uneasy armistice with our Southern heritage.

In that early morning time, Samantha and I confirmed a decision first made on the airplane the day before. We wanted to see Norma. Somehow it wasn't real to us that she was gone, that there could be a world and Norma not be in it. We needed to see her for ourselves, to confirm death's finality and to say goodbye. Our friend Sonny had opted not to see his murdered father in his coffin. He claimed he could then pretend that he wasn't really dead and could come home at any time.

For some reason, maybe because Sam and I had so recently coped mutually and individually with those illusions and delusions that become so apparent in middle age, we craved reality, no matter how painful it was. It was a tangible need to see our aunt and say goodbye to her familiar body one last time.

Momma seemed a little rattled by the thought of going to the funeral home. She had been at the hospital when the unconscious Norma arrived by ambulance. But she went with us, just in case it turned out to be a good idea. With her in a state of agitation, I drove us all in her car. Even though it had been years, the route to Dailey's Funeral Home, where we had said goodbye to so many friends and family over time, was second nature.

Once there, we steeled ourselves for what we were about to do. Momma's face was pink with emotion as the dark-suited attendant ushered us into Norma's room. Who should be there waiting for us, besides Norma, but Momma's other sister, Ginger, and Ginger's oldest daughter, Esther. The room was long and narrow and dimly lit. At far end, forming an altar-like area between two lamps, lay Norma in her blue and silver coffin, dressed in her pink suit she had worn in grand-daughter Helen's wedding. No matter how prepared intellectually you are to see a dead loved one, it is always a shock. There she was. We tearfully embraced Ginger and Esther, moving closer to Norma and to the reality of her death.

I have often heard old people remark at funerals about how the deceased looked so natural, like he or she was only sleeping. The dead people I had seen had never looked natural. They were stiff and waxen, mouths set, faces deprived of the animation of expression.

Norma, on the other hand, and maybe even miraculously, didn't look like we expected at all. She didn't have Granny's tight-lipped stiffness or Papa's wax figurine stillness. Instead, she was soft and luminous in her pink suit. Even her hair, victim of her chemotherapy, was sufficiently abundant for her to look comfortably familiar. Her hands, those knitting, crocheting, canning, card-writing hands, were folded peacefully. Most surprising was her face. She *did* look asleep, her mouth in repose in a gentle smile. As amazing as it is to fathom, we felt better.

The five women drew our chairs up close to Norma, I guess so that she would not be left out of the conversation. Ginger reminisced about Norma's devilishness as a girl, rocking the Ferris wheel carriage wildly and dangerously back and forth when they had once been accidentally stuck at the top.

We laughed through tears that we didn't know what Norma would do without her "nose rags," the converted cloth diaper or recycled tee-shirt she always had with her for her asthma and omnipresent respiratory problems. Ginger and Momma confessed to feeling surprising surges of resentment at Papa because Norma was dead, even though Papa had been gone twelve years.

Papa had tried to dominate Norma, his oldest daughter, and Norma had seemed to let him—and even us sometimes—think he did. Papa always wanted to be loved best, and Norma had a way of making him feel like he was. Both of her sisters had lived their lives in reaction to Norma and Papa. Ginger, the most like Papa in temperament, had married, divorced, remarried, divorced, and remarried and was finally widowed in defiance of Granny and Papa's inescapable but stormy half-century of togetherness.

Momma, the baby, had quietly had her revolt too. We didn't vacation with Granny and Papa at their Smoky Mountain Lodge every summer as Norma did. Norma had Granny and Papa over every Sunday to dinner. We had them for special occasions, birthdays and holidays. My daddy called his father-in-law by his given name whereas Uncle Ewell had called him in the respectful Southern tradition, Mr. Horatio.

Throughout our family's history, we had criticized and canonized them all. Whether one was a doormat or a saint, a bully or a titan, depended on where we were in the story. It is funny how life's story plays itself out that way. At a time like this, however, there seemed to be no distinction between past or present; they coexisted. A death can shed new light on the past, causing you to see the present in an entirely different light. The past, seemingly irrevocably finished, changes because you understand things differently, shifting the present on to a different course.

We left the funeral home changed. We kept repeating to ourselves—perhaps reassuring ourselves in the repetition—that we were so glad to have seen Norma in her casket. It was so unusual—maybe even miraculous since that seemed to be the recurring motif—for someone to look better in death than they had looked most recently in life. We knew that neither of Norma's daughters, nor Ewell, planned to see Norma. For that reason, it seemed important, upon returning home, that we call Della to share what we discovered, to at least offer the comfort of knowing that her mother was going to her final rest looking lovely. Della's voice broke over the phone.

We knew her last images of her mother were grisly. Her husband Ben had executed CPR on his mother-in-law as the EMT's gave instructions over the telephone. In death, the poisons of cancer and chemotherapy overflowed as he tried to revive his wife's lifeless mother. As if that were not horrific enough, their last picture of their mother was with tubes inserted to give her life where there was none.

Della ultimately decided to go see her mother to replace death's vision of horror with Norma's aura of angelic peace.

Our brother's arrival home didn't seem as blighted as Sam's and mine had been. Momma had been tense that a late arrival would necessitate taking two cars to the funeral home for that night's visitation. Different people call that evening's activities different things. My Irish former mother-in-law calls it a wake. My African-American friends call it a viewing. Since the casket would be closed and no alcohol would be served—Norma being a good Baptist church lady—neither wake nor viewing seemed accurate. Visitation, although evocative in my imagination of the Magi, seemed to be the only thing to call it.

That day was tense all around. Daddy has always found an outlet for his tension by doing things, usually initiating some project he had conceived of in a calmer time. Today, he was going to replace the toilet seats in the two upstairs bathrooms. This was a relatively small endeavor compared to some of his other crisis-inspired projects. Two days before my wedding he tore down the ceiling to the downstairs bathroom, never to replace it until years later. The toilet seat project seemed relatively straightforward except for the minor obstacle that Daddy couldn't find a screw-driver.

My father has probably owned a thousand screw-drivers, not to mention other tools, in my lifetime, but mysteriously none was to be found at that moment. This necessitated a trip across town to Sears to buy one. Momma got flushed-faced with the added anxiety; after all, her sister was dead and how could she concentrate on toilet seats and screw-drivers?

Since I had spent so many Saturdays following Daddy to hardware stores as a child, I volunteered to go with him to keep peace. I even promised not to throw up—a childhood problem I had when early morning and too much activity were mixed. Momma looked like she could throw up as Daddy and I drove off. It was almost as if the real life of toilet seats was an intrusion in her time of grief. The screw-driver procured, Daddy installed the toilet seats, and we could return to the business of grieving.

Later that evening, even though we arrived characteristically early, the funeral home was already crowded with well-wishers. Besides our large extended family, Norma's circle was wide. Thirty-five years of colleagues and students at the oldest junior high school in the county, a lifetime of fellow church members, as well as Rotarians and "Alphabet Club" members—as Uncle Ewell called the UDC and DAR organizations—not to mention friends and children of friends, people flowed out of the viewing room, into the lobby and even outside into the yard.

Even Great Aunt Edna was there, even though since her stroke she was stoically senseless in her wheelchair. The stand-offish Burns cousins, children of the sainted Aunt Biscuit, Papa's sister, were there. Papa's surviving brother was there, a homegrown character professionally called Curtis but known in the family as Clevon. He used to publish his poetry and advertise his insurance business in the local newspaper.

Since this was a Southern funeral, some really strange people showed up. One woman, a notoriously dim-witted member of the United Daughters of the Confederacy, asked Uncle Ewell what his relationship was to the deceased.

Then there was one of Momma's old beaus, Lamont. He showed up at the funeral home after having faded into obscurity some fifty years ago. Aunt Ginger said he seemed drunk; he certainly scandalized everyone by loudly recounting, in close proximity of the coffin, a story about a time he, waiting with Momma to go on a date, had held the infant Esther—now a grandmother of 50—and that she had "peed" on his lap. No one could divine why, after so long a time, this boyfriend, whom Momma had dated only because he was tall and whom she had dumped so long ago, would come, a drunk old man, to Norma's visitation, much less to tell such a story.

Sam, Dawson and I gravitated to the outer edges of the crowd, where slips in our own appropriate decorum would be less noticeable, and where we could visit with our friends who came in loving support.

That was, except when Samantha and I were hunting for our flowers. Although we had called and ordered flowers first thing the morning after our late-night arrival, no flowers had arrived from us three when Sam, Momma and I had visited Norma that afternoon. At six o'clock that evening, there were still no flowers. With that same unrelenting but polite ferocity we had employed in the airport, Sam had hunted down the funeral home manager to find our flowers.

Finally, hours later, the red-faced, navy-suited manager came to us to deliver the glad news that our flowers had belatedly arrived. Since the room was crowded with visitors, our flowers would have to wait to be placed, but Sam and I still wanted to see them, to make sure they were appropriate to our role in this drama. We were escorted past the inner sanctum of funeral home offices to a storeroom to see our flowers, among others, awaiting display.

Now, we were already worried about the arrangement since our usual choice of florist had been closed. We had opted for an alternative who seemed acceptable—at least they had designed a lovely arrangement sent to Momma and Daddy on the day of our arrival. Samantha, who handled the call, had instructed them to use the same flowers as in that arrangement—irises, lilies, and roses in a showy profusion, she had said.

But there, hiding in shame in the back of the storage room, was a pitiful excuse for a spray. They had listened to our requirements for no gladiolas—"glads" were so funereal, Momma would say—but that was as far as they had acceded to our wishes. On a relatively blank bed of greenery—flattened palms and lifeless leather leaf fern—accented with only a few nondescript and tiny lilies, a small rose, and a sprig of goldenrod, protruded eight, huge, white mums, refugees from some high school homecoming corsage, missing only the little gold plastic footballs.

These hideous, white blooms were arranged in a circular pattern around a large and slightly crumpled purple bow. The offending mums stuck out from the flat greenery like alien space ship probes, large and pale, occasionally shedding their twisted petals in a trail of tears of shame. Sam's eyes grew wide, and I must have breathed in loudly; we looked at each other in horror at the hideous flowers that would be representing us at Aunt Norma's funeral. Muttering, eyes flashing, Samantha turned on her heel. Luckily for the florist, their shop was closed. I would not have wanted to be on the receiving end of Samantha's failed-flower wrath.

There were no documentable miracles that night, unless you want to count getting through the evening. Uncle Ewell's demeanor was certainly remarkable. He is one of those quiet, long-suffering, coffee-drinking, Southern men, soft-spoken and sometimes melancholy, who would rather, during family get-togethers, sit in the kitchen. He was a judge, after all, but we didn't know how he would hold up in this crisis. Papa had been absolutely terrible—hiding from everyone, using his daughters as human shields to protect him from the onslaught of well-wishers.

But Ewell was another matter. He stood at the head of the makeshift receiving line next to the coffin of his wife, flanked on each side by daughters, greeting, gracious if grieved, everyone who came. Later he said with pride that Norma had chosen him because he was different from Mr. Horatio, and that if people cared enough to come see him, he could stand to see them.

Regardless of how often it had seemed to some over the years that Norma had tried unsuccessfully to remake her husband in the image of Papa, in the end, it was Ewell's quiet steadfastness and Norma's love of that strength that triumphed, as he tendered Norma through her illness, carried her to the bathroom but preserved her dignity, and found words out of his habitual silence to return the phone calls of her well-wishers.

Dawson awoke the next morning, the day of the funeral, with a song in his heart. My brother is notorious for making up songs that range from zany to obscene. We braced ourselves. Dawson's morning creation was a hymn, in honor of all the Vacation Bible School and Granny hymn-singing memories the week had stirred up. There had always been tension in our extended family over religion. Part of Momma's rebellion from Granny and Papa was over Church.

Although they were married at the First Baptist Church, neither Momma nor Daddy could stomach the smug, self-righteous arrogance of the church that had taught Momma as a little girl that only washed-in-the-blood Baptists were going to heaven. Maybe it had been the marriage counseling minister whose only thesis was that the theory of evolution—and by proxy the academic study of biology, Daddy's field—was the root of all evil.

We grew up going to the Presbyterian Church whom even Daddy fell out with when he questioned sending mission benevolence to Biafra when there were hungry folks in our county. We became "the family whose Daddy didn't go to church." When Dawson refused to go through Communicants' Class at the Presbyterian Church, we became Episcopalians.

Granny had been scandalized at worship so close to popery, with acolytes and candles and stained-glass windows and chanted services. Once Granny had asked us what we did as acolytes up there on the altar, other than light candles. Dawson had mischievously responded that, once you had acquired some degree of seniority, you got to bring out the snakes. Granny snorted but got the playfully blunted point.

Mother shrugged at her parents' loudly unstated disapproval, joking that whereas some women changed husbands, she changed churches. Granny never wasted an opportunity to invite us three lost children to any and every special event their little church held. Granny and Papa had long ago left First Baptist and started their own church. It was uncomfortably close to the time that First Baptist integrated, but no one ever had the nerve to mention it.

We had a pretty big clue when Papa wouldn't even go to a Billy Graham Crusade in the football stadium –even though Billy Graham walked on water to Granny—because black people would be preaching. Norma, defiant, took Granny to the Crusade, and then helped her order videotapes of the event so she could watch them over and over, probably as a not-so-subtle torment of Papa.

We acquiesced to going to their church only occasionally, always greeted by the flock of the faithful like the long, lost Prodigals. I sent my children to Vacation Bible School there with their little cousins because the Baptists, regardless of their variety, always put on VBS so much better than do Episcopalians. Our last memories of that church had been of Papa's funeral.

It was in that raucous, enthusiastic, but theologically murky tradition of Vacation Bible School songs that Dawson's hymn was inspired. The night before we had sung, off key to relive our childhood days, "I've got the joy, joy, joy, joy down in my heart!" and its subsequent verses, "And if the Devil doesn't like it, he can sit on a tack!" We roused through "The Happy Day Express" and "Noah and the Floody-floody" but only haltingly remembered the words to "There is a Fountain Filled with Blood."

Maybe it was in an effort to remember those words that Dawson's Muse had been tickled, because giggling, he began,

> "Bathing in the blessed blood of Jeeeeeee-sus,
> Washing all my sins away todaaaaaay.
> Using the loofah of salvation,
> I'm exfoliatin' Satan all away!"

Feeling moved, I started evangelizing, urging my siblings to "Get right—or get left," to "turn or burn" or, climactically, to "get sanctified or get French fried." Sam laughed so hard she cried.

It is one of life's ineffable ironies—or either God's wicked sense of humor—that I am now the wife of a Baptist minister, a theologian, a professor of Hebrew and Old Testament. Me, who had excoriated Baptistness all my life—or at least looked at it with polite disdain in the presence of my kinfolk. I was to find my soul-mate among the rolls of the Raised Right. But, as I was to learn, there are many varieties of Baptistry, and the sort I had been exposed to in childhood represented only one faction, just as those Episcopalians who like to hug and kiss at the passing of the peace and wave their arms in the air and sing "Kum Bay Yah" are not indicative of high church Anglicanism. As Granny would say, "It takes all kinds of people to make a world."

So, I have made my peace with Jesus and reconciled with being a Baptist. Granny would be pleased. I knew by heart the words to the hymn we would sing at the funeral, "Bless'd Be the Tie That Binds." Sam, an Episcopalian and too young to have firm memories of Granny's hymn playing, studied the hymnal, repeating the lines over and over again so it wouldn't look like she never went to church.

That morning, the family was to rendezvous at Norma's at nine to form the funeral cortege to the church. This church had been an offshoot of Papa and Granny's church, moving from in town to the outskirts, trading its hymnals for a "Praise Team," and sending Aunt Ginger back to First Baptist. I eyed the minister of this church from a discreet distance, taking great pains to avoid eye contact with him. Whether it was his very expensive navy suit and affected mournful expression or the fact that he also wore a wireless, microphone headset—looking like a Secret Service agent for God or something—I avoided my siblings.

Later Dawson said the minister looked like an anchor for Team Jesus. I am glad I didn't know that at the time or I might have been inappropriately tickled. Sam and I were predisposed to that.

There had been the time we went to a family funeral out in the country. We were greeted by a funeral home attendant who had a five o'clock shadow at ten in the morning and a voice reminiscent of Lurch on the *Addams Family*. Having ridden for a while, Samantha and I had to visit the restroom, and the comically dignified man had pointed down the hall the way to our destination.

We had been so busy not looking directly at the man to avoid laughing that we really hadn't paid attention to where he pointed. Unfortunately, we turned prematurely and ended up in a viewing room—an occupied viewing room. The unfortunate deceased did not have the benefit of Clinique's expertise—or even an Avon lady—because he was bright orange. Just as laughter billowed forth uncontrollably, who should enter the room but the bereaved family?

Thinking quickly, Sam and I both ducked our heads as if we were crying, and shaking with nervous hilarity rather than sobs, finally found the bathroom. For that reason, Sam and I avoided each other. I allowed myself to be distracted by more cousins whom I had not seen since they were fat-cheeked toddlers. Now they were grown men in beards. I made sure to find the bathroom one more time, happy to find quiet and solitude if only for a brief time.

Momma's greatest fear was the funeral. Here her grief at the loss of her sister would clash with a worship style we didn't share. We could make jokes and make up hymns about it on the surface—that is how our family usually deals with emotional crisis—but ultimately, I knew we needed something from this service, and we all feared we wouldn't get it. Norma's death left an empty spot; no one wanted a queasy, hollow feeling left from her last public appearance.

With a tense sadness, our family entered the church behind Norma's direct descendants. Initially, it did not look good. Instead of a choir loft and organ like we were used to in our brick gothic memories, a raised dais sported a sound mixing board looking like a sort of Karaoke for Christ, with an electric keyboard, bongo drums and a trap set. The windowless sanctuary, in lieu of familiar stained glass or even arched windows, had a projected picture of azaleas in bloom in front of a lake.

Beside that picture was a laser-light-show purple cross, also a projection. Momma stage- whispered that the picture reminded her of the science-fiction cult classic *Soylent Green*. Dawson rejoined, in mock comfort, "Soylent Green is people." I held Sam's hand, partly to steady myself and partly to have someone familiar to hold on to in that alien landscape as we entered the church, crowded to standing room only.

The next miracle dawned slowly throughout the service. It glimmered in the folksy but tearfully authentic appearance of Karl Bennett. Standing behind the plexiglass pulpit, he rendered honest witness to the impact Miss Norma had had on his life. Once a wild and willful teenager, now a respectable police officer in full-uniform-dress-blues and with graying temples, a husband and father himself, he spoke in a feeling-choked voice of Norma's loving belief in him and in the love of God.

The miracle kindled in the testimony of Sally Ann Knowles, once an awkward child whom Norma had fostered into a confident, accomplished woman, community leader, mother and friend. She shared precious relics from Norma's life and leadership as the first woman principal in the county. At the pulpit, Sally Ann read the letter of congratulation Norma had sent her for winning the science fair, the warmly worded thank you note for a shared recipe, and a later letter of recommendation which Sally Ann had applied for her first job as a teacher which complimented its recipient with lavish encouragement, modeling the accomplished life she inspired in others. Our Aunt Norma had not only been beautiful to us her family, but she had lived a beauty that reached out and changed others.

The miracle radiated from Diana and Della who eulogized their mother without idealizing her. They reminisced about childhood escapades, Norma's cooking, and a Mother's love. Although their voices thickened with emotion, neither broke with the tears we shed for them. Instead, their gentle, Southern women's words rang clear and true, Diana's lower pitched voice harmonizing with Della's soprano.

Even the dreadful minister couldn't dim the miracle when he bungled the reading of Proverbs 13 from the King James Bible by ignoring the punctuation and running the words together without any sense. The words could speak for themselves and for Aunt Norma: "Who can find a virtuous woman? For her price is far above rubies... Give her the fruit of her hands; and let her own works praise her in the gates."

Even when he all but held an Invitation in the final prayer, causing Aunt Ginger to hiss on the other side of Momma, nothing could overshadow the life of love we had come to celebrate. The image of the hands of over 500 people in the sanctuary, raised when they were asked who had ever received a card from Norma, burned more brightly than any purple-projected cross. That much love, sent in thousands of 37 cent increments over a lifetime, written by those loving hands, was a far more authentic testimony to the power of God than all the mangled, ministerial prayers.

Instead of a benediction, we all joined hands and sang, "Bless'd be the tie that binds our hearts in Christian love. The fellowship of kindred minds is like to that above," tearfully, clearly, lovingly, in homage to the often undistinguished and unrecognizable ties with which we were all bound.

The miracle burgeoned in the car when Dawson, a self-proclaimed agnostic and an always avowed cynic, quieted Momma's complaints that the minister had tried to save souls over her sister's casket by reminding her that Aunt Norma would have been proud to have led a soul to Jesus, even at her funeral. She had lived her life that way, so why should it be different at her funeral, he asked. I was quietly amazed at the loving tolerance and acceptance of my brother whose opinions were sometimes emphatic and harsh and whose strong feelings were often covered by jest and sarcasm.

The banked embers of the miracle glowed that evening back at Norma's when Ewell, surrounded by his loving kin, recounted stories about his courtship of Norma. I had never heard Ewell talk so much in my life. In my mind's ear, I heard Granny's piano playing, slightly sharp and out of tune, the chorus from an old hymn, "Love lifted me. Love lifted me. When nothing else would help, love lifted me."

Despite the distance of time or miles, the chasm caused by disagreement or disappointment, or even the depths of death, when nothing else would help love lifted us all. It lifted Norma out of her human faults and failings, and us out of our ordinariness and human pettiness. It was the crucible in which all that no longer mattered was burned away, leaving us only with the dear, pure memory of her love for us and our love for her—and for each other.

Despite her accomplishments and inner and outer beauty, Norma was no plaster saint. She was a tiny old lady who could eat more at the Chinese buffet than a lumberjack and still take some home in her purse. She was a breast cancer survivor who insisted on a breast reconstruction at age sixty because she had always been a sweater girl and her vanity wouldn't allow her to live without her boobies. She always bought on sale but there was always plenty of it, and even if that sweater she bought you for your birthday was not your color and cost only three dollars, she never forgot your birthday. She made the best pickles and fig preserves you ever tasted—I still had a jar unopened in my pantry—and could never throw anything away.

She had mailed cards that people received in the mail after her death, her love living past the grave. She was a tie that binds, and in her death, I finally started to learn the words, even though I thought I had known them all along.

Auld Lang Syne

"5…4…3…2…1… Happy New Year!" we yelled, hugging each other as we welcomed the new year and its promises together. This New Year's Eve was different, however, from any we had ever celebrated because we were standing in the middle of Times Square in a crush of a million other people.

From what turned out to be a disappointing distance, we watched what the television always depicted as a glittering and gigantic orb lower with the last passing seconds of the year. In real life, it was about as big as a pencil eraser from our vantage point, but the important thing was that we were there.

Jeremiah and I had decided, before the older boys graduated from high school, that we ought to take a different kind of trip together as a family. Usually, our vacations involved going to see family, spread across the southeast. So, the day after Christmas, we packed up the van and headed off to New York City. There we did most of the tourist things—Broadway, Radio City Music Hall, China Town, Staten Island Ferry, Central Park and the Metropolitan Museum of Art.

We had a wonderful time, laughing and enjoying each other's company as much as the sights and sounds of the city. In the midst of our entertainment, however, we received bad news in a phone call from home. Our beloved dog Bo had been found dead at home by our dog sitter. We wept at the knowledge of our loss, grieving for her and for ourselves. Edward, whose best friend she was, was particularly hard hit. Jeremiah asked him if he thought we ought to go home. Edward breathed hard and blew his nose and thought a minute.

"No," he said stoically, "going home won't bring her back and she won't be any less dead when we get there. You paid a lot of money for us to be here."

Jeremiah looked both sad and proud, a small milestone of manhood having passed between them.

I grew up reading stories about boys and dogs—and girls and dogs, and horses and deer and all sorts of animals. The animal characters of Big Red, Lassie, the Black Stallion, Man o' War, Flag, and Ole Yeller were utterly real to me, and our procession of pets were similarly significant members of my family. Bo was Edward's first dog. When he was about five, I figured that the children needed a dog, but the dog needed to be one that was low maintenance and low key. I researched and studied and finally decided that a pug was what our family wanted.

Puppies of all sorts bring out the child is us all; they are soft and sweet and innocent. Bo was no different. She was like a new baby in our house, inhabiting the play pen in the middle of the kitchen as she mastered house training—which took her quite a while. Her big, dark eyes, velvet-soft muzzle, and up-curled tail were endearing beyond measure. When she was big enough, she slept with Edward, curled up next to him on the pillow, the two of them snoring in counterpoint.

When Edward started preschool, Bo played Nanny to little Anna-Aileene. Bo always accompanied the two-year-old baby out into the play yard, watching her on the swing set or helping her in the sandbox. Once, as I watched out the window to monitor their play as mothers do, I saw, to my surprise, Anna-Aileene shed all her clothes and fill the wading pool. She and Bo were splashing and playing, having a wild things' rumpus of their own.

Bo watched out after the house and cats too. When I let her out into the fenced back yard, she would first do a perimeter check, barking that strange, strangulated bark she had at anything that didn't suit her sense of order. If either of the two cats got out of line, she would chase them, although Skitty, a Maine Coon, outweighed her by at least ten pounds. But mostly, there was peace in our valley, and I would look out the kitchen window to see Bo and Skitty curled up together on a sunny patch of grass, warming in the sun and with each other.

Bo had the biggest adjustment of all of us when we moved from Alabama to Pennsylvania when Jeremiah and I married—even more than the cats did. With her short snout, she didn't take well to the cold and frequently sounded like an asthma patient in distress. The first winter we had in our new home brought a two-foot snowfall. We bought a sweater for her and dutifully shoveled the walk so that we could take her out to do her business.

Comically, she looked out at the snow-banked lawn and launched out on to it. Unfortunately, she had grown fatter in her older age and she sank face first into the snow, her curly tail and her squirming hind legs being the only things showing. We pulled her to safety and kept her to the shoveled path after that, but that didn't really solve the business problem she had. Neither the walk nor the street, sufficient for most of the dogs in the neighborhood, was for her. She went days without going, and we worried she would be ill.

Eventually, we had the bright idea to dig a trench in the snow down to the grass, giving her a path to relieve herself. Sure enough, that was all she needed, and she looked at us gratefully as she squatted.

After the snow incident, Bo was frequently our comic relief. The older she got, regardless of our attempts to give her enough exercise, her once trim figure transformed into something closer to that of Jabba the Hutt. She would follow us out into the yard without a leash because she became too sedentary to run off—that is, unless the Chinese gentleman who lived at the end of the street walked by. Inevitably she would run off after him, tail wagging like a much younger dog. We figured it must be the call of her people.

She also had an embarrassing flatulence problem. When she barked, which still had that strange strangulated sound of her puppyhood, she would almost come off the ground in the exertion. In the exhale of her barking, she had compression problems at the other end, because her barks were punctuated with trumpeting from her backside.

She also developed allergies in her old age, and she would sneeze, showering anyone nearby. Jeremiah, the most frequent beneficiary of her respiratory distress, decided it was some sort of welcome in keeping with her space alien figure, a new way to communicate that we somehow didn't appreciate.

Bo, despite these old-age failings, tried to keep her dignity as head of the household, and greeted visitors warmly. As she had in her youth, she acted as if she were in charge, reigning over the house in her mind. Gus and Emily, our other dogs, deferred to her, letting her eat first. The cats were even tolerant of her when she decided that they were taking things for granted and needed chasing.

We even got a little worried that maybe she was going senile. She took to guarding the food, even to the extent that Gus and Emily were not allowed to eat. We managed her food issues and the other dogs seemed patient with her.

In spite of these eccentricities, Bo loved visitors. She greeted newcomers with a sneeze, and she sat on their feet as a sign of her favor. An old maid herself, it was mostly older ladies she blessed this way. She would sit in a peculiar way on only one haunch, a bit like she was sitting side saddle—again, like the lady she believed herself to be.

We returned home from New York and went out into the back yard immediately upon our arrival. We wanted to see the place where our neighbors had buried our friend. There was her grave in the garden, in a spot where the sun shone frequently to keep her warm. We cried again, and I remembered many other pet funerals I had attended as a child. Later we got a small stone angel to put on her burial spot.

I wondered what archaeologists in the distant future would think of such things—especially my parents' yard, a virtual pet cemetery. There had been Bebos, named for my baby mispronunciation of the line in the lullaby as "bin de bebos" instead of "when the wind blows."

Another dog had also been named for another of my misunderstandings, Cary Moonbeams. Momma used to sing us the song "Swingin' on a Star" when I was a child. In my child's imagination, "Carry moonbeams home in a jar," was instead "Cary Moonbeam's home in a jar." If Peter Pumpkin Eater could keep his wife in a pumpkin shell, why couldn't Cary be at home in a jar, I must have reasoned.

One of our lost was even given a headstone. Zeus was a special dog, a collie. He herded Dawson, Samantha and me and kept us safe through many a childhood escapade. He was a nurturing old dog with big brown eyes and a collie's smile. He fell in love with a kitten we had and carried it around by the scruff of the neck until the poor kitten had calluses on his shoulders and was too heavy for the dog to carry in his mouth. Even when Tom the Cat was older, he was Zeus's shadow.

To keep Zeus company as he aged, we got another collie puppy whom we named Hermes. Hermes was a finer specimen of the breed than Zeus was, but, unlike Zeus, he was dumb as a stump. The dog had a penchant for chewing everything and anything. Left in the car one time, he ate the entire dashboard out of our station wagon. He also gnawed on Daddy's fruit tree saplings, some of them clear to the ground.

Hermes also had irrational fears, especially of cars and thunder. Being afraid of the car was a problem since, without the car, it was hard to convey him to the veterinarian for his occasional visits. Being resourceful children and having the luxury of living out in what was then the country, we once decided to walk the dog to the vet's office, taking the over land, through-the-cow-pasture route.

Single-minded in saving steps, we had failed to account for the fact that there were still cows in that pasture and that collies are herding dogs. No sooner had we gotten into the pasture when their instincts took over and, rather than let our arms be jerked out of their sockets, Dawson and I were forced to let them off their leashes.

Cows are recalcitrant creatures that do not take well to being disturbed. After being herded for a moment or two, the cows must have decided that the foolishness had to stop. En masse, they seemed to turn on Dawson and me, standing there with empty leashes in hand. Up the nearest tree we went rather than be trampled or whatever it was those cows had in mind. It was a while until the cows got tired of grazing under that tree and we got the nerve enough to climb down and collect the now tired and panting collies.

Given strength by our indignation at being treed by a bunch of cows, Dawson and I kept a short lead on the dogs and dragged them across the pasture to the veterinarian's office. The dogs received their treatments or shots or whatever they needed. The trip home was uneventful; the cows had taken up in a distant part of the pasture, and the dogs had had enough herding for the day.

One summer, Zeus went missing. Momma feared that he had gone off to die, as animals often do. We looked in the woods near our house, but we couldn't find our friend. In a few days, some neighborhood boys found a dead dog in a stream bed about a mile away. Fearful, Dawson and I followed them to the spot to confirm our fears.

Sure enough, it was Zeus, his red leather collar offering undeniable evidence. The four of us kids couldn't move the dog that had lain in a streambed and the tropical heat for a week, so we buried him there. I will never forget the smell in that woodland thicket.

When Daddy got home from work and heard of our find, he got this very resolute look on his face. The woods in which we buried the dog lay right in the path of a newly-planned interstate highway.

"I'll be damned if that road gets my dog," he exclaimed.

Shedding his business suit for his habitual Saturday uniform of white t-shirt and khaki pants, he started up the tractor, put shovels and visqueen plastic in the trailer, and set off to retrieve his dog. We children followed in a strange procession down the road and through the woods.

The tractor cut a wider swath through the narrow path and easily moved the brambles we had battled to get there originally. Once we got to the stream, now deeper for the dammed-up mound of our dog's grave, we worked in silence. The sandy soil had absorbed some of the odor, but I could smell death in my nostrils for many days after that.

We unearthed Zeus, wrapped him in plastic and loaded him on the trailer to take him home. Zeus was laid to rest in the piney woods of our own yard. Later, a stone would grace his resting place, saying simply "Zeus, A Friend."

Hermes was not the loyal dog that Zeus had been. In one of his forays to find shelter from thunder—he would just take off running once he heard it—he didn't come home like he usually did. After a few days, we wondered if he hadn't met Zeus's fate, except that he was a young, strong dog.

After a couple of weeks, we got a call from a woman who had traced our name from his veterinarian registration. She had found him and had tried to keep him, but he was too big for her apartment. So, back Hermes came. Shortly after that, we realized that, since the town had moved out to us, having a dog used to roaming just wasn't going to work. We put an ad in the paper, and Hermes found a new home with a family out on a farm. There he could have small children to play with and chickens to herd to his heart's content.

I had a host of cats in my childhood as well. There was Castaway, a stray kitten Daddy brought home, having found her in the woods by the road on the way home. She gave us two sets of kittens, the first of which was a disaster. It was about the same time as my annual class Easter Egg hunt, an event that was part of every child's school year in those days. It always held at our house because our vast yard could accommodate thirty running children, picnics, egg hunt and a kickball game.

Unbeknownst to us, Castaway had just three little kittens in the days before the party. An inexperienced mother, she kept them in the bushes by the back door, but that spot absorbed the full intensity of the morning sun. One of the little egg hunters came to Momma and told her that she had found the kittens but that they were making funny sounds. Sure enough, they were dehydrated beyond our help and died.

Castaway housed her next brood, learning from this tragedy I guess, in the ashes chute behind the chimney, the little door of which frequently came open. Imagine our surprise when three little dusty kittens emerged from their hiding place. We named them Ashes, Soot and Cinderella, in honor of their beginnings. They found good homes and one of them lived to be eighteen years old.

Castaway was not so lucky. She had the habit of sleeping on the tire of Daddy's Lincoln Continental. He usually looked under the car to make sure no animals or children were in the way, but the wheels of the Lincoln had those covers that came down almost halfway down the tire, and he must have been in a hurry that afternoon. Tragically, he backed out of the driveway and felt a bump under the wheel but assumed it was a rock or a limb.

Momma, watching him leave from the front porch, saw the horrible accident unfold, and ran after him in the driveway, screaming for him to stop. Hearing her commotion and putting the bump in its terrible context, Daddy stopped and bolted from the car. Poor Castaway was terribly injured, and there was little to be done. Rather than extend her suffering—even the delay of relief that transporting her to the vet's office would mean—he yelled at Momma to go get the pistol.

Through his tears, it was difficult for him to take aim at the poor, suffering animal, and it took several shots before one was true. A tear-stained Daddy picked us up from school that afternoon to deliver the bad news himself. We hugged and cried and buried her in the yard under the dogwood trees.

The Castaway tragedy was only one episode in my cat saga. Each one had his or her own character and added to our family lore. Phoenix was a kitten we got from friends whose house burned down, his mother having escaped to give birth to her babies in the aftermath of the disaster—hence his name. Aquarius had the misfortune of eating a blue-tailed skink—or at least its tail. As with most skinks, the tail detaches allowing the lizard to escape predators. As an additional defense, the blue-tail's tail is poisonous with an often-deadly neurotoxin. Aquarius didn't die, miraculously, but he held his head at a funny angle and walked drunkenly for the rest of his days.

Kismet was a feral kitten we got from an ad in the paper. She was a sleek, all black Siamese mix, who looked very much like an ancient Egyptian statue of Bastet. She was high strung and temperamental—at no time more obviously than when she gave birth.

Instead of being like most cats who look for their own secret hiding place to have their babies, Kismet yowled and lurked around our feet until we realized that something was going on and that it must be her time. We placed her in the bathroom where we made a comfortable bed for her and left her to let Nature take its course as the books had instructed. Kismet would have none of that.

She had the clever talent of being able to open doors by some gymnastic jumps of her own device. Unfortunately, as she leapt to turn the bathroom doorknob, she was dropping kittens all over the floor. Through the door, I could hear her yowl punctuated by an ominous "schploop, schploop." To get her to stop, I had to sit in the bathroom with her in my lap for her to calm down and finish her job. There, I was exposed, for better or worse, to the miracle of birth more intimately than any film in p.e. class could ever introduce.

Kismet gave birth to six kittens that day. She was as big a failure at tending to her babies as she was at birthing. Sitting there in the musky smelling bathroom, I wished, like Butterfly McQueen's Prissy in *Gone with the Wind*, I could squeal "I don't know nothing 'bout birthin' no babies." The cat didn't seem to want to give me that option, and no one else in the family could summon the stomach to sit in there.

Momma stood outside the bathroom door, fluttering her hands in that way she does when she gets upset, calling out questions through the door. Daddy had things to do, and must have gone out into the yard to accomplish his weekend chores. So, not only did I have to hold the then purring cat as she labored, but I was elected to tear the sacs from around the newborns, to cut their umbilical cords with my fingernails to free them from their placentas, and to rub them with a towel until they took their first breaths.

Unlike Jeremiah, who prides himself in his 4-H and farm experience as much as his European doctorate, I was *not* raised on a farm. This birthing room drama was completely ghastly to me—but as much as I was horrified I was amazed at the wonder in which I was taking part. The whole thing was too much for poor Kismet, however, and she died a few days after the kittens were born. Not wanting them to die with her, I spent hours sitting on the floor of that bathroom in the weeks that followed, holding the small marvels in fur. Six tortoise shell babies crawled for, stumbled to, and mewed at me, their surrogate mother, as I fed them from an eyedropper all during the day.

When their eyes opened, they cavorted all over me as if I were a jungle gym, only to fall asleep, at once as if on cue, in my lap as I did my homework. They learned to eat solid food by licking it off my fingers. All six kittens survived, and we kept a descendant of Kismet for the next twenty years. They were better mothers than their progenitor, but they passed on her odd, raspy, and signature Siamese yowl.

About that same time, we got a dog from the pound, a bedraggled mess with matted fur and worn paws. But she too had wise, brown eyes, was small and cuddly, and when her curly tail wagged, so did her whole back end. We were smitten. Her coat was black with flecks of white, so we called her Pepper. Pepper became a beloved fixture in our family, accompanying us on all our vacations and every family event.

She was a merry little friend who wanted to be human so badly she tried to talk. When she was really excited, usually because we were getting ready to go somewhere, she would come up to us, whole body wagging, and ask "Arrryynngggkkk?" This inquiry meant any number of things, like "Am I going to get to go?" or "When do we eat?"

Given her advanced intelligence, it is not surprising that Pepper became a presidential candidate. Samantha, a creative child of six, decided to hold her own election, thinking she would try her hand at democracy. So, our Pepper ran against George McGovern and Richard Nixon, and we voted in the shower on paper ballots.

Her campaign was unmarred by scandal—since we did our best to cover up the infamous Bibicabad Affair. Pepper, although more intelligent than any dog who had ever lived --including Lassie in our eyes—was predisposed to some noxious inclinations. One of these habits was getting into the cat litter box, and carrying in her mouth—and thus strewing—the undesirable contents through the house. During Samantha's campaign, Pepper left her nasty evidence on one of Momma's Persian rugs, the one from the Bibicabad region. Momma found the unpleasant surprise, and understandably was angry at the canine culprit. Samantha found a way to spin the offense, however, mainly by cleaning up the mess left by the dog, foreshadowing her future work in politics. She won over Momma's sense of humor by insisting that she keep quiet to avoid the potential dishonor. I look back on Pepper's indiscretion and think that there have been many times in my life that it was a good day when something or someone didn't pee or poop on the floor.

The election went off without a hitch, and Pepper was elected unanimously. Samantha made her a crown, since being merely a president didn't seem befitting our beloved dog. Samantha had a lot of crazy ideas like the election. Her caterpillar circus was a big hit until she forgot to let the wigglers go. They died of malnourishment under her bed, which escaped her notice until they started stinking.

My own children's pets afforded some of the same kind of macabre amusement over the years. The most gothic of all of our pet lore had to be the Guinea pigs. Anna-Aileene *had* to have a Guinea pig. We had had hermit crabs and goldfish, and after those malodorous experiences, I was determined to draw the line at mammals. I was not happy about having rodents in the house, but I remembered that a high school friend had owned a pet Guinea pig named Ralph, who slept with her and who was a cherished family companion.

With memories of Ralph, I took Anna-Aileene to the pet store to buy one of her own. We chose a young female with long, silky, reddish and white fur. Anna-Aileene thought she looked like a rosebud, so she was christened Rosie and all was well—at least for a while. Rosie had not been at home with us but a few weeks when Anna-Aileene ran into my room one morning shrieking that there was another Guinea pig in the cage with Rosie. Anna-Aileene, astounded at what seemed like a surprise better than Christmas or the Tooth Fairy, wanted to know where the gift had come from. If I believed the pet store personnel that Rosie was a baby herself, this must be a second Virgin Birth and the newborn was the Baby Jesus of Guinea Pigs, I thought to myself. In that benign but vague way mothers adopt when they don't want to say what they are thinking, I said that I couldn't imagine.

Now we were confronted with a real dilemma. Our first problem was that Guinea pigs apparently can breed almost by breathing the same air as one another. Our second problem arose in trying to determine the sex of the new arrival. If it were a male, it needed to be segregated from his mother as soon as possible. The vet was no help, nor was the pet store. We bought a book and did the best we could, but Guinea pigs' parts are pretty inscrutable. We left Gift, which is what Anna-Aileene named our new rodent relative, in with his/her mother and hoped for the best.

Well, what started out being mildly sacrilegious in a rodent re-enactment of the Nativity descended into Greek, gothic drama, when, lo and behold, one day, there were suddenly three additional piglets in the cage with Rosie and her offspring. We were dealing with Oedipus and Jocasta Pig at this point, and it all had to stop. I promptly scooped up the new arrivals, along with Baby Jesus/ Oedipus and took them to the pet store which purchased them for resale. Rosie, after a few days, either in mourning for her lost family or in a spectacle again of Greek tragic proportions, was found dead in her cage, bringing an end to the horrible saga and our family's adventures with Guinea pigs.

Yet, the Gothic drama did not end there, descending from Greek tragedy into Edgar Allen Poe macabre. We buried Rosie in the azalea bed in the front yard, covering her with stones in a respectable cairn. Unfortunately, our respectable monument was inadequate to guard against the marauding mammals that came into our yard in the night. When we woke up in the morning, a wild-eyed Edward came to me, dragging me to the window.

Out on the lawn were scattered parts of Rosie, eaten and strewn by nocturnal scavengers. The most important goal for us in that moment of horror became that Anna-Aileene not witness what had befallen the remains of her pet. I had a memory of Samantha's rabbit Figgy. He was a large and unfriendly bunny who had kicked his hutch door open one night. His bid for freedom became sudden death when he was caught by similar night-time predators and torn to pieces in the back yard. Dawson felt somehow responsible since he had been the one to feed the rabbit that evening, fearing he hadn't latched the door adequately.

Just as we had then, Edward and I scurried outdoors to cautiously and quickly collect Rosie's remains before Anna-Aileene emerged for the day. It was a secret we kept from her until she was a teenager.

Our dog Gus came to us from Momma. In the spring after Papa died, Momma was outside one morning taking out the trash. She looked up and here came this dog, running towards her as if his life depended on it. As she stood there looking, the odd-looking dog jumped up into her arms like a felon in search of sanctuary. As she stood there holding him and talking to him in that way people talk to dogs—like they can answer—a young man came running up into the yard after the dog.

"Are you his owner?" the man in a tie called out to Momma.

"No, why?" she returned. "Where did he come from?"

Apparently, the young man volunteered, the dog was a stray who had been hanging out at the shopping center down the road. He opined that the poor stray was probably the victim of college students who had bought and then abandoned him when a dog wasn't welcome back home. Turning from the young man, Momma said that she would take the dog in, and that was that.

Momma called the dog Gus. Gus wasn't like any other dog you have ever seen. Lying down, he looked like a fine specimen of a gold retriever or a lab—lovely coat, drooping but attentive ears, squared muzzle, and loud, percussive bark. Yet, when Gus stood up, it seemed as if something had gone wrong. On that retriever's body were stuck basset hound legs. He looked like he was made out of spare parts.

But Gus could run. Daddy was not thrilled about having a dog, fearing being tied down when the empty nest promised new freedom. So, he took this out on the dog, rather than Momma. If Daddy was going to lose his liberty, poor Gus was frequently relegated to the prison of his crate rather than be underfoot—and he could be annoyingly underfoot being so close to the ground. Momma and Daddy's yard had long ago ceased being in the country, and the traffic on their street meant that no dog was safe off his leash.

Yet, occasionally, Gus would break free and dash with amazing speed for an animal with such inadequate leg length. He would cannonball down the road, and Momma would cry, just knowing he was going to be killed. Daddy would run after him or follow him in the car, calling out after him, cussing him and all his ancestors. Gus always came back, but the roads were congested and dogs get run over.

So, Gus lived a life of captivity on a chain, on a leash or in his crate—except for these rare breaks for freedom—until he came to live with us. He had only one other flaw—that there were certain young men who, for reasons known only to Gus, were not welcomed by Gus's wagging tail. These men, including Della's son and Momma's mailman, were greeted by a stealthy nip in the Achilles tendon. Momma thought it might be that these men reminded him of someone who hurt him.

Gus assimilated easily into our household when Daddy's cancer treatment necessitated them being away from home for several months. We already had the happy confusion of four kids, two dogs and two cats, so what was another dog? He already knew Bo, Edward, and Anna-Aileene and took well to Wilson and James, and so he was more like returning family than a new addition. Older now and happy around the children, he seemed content to stick close to home.

Yet, he did show occasional signs of his old claustrophobia. Not only would he not get in a crate, he wouldn't even sleep in a basket. I guess he was haunted by visions of his former captivity. With us, he had more freedom—at least inside the house—than he had in his previous life. He also only took that same mysterious dislike to two people, friends of Edward and Wilson. One was a rough boy who joined the Marines, but he and Gus quickly came to an understanding using techniques he must have learned at boot camp.

Once, Gus tried to make a break for it from our house. Anna-Aileene, rushing out the door to meet the morning school bus, had not properly closed the front door. It must have blown open and the wide-open spaces must have been too beckoning to resist because, when Jeremiah came downstairs to find the door open, there was no Gus to be found.

Jeremiah ran out into the yard, calling and looking, only to see a golden blur making for the woods all the way down the block. Past the woods was a busy highway, and apparitions of Gus's untimely and violent death flashed before Jeremiah's eyes. When we took Gus in, Jeremiah and I, knowing Gus's penchant for escape, made a pact that we would be careful with Gus, but, if something happened, it was just going to be one of those things.

But, that day, agreement or no agreement, it was Anna-Aileene's birthday. Not wanting her to bear the onus of having the dog get killed on her birthday, much less because she left the door open, Jeremiah summoned his reserves and went tearing off down the road after the runaway dog.

Gus must have thought it was a game because he stopped for Jeremiah almost to catch up with him and then turned sharply and scampered into the woods. They had made a big loop through the neighborhood, but Gus still headed ominously towards the highway. Gus headed down the sidewalk at a home stretch pace, and Jeremiah decided that if he were going to catch the dog, he was going to have to outsmart him. So, Jeremiah cut through yards and the woods, and intercepted the escapee.

Meeting the oncoming rocketing racer on the sidewalk beside the highway, Jeremiah, in an effort of desperation, launched himself in a flying tackle towards the wayward dog. High school and college pick-up football games—or greased pig chases—must have paid off because Jeremiah, cursing as he fell, landed on the dog, holding on tight. Gus quit running, the game over. Jeremiah struggled to his feet, clutching the awkward dog, and limped home. Anna-Aileene's day, unbeknownst to her, was saved by a Daddy's soft heart and ability to sprint.

Jeremiah also inherited my cats when we married. It must have been true love for him, since Jeremiah is allergic to cats, having been asthmatic as a child. Yet, there they were and he was too tenderhearted to suggest that we do them in. The most miraculous attachment was Skitty. Skitty had been born in the wild some years before in the debris pile that accumulated behind my house during its construction. Her mother and siblings had been easily trapped and taken to the animal shelter, but Skitty proved elusive.

So, I kept feeding her, finally successfully catching her later in the next year. Then I didn't have the heart to take the beautiful animal to be destroyed—as I knew she would be—so I took her to the vet to be spayed and get her shots. Skitty, called so for her skittish ways, never came in the house and, most times, ran from you when you came too near. She wasn't really our cat, but rather the cat that lived at our house. When it came time to move, I was really torn about what to do. I couldn't in conscience abandon her, nor did I want to trap her to have her put down. Jeremiah, the big softy, said she would just have to come with us.

So, Skitty, with Sassy and Bo, the children, us and all our belongings made the 900-mile journey to our new home in her own blue plastic cat carrier. Caught and drugged—Jeremiah's skill with animals once again proving invaluable—she made it almost all the way to our new home in the outskirts of Philadelphia before coming too about an hour before our arrival. "I-wanna-get-out-nowwwww," she would yowl.

Upon arriving and getting settled, we left her in the cage for a few days so she could get used to the sights, sounds and smells of the new place, feeding her through the little trap door of her prison. Once released, she hid in the bowels of the house, and we feared that she would hide forever. Eventually, she did emerge, and then only at night, when Jeremiah was unwinding with his late-night news shows. She would follow him on his evening walks. There they became friends—or at least allies.

Somehow, Skitty escaped from the house and went missing just before Thanksgiving. Jeremiah combed the woods near the house calling for her, but there was no sign. We feared that the allure of the new world was too much for her and she had gone native. A month later, who should scratch at the sliding glass door but Skitty, an early Christmas present, ready to come in after having had whatever adventures she had had.

She didn't ever leave the house much after that. Every night, she would sit with Jeremiah on the couch and watch the news, gradually getting closer and closer over the years, until finally, she would sit right next to him, her head on his knee. He never really did like cats, and she made him sneeze, but who can turn away a love like that?

So, even though our New Year's celebration in New York was marred by the loss of our friend Bo, she is ever with us in memory, joining the roll call of other sainted pets from years past. Some folks will say, your pets aren't people. Yet others, like my former mother-in-law, despairing that she would ever have grandchildren, had a bumper sticker that encouraged passersby to "Ask me about my dogs." Her dogs were her family after my father-in-law died in a way that no human could ever be.

I have known people whose pets had a place at the table and who took "walks" in baby carriages when they got too old to walk alone. Jeremiah's Uncle Bernard bought a golf cart because his beloved collie Sunny was too arthritic to accompany him on his rambles through the woods. I love my pets, but I am not that bad.

When one of my childhood cats kept having accidents on my great-grandmother's sofa because she was not pleased with something, Momma warned us that dead cats don't have accidents. She never did any such thing, but we knew there was a line between man and beast. Often though, we wondered on what side of that line we fell when we irritated Momma enough.

I am fascinated by Koko the gorilla, I guess as a residue of my childhood admiration of Jane Goodall. Koko is the ape who was taught to "speak" using the sign language of the deaf. Her fame has spread far and wide, especially to young children, through several documentaries, a book and even a web page. Koko now has the vocabulary of a six-year-old child, makes up new words in the absence of adequate vocabulary, tells stories, expresses feelings, and recounts events.

Koko also had a pet kitten whom she named All-Ball because it slept balled up in her lap. All-Ball happened to escape the safety of their cage one day and got run over. Koko grieved for her little friend. The public, seeking to comfort the amazing ape, sought to assuage her with gifts of new kittens. She finally chose one, a tailless one like All-Ball, whom she named Lipstick. If Koko is any sort of mirror to humanity, it must be an essential part of our personhood to love and protect those things that are smaller and more vulnerable than ourselves—whom we love just for being and who love us in the same way.

I think the pageant of pets I had in my growing up years and beyond is also a measure of who and what I am—or what any of us is. My ability to measure time in my life is marked by their time with us. With our pets, we can be children and parents at the same time, frolicking with our furry family members while learning lessons about nurture. Maybe animals teach us about being human, offering us a chance to drink deep in that ageless cup of kindness we sang about at New Year's.

School Days

IF YOU ASK MOST people when the New Year is, they will probably first look at you like you are an idiot or look for the hidden camera, and then respond with the patently obvious answer of January 1.

Actually, the question does have more than one answer. If you are Chinese, the new year begins on the first day of the first lunar month. That could be as late as February sometimes, depending on the moon's cycle.

Jews celebrate the new year with Rosh Hashanah in September or even October. In the Christian Church calendar, the acknowledgement of a new year's cycle begins with Advent in November or December.

For school teachers, however, the year begins the day after Labor Day, and we measure our lives in school terms. Instead of champagne and confetti to mark our new beginning, teachers, regardless of what level they teach, stock up on pencils and dry erase markers, construction paper and Kleenex tissues. Rather than resolutions to accomplish, we make lesson plans, blocked out through the weeks of the school year.

With the same expectancy as those who watch the bejeweled ball descend at Time Square, teachers look at pristine grade books, awaiting the achievements of another crop of kids. We decorate our classrooms with bulletin boards and posters in anticipation of the arrival of the children. Having spent the week before the students arrive in meetings and preparation, most of us cannot sleep the night before school starts for the butterflies in our stomachs. You would think we were going to Disney World—and that we had never really grown up.

I think the bug bites some of us early. Most of the little girls I grew up with played "school," but not everyone had a grade book for her dolls like I did. Momma schooled me at home instead of sending me to kindergarten; it was not mandatory at that time, and I was young in my peer group with my December birthday. I sat on the tall stool at the kitchen counter with a large pad of art paper and crayons in front of me and learned to write my ABC's. I remember the triumph of learning to spell "beautiful."

Sheltered like that, starting school was actually a little traumatic. The noise and chaos—not to mention the strange smells—of the school building were scary. I had grown to the ripe age of five in relative solitude, with visits to cousins, grandparents, church, and the public library as my main interactions with my fellow human beings. Teeming crowds of anonymous children on the playground were overwhelming. I told my mother I was not sure I wanted to eat with strangers.

Despite the new blue and white striped seersucker dress, new Mary Jane shoes, and new taffeta ribbons in my pigtails, my first day of school was a disaster. It went well at first. Daddy had escorted me from the car through the hazards of the playground into my new classroom at Marjorie Rawlings Memorial. I had arrived with my transformed cigar box filled with big fat color crayons, fat yellow pencils with pristine erasers, scissors and other school necessities and successfully deposited it in the cubbyhole under the desk with my name on it.

I can still smell the special aroma of that box when you opened it, with its odd mixture of tobacco and crayons. My Mary Poppins lunchbox was placed on the shelf with all the others, lined up neatly in a row. Daddy left, and I remember feeling only a little bit queasy. My teacher, Mrs. Myrtle McDaniel, was soothingly matronly in her crisp cotton print blouse, dark skirt and Hushpuppy shoes. She looked like somebody's grandmother, and I guessed I would be in good hands.

Things went pretty well until lunch time. We started reading the first day, and I was excited. Mrs. McDaniel opened the giant book—large enough for us all to see from its place at the front of the class—whose first word was "Look!" The illustrations depicted Baby Sally with Daddy's galoshes on, splashing in a puddle. Brother Dick, always the goody-goody, was telling Mother, but sister Jane was laughing.

That seemed normal enough, and I felt confident about reading based on my kitchen counter lessons. I survived marching in line out to the playground for recess. I feared getting lost in the cavernous old building and never finding my way back again, so I stayed carefully close to the child in front of me. I had waited my turn for the swings and even climbed the jungle gym, being careful not to get my dress dirty.

Lunch time came and we lined up to wind our way downstairs to the lunch room. I guess I was preoccupied with my fears of the unknown as well as my anxiety about eating with all those children in one place that I didn't listen to the instructions. We were supposed to enter down the right-side aisle and exit down the left. That was fine. The part I missed was where to throw our trash, using the can closest to us for efficiency.

For some reason, I missed seeing the one near the end of our long table and ventured down the center aisle toward the front of the lunch room. Unbeknownst to me, there had been an accident of some sort which had to be mopped up, leaving the tile floor very slick. As I approached the trashcan, my feet slipped and I fell forward, hitting my mouth on my lunch box. A nearby teacher rushed towards me, helping me back to my feet, wiping my tears and my bloody lip. Gently, she said that she thought I belonged back there with my class and returned me to my table.

I was humiliated. In those days primary grades only went for a half day for the first two weeks of school to get children acclimated to the school day. School ended shortly after lunch, and I told Momma once we were reunited that I didn't think I was ever going back.

I did go back, and I have been going back in one form or another for over forty years. The schools changed, and my role changed, but every September rolls around with the same anticipated journey. My decision to become a teacher was not an immediate one, however, despite my playtime grade books. By high school, I had fantasies of walking in the steps of Jane Goodall in the jungles of Tanzania or following the likes of Joan Baez on the stage in song and protest.

But I loved learning and literature. I had spent most of my childhood with my nose in a book. Our public library was an old building with oiled oak floors that creaked when you walked over them. Four stories tall, the building offered floors dedicated to different purposes. The basement was for the children, a cool cave with low ceilings and braided rugs to lie on to read. The main floor was for circulation and welcomed you with its banks of card catalogs, filling the walls on both sides of that enormous room. Now there are no more card catalogs, only databases on the computer.

Reference resources were housed conveniently near the circulation desk so that the librarians could easily help students and check out books. The next floor was my favorite floor—the stacks of fiction. I would wander along the tall stacks, selecting books off the shelf at random for the sheer joy of discovery, pretending I was in some medieval labyrinth. My eclectic tastes were fed as Daddy read us Kafka and Ambrose Bierce, and Momma read us Homer and Robert Louis Stevenson.

Rarely did our family dinners end without someone having to consult the unabridged dictionary that lay on the accessible bottom shelf of the nearby cabinet. We were even known to interrupt family vacations to find a local public library in the middle of nowhere to look up how a word should be pronounced or used or what its etymology was. It is little wonder then that English was always my favorite class.

Growing up, I spent many hours in the window seat haven in my bedroom, looking out on the world below, snuggled up with a book. The safe fortress of fiction peopled my imagination with characters from Dickens or Hardy, and filled my heart with the poetry of Coleridge or Whitman. I devoured each new work like someone starving in the wilderness. Geometry and algebra may have mystified me, but the secrets of the written word enthralled me.

During my senior year, I gave a presentation to my English class on Voltaire's *Candide*, since I had read it in French as well as in English. After class, my teacher looked at me and said with sudden seriousness, "You really ought to think about being a teacher, you know." Embarrassed, I laughed, and asked her if I could trade my copy of *The Mayor of Casterbridge* for *Jude the Obscure*, since I had finished the former the night before. She laughed and shook her head at my single-mindedness, knowing in her wisdom what I didn't know then—that my focus on fiction would turn into a calling. It isn't surprising that I majored in English with a concentration in literature in college.

Momma credits her influence on my decision to become a high school English teacher. She forbade me from graduating from college without a marketable skill. I didn't want to major in education, but I could take courses to satisfy requirements for certification. That added an education minor to my very practical English literature major and humanities minor, satisfying Momma.

I hated most of my education classes because they seemed to focus on irrelevant generalities or superficial specifics, yet I began to give teaching serious consideration. After all, it made good use of all my character flaws: I am a bossy, big sister know-it-all. I did my student teaching at the high school from which I graduated—and, historically, from which my siblings, my mother and both of her sisters graduated.

The same teacher who had recognized my passion for *Candide* pulled strings to allow me to intern with her before she retired. At first, it was a little like living in limbo, since most of the other teachers remembered me as a student rather than recognizing me as a peer. Then there were the times I was stopped in the hall and required to produce a pass or charged only the student price for milk in the lunchroom. Yet, the school that had been a bit uncomfortable for me as a student was ideal for me as a teacher. Its red brick solidity welcomed me every morning. Its black tiled halls, still fragrant with the spearmint-smelling green stuff they throw on the floors to attract dirt, were familiar and comfortable. As I entered into new territory professionally, it was reassuring to come to a building I knew like the back of my hand.

I got my first job accidentally. One of the teachers at the school where I did my student teaching had a nervous breakdown; her husband had left her, having first cleaned out their bank account. I was hired to take her place midyear. After the first week of taking her classes, I found myself wondering if the job hadn't contributed to her emotional collapse.

First, I had four different preparations: a remedial and two standard ninth grades and remedial and standard tenth grades. Next, the classroom was situated on the third floor right next to the boys' bathroom, facing the searing afternoon sun in a building that wasn't air conditioned. The building had those old-style windows that swing open with a hook on a pole, and tall eighteen-foot ceilings in defense against the heat. Neither the ceilings nor the windows nor the fans I brought in did much good, and I frequently went home looking more like I had run the track than taught English all day. I learned to teach over the whir of four oscillating fans without yelling and losing my voice.

Yet, the heat took its toll. The stifling heat and something from the lunchroom invariably combined disastrously by the end of many a day. At least once a week, someone would get sick but not quite make it to the bathroom, losing his lunch right in front of my door. If that weren't bad enough, the pranksters who weren't satisfied with leaving dead squirrels in the bathroom regularly tried to flush an M-80 or some other contraband explosive device down the toilet. With the explosions, my reluctant scholars would be lost for the remainder of the class period.

Although I have a missionary zeal about teaching, about literature, and about children, being a teacher exposed me to the full spectrum of humanity, introducing me to a side of life I might just as soon not known about. That first class was an eye opener. I had several boys who chewed tobacco and would spit into cups which they left under the desks. I didn't have friends who partook of that sort of tobacco product, so the first time I dumped the desks over to empty the trash on the floor to help the custodians, I was horrified by flood of nauseating amber spit that spilled on to the floor when the cups were upended.

The next day, I told my classes that whoever was caught with one of those spit-filled cups would have to drink the contents. The boys looked at me in disbelief and indignation, chins lifted defiantly. Sure enough, one had to test me, and I had to carry out my threat. On that day, it was a good thing we were close to the boys' restroom because the offender promptly got violently ill. I didn't find any more spit cups after that.

Nor did studying John Milton prepare me for the depths of human poverty, ignorance, and misery I encountered on a regular basis that year. There was Tammy, a pasty and pudgy faced child who struggled with her work but who was eager to please. Frequently, even though her class was in the morning, when I walked past her desk, I was overpowered with body odor.

When I was able to determine who the offender was, I went to the counselor to ask for advice as to how to handle her problem. She suggested I send the child to her on some pretext, and she could broach the subject discreetly. It turned out that Tammy and her family lived way out in the country at the county line in a shack with no electricity and no running water. This wasn't Appalachia after all; our school was affluent and boasted double digit National Merit finalists each year. Such conditions astounded me in the waning years of the twentieth century. The nurse and I bought Tammy a supply of deodorant and hygiene products, and that took care of the odor predicament.

Tammy's difficulties were quickly to be topped by those of Schedule (pronounced Sha-doo-lee), whose name first attracted my interest. I wondered what universe created a mom who saw that word and thought it was a fitting first gift to give her child. Schedule secured my immediate attention when she came forward in the middle of class one day. Schedule was a tall, ungainly girl, towering over me and outweighing me by at least a hundred pounds. Insisting on drawing me aside in confidence, she whispered that she needed to tell me something.

Ever suspicious of mischief, I must have frowned.

"Pleeeease," she said, "It's an emergency."

I knew that teenage girls have embarrassing emergencies, so I conceded to her need for privacy and leaned closer for her to whisper in my ear. I was not prepared for what she said, however.

"I think I am having a miscarriage, and I need to call my grandmother," she said.

I must have started because she drew back. Looking her in the eye, I asked her if she were sure. She nodded. I flew into action, sending her immediately to the clinic and getting another teacher to watch my class while I went with her. The nurse wasn't there that day, and even though the gray lady volunteer and I were skeptical, we couldn't take that risk. We located the grandmother and off went Schedule into her care. I said a prayer for her and for myself as she lumbered down the steps.

This drama was to happen twice more that year, but with each subsequent episode of these imaginary miscarriages, I got wiser. By the time of her third whispered trauma, I had the nurse lined up to talk to her. I had also done some research on my own about poor Schedule. According to her records, she had never passed sixth, seventh or eighth grades, but had been sent to high school because she was "above the physical norm." Now it made sense why she never wanted to read out loud and rarely did any of her work. I doubted whether she could read.

When I went to the counselor about this educational disaster, she shrugged. Social promotions were the system's way of sweeping problems under the rug. Since she was tall and physically mature, her self-esteem would suffer if she remained in middle school with younger-looking children, they reasoned. I wondered what it did to her self-esteem to be in high school and not be able to read.

But that wasn't all she didn't know how to do. The nurse later reported back to me that's Schedule didn't understand about her monthly cycle which, in many adolescent girls, could be wildly irregular. Since a recent family member had suffered a miscarriage, she assumed that every period she had was a miscarriage. The nurse explained to the child about her cycle so that she wouldn't be in a panic every time it came. I thought about Granny who at seventeen wanted to write a book called "The Cares of the World." If she only knew.

Sometimes, however, I felt like I made a real difference that year. Joy was a bright spot in one of my ninth-grade classes. With a broad smile revealing a mouth full of braces, she informed me my first day that she loved to read and to write poetry. She kept a poetry journal and asked me if I wouldn't mind reading it periodically. I was thrilled.

At first, the poems were your typical adolescent attempts about love and nature. I made positive comments and offered suggestions about reading. We bonded, and she regularly hugged me goodbye as she left class. As the year wore on, however, Joy's perky demeanor and broad smile dimmed. She got thinner and didn't wear makeup any more. In the spring, she didn't go out for the track team even though she had been a star of the freshman team that year. Her poems got darker and darker. She quit combing her hair.

At first, having been attracted to dark romanticism myself, I thought it was just a phase. When the poems were about nothing but death, however, I panicked. I decided to risk violating Joy's trust in me by sharing her poetry with her mother. I had no idea what I was going to say, but I couldn't take the risk that something might be dreadfully wrong with that precious child. My own experience taught me that teenagers can and do commit suicide.

That next week, one afternoon after school, her mother and I sat in my hot classroom, and she read the poems that her daughter had written as I sat quietly by, hoping I was making a mountain out of a molehill. Mrs. White's tears told me that I wasn't. As she closed the journal, she poured out the fears she had harbored as she had watched her daughter change from a happy-go-lucky child into a morose and sullen wraith. They had watched and waited and feared—until they got my telephone call and Mrs. White read the journal. If watching Mrs. White confront her daughter's problem was daunting, the next step we took that afternoon was terrifying.

Finishing up a make-up test, Joy came to my classroom to meet her mother, who had pretended to meet me on some other pretext. When she entered the room and saw our tear-stained faces, Joy knew. Her face clouded for a moment, and I dreaded the defensive indignation she would loose on us both. But instead, a flood of pent-up tears broke, and she rushed to her mother like a lost child reunited at last.

Mother and daughter left the classroom, arm in arm, and I sat at my desk for a long time, grateful and humble that my gamble had worked. As is the case when you teach ninth graders, you often lose touch with them even before they leave high school. They think they have outgrown you for the greater challenge of senior English. Part of it, I think, is that they hope no one will remember who they were or what they were like at that age, and eschew too many reminders.

Yet, the week before Joy graduated, she came to see me, to thank me for saving her life. That moment was reason enough to be a teacher.

For every good parent, however, there are the enablers, the devotees to the cult of self-esteem whose precious children are never to be corrected. Now they are called helicopter parents who see their children as investments to be nurtured from the womb until they pay off after graduating from a prestigious college. Employers have even complained that these parents have started attending their grown children's job interviews, asserting that proactive role that that has robbed their children of self-reliance and responsibility.

Danielle had that kind of parents, although we didn't call them that then. Danielle was a bright girl for whom everything had always come pretty easily. She encountered the same problem most bright ninth graders do; middle school excellence is frequently achieved with only a modicum of work. Like everything else in life, the next step-up increases in difficulty and sophistication, like the difference between riding a bicycle and driving a car. Danielle was having trouble making the transition and meeting the more rigorous academic expectations of high school.

Her parents were dismayed by Danielle's lapse in performance and promptly made an appointment to meet with me. They were highly placed professionals who had gotten to their positions of esteem by hard work. Their daughter had been given every advantage so that she would not have to claw her way to the top as they had done.

Their demeanor was icy when they entered my classroom. They proceeded to let me know their daughter's stunning academic vita, including all the summer programs in which she had participated over the last several years. I agreed with them that their daughter was indeed a very bright girl. Given the premise of her genius, however, they went on to insist that the problems she encountered in my class must be because of my defective material and instruction and demanded to see the vocabulary work with which she seemed to have the most trouble.

I showed them the program, a demanding series which required students not only to learn definitions of words, but all the nuances of meaning. The tests assessed their critical thinking skills as well as their rote knowledge of the words. I acknowledged its difficulty and suggested some strategies for studying. They poured over the tests and the words, asking accusatory questions, to which I responded calmly and forthrightly. When they couldn't seem to goad me into anything, they left with the same strained, dissatisfied look on their faces with which they had arrived. I had the feeling there was something they thought I was supposed to do to fix the problem, since it had to be my fault, not theirs—or Danielle's.

Despite her parents' attentions, Danielle's performance did not improve. Her parents followed up their visit with weekly memos informing me of what I was supposed to be doing to meet their daughter's needs. Danielle's difficulties had expanded from vocabulary tests into other aspects of her work in my class.

Eventually we had another conference which exceeded the first in hostility. The pair entered, enraged. I was damaging their daughter's self-esteem. Shaking her finger in my face, Mrs. Adler all but accused me of villainy, stuttering in fury at my insolence in bringing her child's grades down. Her daughter was working hard and I was supposed to appreciate it. How could I keep giving her these bad grades? How could I claim to be a mother? she challenged.

I remember thinking that she didn't know whose granddaughter she was wagging that finger in front of me as I recalled Papa's claims of having bitten a man's finger off in a fight. Instead of getting my Horatio up—as we call getting angry in my family—I clung to my calm and stood up slowly.

I told them quietly that I was always interested in working with parents to help their children. Students in my classes were not given grades; they earned them. I also could appreciate that Danielle was working hard, but ultimately the outcome was the proof of the quality of that work. I patiently employed analogies of engineers and bridges and surgeons and patients and the irrelevance of the hard work if the bridge collapsed or the patient died.

I continued that if they were indeed desirous of finding ways to help Danielle find her way through this challenge, I was eager to help. If they were there to insult and abuse me, I would have to excuse myself. I told them that it was my experience that when parents made their children's schoolwork more the child's responsibility than the parents', the students usually did better in time. They had obviously done well in school and reaped the benefits. It was Danielle's turn to work hard and harvest success.

I gathered my papers, and made a move toward the door. The Adlers had a stunned look on their faces, and stammered. I thanked them for their time and left. I left with the sinking fear that standing up for myself would get me in terrible trouble. Luckily, nothing came of it, but I vowed to myself never to have another parent conference without a witness.

Danielle stumbled through the rest of the year, gradually adjusting to the exactitude of high school work and bringing her grades up to a respectable B+. I only occasionally received imperious memos from her parents. She moved on and I added my experience with them to the annals of my pushy parent collection.

Along with its pathos and exasperation, teaching—like living—is also hilariously funny. After all, we are members of a ridiculous species, and I teach humanity at one of its most awkward stages: adolescence. The result is material any stand-up comedian would covet.

The intellectual gymnastics some students will go through to try to get out of work is hysterical. Ultimately, if they had exerted half the effort expended trying to avoid work in actually doing the work, it would have been finished in half the time. Invariably, on test day, a student will raise his hand and ask if spelling counts. I answer his question with a question: if I say no, will he misspell things on purpose?

In my later years, the benefit of life's wisdom comes pouring out of me at those moments. That is when I regale the offending inquirer with the true story of the poor young man in business school. This young man had studied hard and graduated with honors with his MBA. He took the CPA exams and passed them all. Proudly, he composed his resume and blanketed the city's accounting firms with them. With his credentials, he was confused when weeks passed and he heard no response much less received any invitations to interview. Finally, he got a letter back in the mail. Actually, it wasn't a letter exactly; it was a copy of his resume from which he read the words now circled in red announcing his goal to become a certified *pubic* accountant. Spelling counts, I tell my students.

Lazy thinking and misuse of the language provide some of the best anecdotes of human inanity in the classroom. In one class I taught, we did a unit on philosophy. After reading and studying the spectrum of western thought, students were to select a philosopher and write a paper about how his thoughts survive in our world view today. Kirk proudly chose Plato. After all, there was more than enough written about the great Greek cornerstone of western ideas, and this paper should be a cinch—an easy *A*.

Imagine his chagrin when he received his graded paper back with a big, red *F* on it. Irate, he burst up to the front of the class, slamming the paper down on my desk. What could be the problem, he demanded. After all, Kirk was usually an *A* student.

I asked him to read his opening paragraph aloud. Underlined in that paragraph was Kirk's assessment of Plato's legacy, including the "fact" that Plato was a devout Christian. I explained to him, trying not to laugh, the illogic of his chronology. His response was that if this were a math test, he would get partial credit since he only made one error; therefore, he should get, at worst, a *B*, but most certainly not an *F*.

Trying not to get angry myself, I countered, if on his math test, he had used the formula for the circumference of a circle to solve all the problems asking for the area of a circle, he would have gotten all the problems wrong and received the *F* he deserved. The problem with the hypothetical math test as well as his essay was a total failure to comprehend and apply—in this case, his philosopher's historical context much less the legacy of his ideas. Yes, Platonic idealism did impact Christian thought. One need only read the Gospel of John to see it, but Plato could not have been a Christian, devout or otherwise, unless he were clairvoyant.

Somehow research seems to be the undoing for young students. In a hurry to complete the assignment rather than learn anything, as young Kirk was, they take short cuts or get creative. Today, with the ease of Internet research, plagiarism is an unfortunate norm. At least Kirk couldn't be accused of that. Neither could Sapphire.

Sapphire was researching the death penalty for a persuasive project. She was to investigate the merits of the death penalty versus life in prison for society's ultimate crimes. The comedy of her paper came not in her conclusions but in the descriptions of the primary issues. Electrocution she described as "the fast flourishment of excitement through the body." I wondered if she were talking about an execution or an orgasm. Life in prison's downside was described as "living your life in a nutshell." Hamlet may have been capable of being king of infinite space but for his troubling dreams, but I doubt that Sapphire was alluding to Shakespeare.

The saddest malapropism witnessed in my career was not so much a misuse of the language but a horrible slip of the tongue. Herbie was a shy boy, a gangly red-head whose greatest talent was long distance running. To fulfill the required oral book report, he had chosen to read *Moby Dick*. Now, since I have never gotten past chapter two despite several attempts at reading that American classic, I was impressed that he had chosen the work, much less read it. It sure beat the perennial presentations on Hardy

Boys mysteries by those who had forgotten to read anything and dredged something up from their past.

On his appointed day, Herbie nervously approached the front of the class, clutching his notes tightly in his hands. He anxiously addressed the class, stammering, "The name of my dick is Moby Book."

Simultaneously, his eyes went wide and all his classmates inhaled sharply. They all looked at me. I affected a serious but benign look on my face and nodded at him to continue as if nothing had happened. Instead of continuing his presentation, the poor child, his face as red as his hair, groaned and bolted from of the classroom. Apparently, he went straight to the guidance counselor and changed his schedule because I got a drop slip in my box later that day. He couldn't take the possible horror of returning to the class to endure the cruel questions of his classmates as to what his private parts were named, I guess.

Students are not the only ones responsible for foolishness in the classroom. Teachers can be idiots too. There was the social studies teacher Samantha had who, a virtual Holocaust denier, taught the class that the Nazis had actually sent the captive Jews to showers to open their pores so that the poison gas would be more fast-acting. This was the teacher who had never heard of Joseph Mengele.

While not so misguided, I too had my share of gaffes in the classroom. The worst was the result of a logic lesson gone wrong. I was trying to demonstrate to my class of seniors some finer points of the rules of deductive reasoning in the concept of distribution.

In a syllogism, the major premise usually states something to the effect that "All M's are P's," I explained. The minor premise follows with "All S's are M's." With the syllogism constructed this way, we can conclude with confidence that "All S's are P's."

The concept of distribution gives us that assurance because it describes the inclusion or exclusion of every single member of a group or class. Thus, I continued with my students, in this syllogism, by saying "All M's," we have included and excluded the members of the group, therefore defining the limits of M-ness. Since that is so, transitively, the S's fit in the M group who fit in the P group. The P term, however, is not distributed since we haven't included or excluded every single member of its group or class; we haven't defined the limits of P-ness.

Now, to add to my Freudian slip, I was largely pregnant at the time. They looked at me, waiting to see how I would react, and I looked at them, hoping they had been ignoring me. They weren't, and the sheepish grins were already sneaking across their faces. Looking at my extended belly, I muttered to myself that I guess I *had* defined the limits of "p-ness" and burst out laughing. After that, there was no logic to be taught in that classroom. I sat down and we laughed for the rest of the class period.

For all the foolishness teachers may be guilty of, teachers are also beacons of humanity and civility in a chaotic world. My fifth-grade teacher Mrs. Carpenter was one such light. Although schools had been racially integrated at the student level since the year before I started school, teachers had not yet crossed the racial chasm. That year they did.

Mrs. Carpenter was a tall, slim woman, impeccably dressed and unutterably dignified, beyond the norm of teachers in that day of double knit and earth shoes. She had a low-pitched voice with a deep drawl, and when she read out loud to us, we were mesmerized. She had her share of difficulties that year. First, two boys snuck back into the classroom late one Friday afternoon and urinated in a bucket in the coat closet.

In the heat of the un-air-conditioned room over the course of the weekend, the odor grew horrendous. When we returned Monday, the atrocity was readily apparent all the way down the hall. Some boys were snickering. Our class was ushered into the library to start the day where Mrs. Carpenter eventually returned to us to explain the foul stench.

"Someone has urinated in the coat closet," she said.

Quizzical looks were our response. Then from the back someone yelled out, "Somebody peed." Her response was a withering glance in the direction of the offending explanation.

She was not spared the stink of racial prejudice either. Mazie Stokes was the toughest little girl in the fifth grade, contraband gum *in* her mouth and profanity spewing *from* her mouth. For a lot of us at that time, our exposure to blasphemy was sneaking and looking up bad words in the dictionary or eavesdropping when daddies had to do plumbing. Nowadays, vulgarity among children may be normal, but in my day, a little girl who said "shit" when she struck out in softball was an anomaly.

One day, Mrs. Carpenter corrected Mazie for some infraction, and she snarled back, "You can't do that to me, you stupid nigger."

The silence that followed was deafening. No one breathed. Mrs. Carpenter stood there for a moment and then, in a low and dignified voice that had an edge of weariness as well as ice in it, she asked Mazie to come to the front of the class. Mazie burst into tears, thinking she was going to get a paddling, but walked slowly to join Mrs. Carpenter at the front of the room.

Mrs. Carpenter had meanwhile taken out a dictionary. "I would like you to look up the word *stupid*, Mazie," she said. Sniveling, Mazie complied. "Read the definition aloud please," Mrs. Carpenter directed. Between sobs, Mazie read the definition aloud. "Does that describe me or any of your teachers?" the teacher asked.

"No," wailed Mazie.

"Now, look up the word *nigger*, please."

It not being an unabridged dictionary and it being 1968, that word was not in our dictionary. When the crying Mazie could not find it, Mrs. Carpenter turned and explained to the class—who had scarcely breathed during the drama unfolding in front of us—that words not found in the dictionary were not to be used in polite company by civilized people. Since we were civilized and our parents expected us to be polite, we were not to use words like *nigger* ever again.

No one in that room moved as Mazie closed the dictionary and walked back to her seat. Mrs. Carpenter picked up our Warriner's *Grammar* and continued the lesson interrupted by a little girl's and a society's bigotry. Mrs. Carpenter was my hero, and my parents requested her when Samantha was in fifth grade.

So, for better or worse, for ninety per cent of my life, my life has answered the call of school bells. The years have been measured by lunchboxes and book bags, first day of school dresses and opening day butterflies, boxes of chalk and stacks of papers graded. Yet, for me these gauges of the passage of time are as natural as the tides or phases of the moon.

Invariably, at a party or somewhere, someone will ask me why I would want to be a teacher in the first place, especially in high school. Kids, these days, someone will say. I usually try to make a joke of it, saying that I don't think I could teach people who cannot zip their own zippers or wipe their own noses, so that rules out elementary school. People think they know about my profession because they once attended school. Or there is the, "I wish I had a job where you get summers off." I don't even try to answer those people.

In seriousness, it is the calling of my own humanity that led me to the classroom. Some may say that those who cannot do, teach. I would tell those scoffers that teaching enables all the *doing* in the world. If all the teachers in the world suddenly disappeared, very quickly our ability to do everything would cease, and proverbially Atlas would shrug.

Sometimes, we teachers sit around the conference table and talk about our dreams. Some laugh about what they want to do when they grow up. I may be still growing up at fifty-something, but I have found what I want to do. Regardless of the foolish ignorance of students or the willful folly of their parents or the human foibles we all share, teaching is more than a job; it is a life. And, maybe the most important part of it is that not all the learning is done by the students.

Snake Charming

THE TELEPHONE CALL CAME at four in the morning. Its insistent clamor stabbed through the security of my sleep, jolting me awake with an ice-cold pang in my stomach. After all, little good news ever comes in phone calls in the wee hours of the morning. I reached from under the comfort of the covers to answer the phone and silence its intrusion into the morning stillness.

Daddy's voice was on the line. "He is dead. He has shot himself. Your Papa is gone."

The words sliced into my consciousness, registering, bringing that same cold feeling to my brain as filled my stomach.

"Where are you? Where is Momma? Is Momma okay?" I knew she wasn't okay as I asked the question.

'Momma and Daddy had gotten a similarly disquieting call from Aunt Ginger an hour earlier. Since Granny's death, she lived with Papa, being a widow herself. That night, her sleep had been disrupted by a loud and unfamiliar sound, difficult to interpret in her baffled slumber. The mysterious pop was followed by hands reaching down and dragging her out of her sleep, hands of the night nurse shaking her awake. Artemesia had heard the sound too, running into her patient's room to check on him.

She found him on the floor beside Granny's dressing table, as he had slumped from off the stool. It wasn't readily apparent what was wrong at first; the gun's caliber was small, and its damage, though deadly, wasn't visible at first glance. Thinking maybe he had gotten up to do something, sat on the bench, and passed out, she shook his shoulder as she would later shake Aunt Ginger. Unresponsive, he rolled over on to his back under the force of her push, revealing his bloody and bruised mouth and the growing pool of blood under his head. The pistol, still clasped in his hand, glinted in the light of the lamp she turned on.

Later, Momma would agonize about that pistol. She had known it was in the drawer along with precious relics left untouched since Granny's death five years before: Air Spun face powder, Juicy Fruit gum, emery boards, and My Sin perfume. She had startled at its cold steel intrusion into the soft and sweet-smelling memories left in the drawer.

She also knew why it was there. Papa had always said he would rather shoot himself than have a colostomy. When he was diagnosed with colon cancer, he had been able to convince the surgeons to use less radical means to stop the cancer's progress. It was more important to him to save his dignity than his life. After three small surgeries, the only alternative to a slow and horrible death became the colostomy he had sought to avoid.

His pain, which he described as being clawed from the inside out by wild tigers, despite heavy doses of narcotics, was becoming unbearable. Papa's ability to down a fifth of Scotch in an evening and remain utterly lucid and appear coldly sober was now a detriment rather than an attribute. Momma had moved the gun, laying it casually on top of the refrigerator in the utility room off the kitchen. Later, the gun was no longer on the refrigerator where she had put it. It was back in its drawer.

I don't really remember getting dressed or telling my husband. I know I called Dawson and Samantha. It has always seemed to be my job to call people and tell them bad news. There is always that moment of hesitation in telling someone something so dreadful, especially faceless over the telephone. I don't know whether it's better to just blurt it out and come straight to the point or prepare them first that you have bad news. Either way, it is never good. Their stunned silence echoes across the line like a slap in the face. It had been the same when Granny died. I had to call Cousin Hamilton to tell him his aunt, my Granny, was dead. Dawson, upset at the news, had snapped at me. I had had to tell my friend Arlene on the occasion of both her parents' deaths. The words always leave a sour, dry taste in your mouth.

I don't remember the drive to the house that morning. Strangely, I do remember every nuance of the ride from the hospital back to the house when Granny died. Fear must have blurred my senses and dulled my good sense that cold morning. When I got to Granny and Papa's house, an ambulance was pulling away. To my surprise, police cars were in the driveway, their blue lights casting a surreal glow on the morning gloom. With a shooting the police would have been called.

As I crossed the yard on the walk I had swept so many times as a girl, I could see in the January predawn light an officer sitting in the front seat of his cruiser, filling out his report. I didn't knock on the door but went right in and found my family huddled together, faces pale and tear-stained in the growing morning light. The wood floors creaked and caused the grandfather clock workings to vibrate in their familiar way. The clocks were stopped. The noise of their chiming had always bothered Papa.

But, for the familiarity of the room, there was something foreign about it too. A blue-uniformed policeman was standing in the living room, talking to the family. Thankfully, it was Karl Bennett, the family friend who would eulogize Aunt Norma at her funeral a decade later. To have to share details as intimate as a suicide with a stranger would have been too much for Momma. Aunt Norma, despite her grief, was graciously thanking Karl for his pains and his discretion. I could tell instantly that both Momma and Norma were afraid that Papa's suicide would make the newspaper and that Papa's memory and public persona would be tainted by such a death. Papa's memory was tainted by plenty of other things, but none of them ever made the newspaper.

Papa's temper had dominated us all. Despite his totalitarian command over so much of his daughters' lives, Papa was one of those people who could charm you into believing that doing what he wanted was what you wanted anyway. His whimsical and often self-deprecating humor disguised his willful need to have everything his way. Why else would Granny have tolerated his infidelities, much less the little blue-eyed girls with a gap between their front teeth just like his, belonging to that lady who worked in Papa's store? We all, at one time or another, found ourselves going out of our way to make Papa happy, and then wondering what in the world we were doing.

Sometimes, it may have been out of fear of riling him. His rages caused blood vessels to burst spontaneously in his eyeballs. Even as small children, the threat of Papa's eyes bursting could hush us into compliance or make us scarce during Papa's naptime if we were at Granny's house.

The legends of his fits were always in the back of our minds. He had walked out of his father's home at fourteen in a fit of temper and ended up in Maine. He had bitten the ear off of a mule that wouldn't plow and the finger off of a man in a fight. Then there was the time that Papa took a swing at his own brother in a downtown restaurant over some petty disagreement. He had even huffed out of our house one time when he thought that Daddy had insulted him.

The incongruence of Papa's charm and fury kept us all off balance. This confusion bred a sense of shame that runs deep in my family and is the root of a lot those things we don't like to talk about, I think. Papa's temper, like the rest of his periodically uncontrolled passions, was our secret, guarded first by Granny and then by us all. In the wake of one of his tantrums, his eye an angry red against the sky-blue, we all were to act as if nothing had ever happened.

In his death, his daughters faced another incarnation of keeping secrets and of those conflicting feelings Papa always inspired. Had Papa just had enough and taken his life, angry that he couldn't beat the cancer like he had always beaten everything else? The only time he had not had his way was when Granny died. It hit him so hard he could never even talk about it directly, referring to it instead as "that thing that happened to me." Was he striking back at death, throwing the first punch rather than waiting for death to take its own sweet time?

Since we would never know these things, we could only agonize and speculate, feeding more on our own fear and hurt than on real information. Besides these inner battles, we faced public uncertainty, too. If knowledge of his means of death were public, how were we to act about it? Were we to be shocked and surprised? Because we weren't. Were we to be angry? Because we were.

It seems to me that those left behind in a suicide share a different sort of grief and guilt than those who lose a loved one to an illness. There is always that question that hangs unanswered as to whether you could have done something to prevent it—like hide the gun in a better place. Those who suffer through a suicide also feel a special shame; why weren't we enough to hold him here? What could I have done differently? So, each of us nursed the wounds that our grief opened.

It was not that we didn't understand and even condone Papa's decision to end his life. He was ninety and ill. His last days would hold pain and indignity. Admittedly, there are worse things than being dead at some point. Hospitals made Papa crazy. He had just had his last surgery, after all, and had to spend a short time in an extended care facility. To him, the noises and smells of sickness and age were worse than any prison. He had pitched his last fit to get out of that place, and his daughters had had little choice but to bring him home.

I had seen him that last day, stopping by for a very brief visit to let him kiss Edward. We had been to the park to play before stopping by. Edward's ruddy face glistened with his play's exertion and the day's humidity, and he had that earthy, little boy, puppy smell. His dark eyes were bright with the anticipation of seeing his Papa.

In contrast, Papa's large and usually robust frame seemed a hulking wreck, slumped in his recliner. His skin was pale, and he smelled damp and sour when I bent over the kiss his forehead. His blue eyes that lifted up to see Edward were cloudy and nearly colorless. In a supreme effort, he patted his great-grandson.

"The Lord is my shepherd. I shall not want," he said.

"I love you, Papa," Edward reminded him, looking suddenly very serious.

"I love you," Papa returned with great effort, his normally booming voice a whistling whisper.

Edward's every footstep had jarred the sickly silence of the house. A little boy's noise would have normally been a welcome diversion, but not that afternoon. We left right after that, not knowing that it would be the last time we would see him alive. Momma said that the rest of the day and into the evening Papa had continued to recite the twenty-third Psalm. In retrospect, I wonder if he were setting his emotional table beside still waters to give him the courage to take his journey into the valley of death.

Given the state Papa was in and what he had to look forward to, we rationalized, who wouldn't opt to end it? He had always lived life on his own terms, so it was no surprise that his death was, also. Intellectually, we could support it. Emotionally was another matter. Our imaginations' video of his last moments—the struggle to get out of bed, to walk to the bench and sit down, the effort to open the little drawer full of death and memories, the strength to raise the pistol to his mouth, hold it still and pull the trigger—haunted us all.

What did he think and feel in that last moment? Did he see Granny standing at the gate, waiting for him, as he had described in a poem he wrote for her birthday weeks before? Was his determination tinged with any regret? Did it hurt? All of these questions would never be answered and held us all in a sort of purgatory for a long time.

But, to the world, we were brave and supportive. The suicide was not made public, and his obituary stated diplomatically that he had died after a long illness. Privately, I told some of my friends to help me deal with the reality of it, much to Momma's chagrin.

It was decided that the little children were not to be told. I didn't think telling a six-year-old that his great-grandfather killed himself was appropriate, but it seemed to me another secret our family would hold, another elephant that would sit in our living rooms and tread through our conversations without ever being acknowledged openly.

My memory of the funeral is alternately a blur and sharply focused now. It seems odd in retrospect for so many of the details of Papa's funeral to be so vague while all of Granny's are as sharp today as if we had buried her yesterday. I do remember not shedding a tear at Papa's funeral, and I remember thinking how weird that was. Momma and her sisters wanted to hurry the funeral along, hoping that the sooner we got Papa in the ground, the better chance we had of avoiding anyone bringing his cause of death to light. It also took a while for folks to get back home.

There was Dawson who had to rearrange trial dates before he could get back home. Momma excused his pregnant wife from coming to the funeral. In her condition, she didn't need to be exposed to the horror of death by one's own hand, Momma said. It also could have been that the pregnancy was a good excuse to not have to deal with the daughter-in-law with whom she enjoyed an uneasy relationship. Momma did enjoy noticing that the baby born that next May was a blonde and blue-eyed cherub with a gap between his front teeth and a temper like Beelzebub just like Papa.

The church was full. Papa had been an important figure in our town, after all. We grandchildren had crowded in on the second row of the pews. The first row was reserved for Momma and her sisters, Uncle Ewell, and Daddy. Momma always said that sitting on the front row at a funeral was something to be avoided, but there was no avoiding it then. Besides feeling crowded, I can also recollect the oddly appropriate gun-metal grey coffin.

I saved the program from the service. It records that a soloist sang Papa's favorite hymn, "How Great Thou Art," and Dawson gave the eulogy. I don't remember what he said, only that at one point his voice got thick and his face was blotchy as it did always when he got upset. Someone read Papa's latest poem to Granny, about her standing at the gate waiting for him. It was supposed to comfort us to think of them reunited, I guess.

Instead, in my head, I heard the lyrics of the song he had written which I had set to music as a more accurate picture of what brought us to the church that morning. Papa had written this ode some years ago, when sadness had overcome him on a visit back to his boyhood home place in the long-ago abandoned community of Sparksville, Georgia.

He had just come from the nursing home where his older brother was dying, prophetically of intestinal cancer that Papa would suffer from, and he had stopped at the house before heading home. It was about sunset, and the combination of his brother's failing health, the dilapidated house and run-down land with the dying day and the implied threat of his own mortality combined to give him, as he described, "a powerful case of the blues." The final stanzas came to describe his last days:

> "My steps are weary;
> My hair has thinned.
> Lord, when I walk, it's against the wind.
> Oh, how my old joints are achin'
> And, there's no relief in these pills I'm takin'.
> I've got those Sparksville Blues.
>
> Here comes the train ramblin' down the track,
> Singin' that tune, 'I don't wanna come back.'
> Dusk has fallen all on this earth,
> The saddest day, since my birth.
> I've got those Sparksville Blues.
>
> But I'm all packed for a long, long journey.
> And this adventure costs me no money.
> It's a trip I was born to take.
> I think I'll get started before daybreak.
> I've got those Sparksville Blues."

On the day of the funeral, I told Edward what we were about to do. While my cousins Diana and Della had decided for their children—some of them much older than Edward—that they were not to go to the funeral, I had given Edward the choice. He had had a very special relationship with his great-grandfather and, although I felt naturally protective of him, there was no way to protect him from the reality that one of his favorite people in the whole world was dead. Funerals are for the living, and if going could help him start to process living without his Papa, I reasoned, he ought to be able to go.

We all met that morning at Aunt Norma's house to process to the church together. Edward was dressed in his suit and ready to go, his hand clasped tightly in mine. Yet, when he saw his cousins playing chase and jumping on the trampoline in the yard, he looked at them and then at me with longing. I told him that I had play clothes in my bag, and he could go change and play if he wanted to.

He hesitated, his face a battle of mixed feelings. He loosed his grip from my hand, and he took the offered clothes and tennis shoes, disappearing into the crowd gathered at Aunt Norma's. I caught sight of him, laughing and running, out of the rear window of the limousine as we left for the church, his innocence preserved for a bit longer.

As a teenager he would express regret that he didn't go, feeling guilt that somehow he hadn't done what he was supposed to. I had finally told him that Papa had killed himself, even though, if Momma had had anything to do with it, it would be a secret to this day. I had had enough of secrets by that time in my life. Edward, as is his way, seemed to understand both my efforts to let him remain a child a little longer and his Papa's choice not to remain in pain.

Papa's messy death left Momma, Norma and Ginger in emotional disaster. Momma had barely come to peace with Granny's death five years before, its suddenness pulling us out of a football game and our sureness. Papa's needs had distracted us all from really dealing with the totality of our loss. He had to be fed, and he had to have his shirts ironed, and he had to be entertained so that he wouldn't want to marry that lady at the store with the now grown blue-eyed daughters whose gapped teeth had been fixed by orthodontia he had paid for.

His estate was a debacle, too, despite the high-priced lawyers he had had working on it since Granny's death. He had spent a lifetime earning it, and it would have suited him just fine to take it all with him. But there was no doing that, and, since he couldn't, his next priority was to prevent the government from getting any of it. Momma and her sisters were intelligent and educated women, but the tangle of regulations and trusts tinged with the shame of how and why they would be coming into all that money, baffled them. The bungling lawyers seemed to be no help. Perhaps it was the fact that nice Southern women never talk about money.

Perhaps, again, it was the snarl of mixed feelings Papa always seemed to rouse—this time about the money he had held over their heads when he wanted to have his way and charm wasn't working. The chaos of Papa's estate wasn't as easy to clean up as the blood on the bedroom floor. There was the matter of the large bequest to the lady at the store and her daughters. If he had killed himself to avoid indignity, Papa seemed to have left a good bit of it behind.

That's the trouble with suicide. It adds disarray that never seems to get put right to the natural pain, loss and fear you encounter with death. There is always the not knowing that clutters and confuses beyond the normal fix our finitude puts us in. Even when they leave a note, you still can't know the answers to the questions that plague you in those still morning hours haunted by the ringing of the telephone.

Papa's death wasn't the first self-inflicted death I had experienced. The summer before my senior year in high school, I had started dating a boy named Caleb. We had flirted in the ninth grade, but he was shy and awkward, and I was terribly innocent. We were both in the band; he played the trumpet and I played the flute. Unannounced at the homecoming game, he descended from his row in the stands and presented me with a mum—one of the floral monstrosities with the little gold, plastic footballs affixed to the center—before the game.

Confused but pleased, I pinned the thing to my wool band uniform, thanked him, and he went back to his assigned place in the stands. Caleb had a dark allure—tall, broad-shouldered, and poetic. After that football game, he passed me notes to me in science class with some of his poems in them. We both played guitar and talked about playing together. He seemed like a wild thing, though, and I was a bit afraid of him. Shortly after Christmas, Caleb withdrew from school to finish the year at military school.

In the spring at the end of our junior year, he came back. Taller, trimmer, straight and strong, long hair cut short, he appeared at school at the top of the stairs as I was starting up. I startled at seeing him and must have stared at him. He laughed and gave me a hug there on the stairs, surer of himself than he had been on that long ago night at the football game. The military school wasn't for him, and he came home. He was at school to re-enroll, home to stay.

We parted on the stairs so that I wouldn't be tardy to class with promises to get together. The two and a half years at military school had matured his Byronic good looks with a soldier's confidence. I couldn't stop thinking about him.

He called soon to ask me to his family's house for dinner to celebrate his seventeenth birthday. It wasn't the usual first-date invitation, but I knew his sisters and his parents from band, so it felt natural. After dinner, Caleb was eager to listen to the Aerosmith album I gave him, and asked me up to his room. His room. My stomach went up into my throat. That was forbidden territory, the location of A Bed, about which Momma had extracted stern promises.

I had dated other boys, one for almost a year, and I had never been in their rooms. Part of me felt like Momma's fears were outdated and ridiculous. It reminded me of Granny's daddy who had demanded on his deathbed that the girl Granny vow never to engage in mixed bathing. After all, if men swam with women, someone somehow might get pregnant. She had sworn to obey, but in later years guiltily gave in to the natural recreation so many enjoy without threat of conception—swimming. She had escaped unscathed and was undoubtedly a virgin when she and Papa married.

Caleb and I were just going upstairs to his room to listen to music. We would be fully clothed, his door would be open, and his little brother, with whom he shared his room, would be with us. I felt guilty but went upstairs any way, and we listened to the album. Mommas have a way of being right in their way. Sitting on the floor, leaning up against his bed, playing Candy Land with Buster, his little brother, he and I kept looking at each other as the songs' suggestive lyrics wove in and out of our topicless conversation. We knew where we were.

As my Granny before me, despite my foray into the forbidden, I went home unbesmirched that evening. But, as the summer ripened, quick kisses goodnight after a ride home from Monday night band with Daddy standing behind our closed front door gave way to leaving movies early to go parking down out-of-the-way country, dirt roads.

Besides the dangers Momma warned me about, parking was fraught with other perils. In the subtropical heat of a Gulf Coast summer, you had two choices, both with problems. If you opted for ultimate privacy and kept the car windows rolled up, you quickly got wringing-wet-sweaty and the inside of the car got so humid it would threaten to create its own weather system. If you opted to avoid heat exhaustion and clothes that looked like you had run a marathon in them (which would be an incongruous condition if you were actually in the air-conditioned movie theater like you were supposed to be) and rolled the windows down to catch a breeze, you were soon eaten alive by mosquitoes. I used up a lot of Caladryl that hot summer.

As the summer waned, our romance waxed, but soon August heralded the start of school. Looking back on it, although he had impeccable manners and was a gentle soul, Caleb must have had a smoldering problem with authority that I didn't understand. I was innocent at that time of dark places and deep-seated discord. Our conversations were about music and moonlight, those that we had, that is.

As a prelude to my senior year, Momma agreed to let me spend several nights with Katie, my best friend, even though her parents were out of town. Our friendship always reminded me of the little girls in *The World of Henry Orient*. Our world was like a musical out of the forties, fantastical and fabricated. Katie would play the perky blonde Debbie Reynolds-type who could tap dance and sing; I would sing the torch song and look like Ava Gardner. Both of us were anachronistically out of our element in the seventies, so innocent that we really didn't grasp what the "it" was when the popular poster said, "If it feels good do it."

We were trying, however, to grow up, and rebelliously fixed ourselves a rum and coke that evening as the strings swelled from the stereo with strains from *Brigadoon*. Emboldened by the rum, I decided to call Caleb, whom I hadn't talked to in days. That was another thing Momma said that nice girls didn't do. But I was worried his silence was because he was not really interested.

He seemed relieved to hear from me, and I chattered about being sunburned and about my latest bout of bug bites being about healed. He laughed that low, rumbling chuckle of his. He was going to the beach the next morning with his sister and her best friend as a last outing before the two girls left for college, but he would call me when they got back. My heart pounding like it usually did when I was around Caleb, I hung up the phone. Rummy and romantic, I slept sweetly that night.

The next morning, I went to my summer job at the Parks and Rec. I fought to keep my mind on the children as we camp guides lead them through outdoor activities and games. Not being all that coordinated, on a good day it took a good bit of my concentration to keep track of my feet. Distracted, I made mistakes, and my co-workers shot grim looks at me across the sea of little heads playing kickball.

Later, we adjourned from the field of battle for the much cooler art studio. I was deeply engrossed in the middle of a lesson on perspective, when suddenly Momma appeared at the door, tentatively opening to heavy doors and slowly peeking her face through the crack. My supervisor Mrs. Rumsford had a notorious temper and did not suffer interruptions well.

As discreetly as I could, I started the children on a drawing exercise, and I slipped out to see what Momma wanted. Immediately, I was fearful that something had happened to Papa or Granny, but I reasoned that if that were so, it wouldn't be Momma coming to get me. Through the double set of double doors, I emerged to find Momma with a grave look on her face.

She took my shoulders, firmly but tenderly. "He's dead, honey, Caleb is dead." In disbelief I must have echoed her statement as a question, to which she responded, "Yes, he o-d'ed."

I must have wailed and fallen to the floor because Mrs. Rumsford was soon outside with us to ascertain what had drawn me from my job, and what the noise was about. "Her friend o-d'ed," Momma said to him from down on the floor as she tried to cradle her crumpled daughter.

"Is he going to be okay?" Mrs. Rumsford asked, sounding as if she were very far away. I remember her next words clearly; "No, he's not okay. He's dead."

In the shock of those words and the thirty years since, a lot of details of the rest of that day and the days after are blurred. We went to Caleb's house that afternoon to help and be helped, and learned more information than Momma had gotten from Uncle Ewell who had heard the 9-1-1 call to the Ramsay's house on his police scanner radio. Buster had gone to Caleb's room to wake him up, but he couldn't rouse him. His momma had gone in, but there would be no waking Caleb. She had called the ambulance, even though it was too late.

Police were called, and as they investigated, under the bed they found a bag with airplane in it. Apparently, Caleb, had experimented that night with intoxicants, an all-too-common way to get high without the risks of purchasing illegal drugs, we were to learn later. The risk was far greater than arrest. He must have simply breathed too much, and his heart stopped. As Momma and I entered the Ramsay's house, I experienced the most humbling moment I have ever had or ever will have. Mrs. Ramsay put her arms around me and tearfully said she was sorry. She, a mother who had found her dear boy dead in his bed, told *me* she was sorry. I felt utterly insignificant in the face of her loss.

As we are wont to do in the face of death in the South, we fell to cleaning; Mrs. Ramsay said she couldn't bear for people to see her grime. With wooden movements that familiar tasks allow, Momma and I vacuumed and mopped and dusted and straightened. We washed the dog. We made the beds, not daring to go into Caleb's room, though. Buster would sleep with his sisters. It would be a while before anyone would go in there again.

While we were there, Mr. Ramsay returned from making the arrangements. Interment would be private for the family the next day, but there would be a memorial service the day after. As he outlined the details mechanically, he tearfully looked at the family portrait that they had just had made. It was too much, and the tall man—whose height he had passed on to his now dead son—slumped and quickly left the room.

Others would later tell me that they would retake the picture in the coming months because Caleb's death was too much for his father. The Ramsays would also move to Oregon, maybe in an effort to leave that house and its pain behind. I always wondered if they really did leave it behind. How would Buster ever leave that morning behind when his big brother didn't wake up? It seems to me that pain never leaves, wherever you go or whoever is or isn't in the family portrait.

I didn't have a black dress to wear to the memorial service, so I wore a dark brown one of my mother's. Wearing the unfamiliar dress made me feel like I was someone else. Clutching Momma's hand and later seated tightly between her and Katie, I sobbed through the service. My eyes and brain felt water-logged and swollen, numbed and sluggish. It was hard to breathe.

The days following were similar, although at some point, I quit crying. I felt like a robot, an alien in my own life and body, guilty to be alive when one who had been so vivid was dead. Having not gone to the burial and having lost touch with his damaged family, I never knew where Caleb's grave was located. I could never bear thinking of him being in the ground any way.

When I could endure thinking about him without it spinning me into a deep, dark hole, I would see him sitting on the floor in his bedroom with Buster in his lap, playing Candy Land and listening to Aerosmith. It wasn't until decades later when I was at the cemetery for Vivian Turnbull's funeral, I finally found him. His headstone was simple, but my feelings were not. I felt an aching emptiness and the rush of old questions never to be answered and an old pain that had never really healed.

Sometimes, though, even when you have some of the answers, it doesn't make it any better. In fact, it can be worse. As the tempting serpent offered, knowledge wouldn't kill you, but it sure could set off a series of other consequences that may make you wish for ignorance. A friend of a family friend knew a boy who left a long diatribe of a suicide note before he turned on the car in the family garage. The next day, when one of them showered, a steamy message, from him perhaps, said, "It's all your fault."

That family was utterly broken by the boy's self-destruction. The marriage failed; the sister was hospitalized off and on through her teens. Having him tell why he killed himself was a crueler blow than the death itself. It was as if hurting himself wasn't enough.

And then there was Michael, a former student of mine who had gone on into the Peace Corps, serving in the Middle East and Vietnam. He later took a job to defuse landmines and munitions left behind in Vietnam to destroy those that war had spared.

One evening, after putting his children to bed, he sat down with his wife at the kitchen table, pulled out a pistol, and blew his brains out. He had been battling himself for a long time, we learned later. The mangled bodies of children left behind, the plaguing uncertainty of old mines' triggers as he defused them, and the fruitlessness of fighting for peace overwhelmed him. He left his wife a letter which she found on her pillow later explaining his state of mind and begging her forgiveness.

Samantha was really torn up about Michael's death even though it had been over a decade since she had last seen him. She had dated his best friend back in high school. Back then, Michael was a beautiful, dangerous, wild thing, the way boys can be. He read Coleridge and drank Jack Daniels, drove an MG and wore flip-flops before it was fashionable. Sam ran into him in an airport the last time she saw him as she chased her daughter who had escaped the confines of her stroller. The thought of a boy who was so intensely alive ending as a lonely and frightened man at that bloody breakfast table haunted Sam. Knowing why he did it didn't help much. He was still dead, a waste of life. Sometimes we don't want to know the answer, I guess.

I wonder if Daddy would rather not know the answer to his mother's death either. Daddy's momma died when he was nine. His memories of the event recounted to us in childhood are few and dim. As a child, I had overheard Aunt Flossy, his sister, tell Momma things about it. The death had not been immediate but had taken a few days. They had visited her in the hospital, but she had not been able to talk to them.

Her cause of death seemed to change with each telling, however. We attributed it to Flossy's overdeveloped sense of drama which filled in the gaps of her ignorance, since she was only a couple of years older than Daddy. Daddy had been inconsolable at the funeral, throwing himself on the casket. After her death, Daddy's father, a sloppy alcoholic, was incapable of his children's care, so Daddy and Flossy moved in with their oldest sister, Endora.

After the move, Daddy's childhood ranged from the idyllic innocence that cradled rural America in the forties to an angry sense of abandonment and deprivation of a child who sleeps on the couch in his older sister's house because his momma is dead. I had grown up with Daddy's anger about his childhood, having heard him wish more than once that he could burn his hometown down. Most of his anger focused on his father. His sisters had done the best they could; taking on a smart-aleck nine-year-old to raise could not have been easy.

The symptoms of Daddy's brain tumor had manifested themselves before the technology which later detected it was available. Unable to determine a physical cause for his troubles, the doctors sent him to a psychiatrist. Predictably, the tired Freudian diagnosed Daddy's unresolved conflict with his father as the source of his ailments. Although he privately thought the diagnosis was ridiculous, Daddy didn't want to be guilty of not pursuing a cure to the various and seemingly unrelated complaints he experienced.

So, one Saturday morning, Daddy packed up the whole family and we went to reconcile with his father. This figure was such an alien to our family that we really didn't even have a name for him—not Grandad or Papa or anything. Daddy called him by his first name when he spoke of him. But, accustomed to being packed into the car on Saturday mornings for one adventure or another, off we went, hopeful and expectant.

In the subsequent years, we spent time with Daddy's sisters and their families. His father even came to visit us several times. When his father died, Daddy, as the son, took charge of the arrangements and paid for most of it, as well as the remaining hospital bills. When he learned that his mother never had had a tombstone, he saw to it that she had one and that the cemetery where she was buried maintained her grave properly. He and his sisters went to see it set right with a small ceremony. That should have been a clue.

In the intervening years, as he gathered genealogical information, Daddy came across his mother's death certificate. Under the cause of death, there it was: suicide by drinking a toxic substance, probably lye. Suddenly the early but lingering death, the inability to talk, and her daughters' wrecked lives made sense. Yet, if those small details found a new logic, everything else lost its reason. Daddy's cooled anger at this alcoholic father flashed hot again. He must have driven his mother to desperation, Daddy thought. Although we had the truth at last, all that had seemed to be put right and healed and forgiven was broken again in that truth.

Me, I don't know if I would not have been angrier at his mother than his father. After all, she left her nine-year-old boy behind with an incompetent alcoholic. There will never be an answer to what kind of despair drives a mother to do that.

The survivors of suicide must resolve their quandaries the best they can. Regardless of how you pursue it, you are left with either the sour taste of truth or a stale whiff of denial. Those of us left behind have to wonder if that same force that drove our loved ones to self-slaughter might someday drive us to the same thing. Statistics back it up.

Look at Hemingway's family. His father killed himself. Papa Hemingway put a shotgun in his mouth. One of his granddaughters, an actress and model, took her own life. After Caleb died, I had wished I were dead. Nothing was ever to be the same, and I didn't want to be here if it wasn't. I remember feeling so tired of living but so afraid of dying. I don't know what kept me from following him.

Hamlet's conscience gave him pause. Voltaire's Old Woman in *Candide*—who, after having been ravaged and savaged as her family was slaughtered and who had a butt cheek chopped off to feed an army in a siege—asked the same question about why we endure life's hardships. She describes life as a serpent that we embrace even as it eats our very hearts. Perverse creatures, we seem to love the very source of our pain and destruction.

If we then choose to live, anguish and all, we have to learn how to live with the memory of those who chose not to, another serpent coiled in our bosom, knowledge of their imperfections hurting us and their memories. When the recollection of those who left us brings with it the smart of abandonment, we have to reconcile seemingly incompatible parts of ourselves—our child's heart with our grown-up mind.

An adult may not understand why his mother would leave him, but a child forgives her because he loves her. A child may feel forsaken, while an adult may rationalize the act as a final assertion of self even as not being. The coexistence of their rejection and our acceptance of it becomes a measure of who we are. Their lives—and their deaths—become the serpent we cling to because that knowledge is what we have left of them, just as our own life, grief and all, is what we have to try to charm into what we can.

Harvest Home

I WAS IN THE UPS store to send a package when my cell phone rang. By the ring tone, "The Flight of the Valkyries," I knew it was Sam. I answered with a smile in my voice at the funny looks I got from those around me in the store.

"Where are you?" she asked, at which time I told her where I was and what I was doing. "Call me back when you get home. I have something we need to talk about."

My stomach sank. Calls like that never bode well. I finished my errands quickly and hurried home.

Once home, I immediately dialed Sam, and breathlessly asked, "What's wrong?" when she answered the phone.

"It's Momma," she said.

Now, of late, Sam and I did a lot of talking about Momma—and Daddy for that matter. As our parents were aging, our anxiety about their well-being was escalating. Part of that same energy that was still being exercised in parenting was now starting to be funneled into a new thing to worry about—Momma and Daddy. Although our parents were still pretty vital, both Sam and I had decided that they had reached that stage of being old and peculiar. They repeated things. They told you to call back so that they could finish their *Gunsmoke* rerun. They talked about aches and pains and doctor visits.

To me, just like being grown up eludes an easy definition, what being old is has begun to also—especially the older I get. When I was in my teens, fifty was ancient. In my late forties, it looked younger all the time. Staring down sixty, who knows when you get old? Jeremiah and I tease that 85 seems like a ripe old age. All those things that we don't do now because they aren't healthy, like smoking a pipe for him, we will do when we are 85. The logic is, what is the behavior going to do, shorten your life? I will probably feel very differently once I get to be 85.

Sam's phone call brought that home. She had just gotten off the phone with Momma who had revealed, after a delay of some weeks, that she had been diagnosed with Parkinson's Disease. Sam broke down on the phone. I felt immediately empty, like a ghost trying to reach a corporeal form again. Suddenly, my Momma was too young to be threatened with illness, too vital to be branded with a debilitating condition.

But the diagnosis made sense. The variety of symptoms she had been experiencing over the last year or so that had been attributed variously to aging, now seen in a totality, also made sense. What didn't make sense in my child's heart that suddenly spoke more loudly than my adult's mind was that my Momma should be ill. Daddy could be sick or injured—even catastrophically as was his flair—but not Momma. Daddy always bounced back, miraculously. Now my Momma was threatened not just with the foibles of aging but with illness—and things that were imaginably worse than being old.

But it isn't really being old that is so worrisome. I have always liked old people, old places, and old things. I blame it on my name which means "old one." My home is filled with old furniture—not quite dignified enough to be called antique, but vintage instead—which Jeremiah and I have restored: Granny's dining and living room suites, Great Grandma Dump's bedstead, dresser and, most importantly, rocking chair, Aunt Edna's wicker porch furniture, his Papa's tool bench. My house looks like a catalog show room for Sears and Roebuck from 1929, where if you look at the reproduction of that famous book of dreams, you will find most of my furniture. Our walls are graced with family photos of old, from nineteenth century daguerreotypes to Polaroids from our childhoods.

Old places are as alluring. Both Jeremiah and I are more at home in the mountains than the beach, the Appalachians being the earth's oldest mountains, worn down by the cycles of seasons and centuries. Although I was born in the sun belt, the mountain breezes through the white pines have always whispered my name. I sleep better there and dream fantastical dreams. I have always made it a point to go to ancient places in my world travels as well. I tried to imagine the stories that could be told by the rocks at Jericho, the huge bluestone plinths at Stonehenge, or the worn stone steps at Durham Cathedral. Just like in the mountains, in these places, voices of times past seem to murmur their mysteries to my mind's ear.

I guess it's no wonder that, ever since I was a little girl, I have always enjoyed being around old people. I didn't know what the fascination was based on to begin with, although I have it pretty well figured out now. I guess that contradiction of vitality in decrepitude piqued my curiosity.

Maybe it was just that they had interesting stories. I had grown up with stories of Papa's Grandma Wilkins who had threatened Reconstruction bringers of war-widow charity with a shotgun. She warned them not to come back even if they saw buzzards circling the house. Grandpa Wilkins ended up coming back to life, walking all the way home from the Yankee prison camp in Pennsylvania and surprising his daughter Temperance who couldn't believe he was her daddy. Her daddy—or all that she knew of him—was in the trunk, in the form of a portrait put away when they thought he was a war casualty. My earliest memories of the aged are colored by trips to Great-Granddaddy's—Papa's daddy—for family reunions.

He was in his nineties when I was born, and by the time I could remember him, he was nearly a hundred. He had an old man's whispery, whistley voice, already softened by his Deep South drawl. He always wore a dark blue three-piece suit and a felt, center-creased dress hat with grosgrain ribbon trim, no matter the occasion. They said you could always tell the weather of Grandaddy's mood by how that hat sat on his head. If it were cocked back on his head, it was fair, but if it were pulled forward over his brow, storms were on the way.

If Papa's stories were true, Grandaddy had quite a prickly personality, but I never saw it, and I usually found my way to his lap. Settled there, he let me hold and listen to his gold pocket watch, an antiquity that fascinated me in a wristwatch world. He told me stories of his life and sang me songs. I especially liked the sad tune of "Two Little Boys in Blue" about two boys who loved the same girl. When I got too big to sit in his lap, I sat on the footstool beside him. I found his stories much more entertaining than the strange cousins who usually ended up having scuppernong wars, throwing the unripe grapes at each other in the sweltering Georgia heat.

Grandaddy had a housekeeper named Lily. She had the biggest feet of any human being I had ever seen. She too had a reputation of being irascible, but she and I loved each other. If it got too hot and buggy out in the yard with the relatives, I sought the cool quiet of the house.

The old kitchen had an ancient linoleum floor and a sink with an old, disused pump handle to one side. They had had modern plumbing installed, but no one ever took out the old pump. Nothing had any paint on it except the kitchen table which stood out in its clean whiteness, its white metal enamel surface cool to the touch. At that table, she would give me sewing lessons, and we made little aprons for me to wear to help her in the kitchen. I still have one of them, with her small, straight stitches punctuated with my large, awkward ones. She also kept a store of candy for me, boxes of Cracker Jacks or gelatin orange wedges.

Everyone else was a little scared of Lily, her being so tall, her skin so dark, and not having any teeth. I just remember being enveloped in the clean smell of fresh ironing as I hugged her hello. Once I brought her a pair of "earbobs"—which she loved—and she cried. I think I heard that she ended up in a mental institution when she tried to stab someone with a butcher knife. I never saw anything to presage that in the refuge of her kitchen—just a kind old lady who was sweet to me. It never dawned on me that she wasn't kin; it never dawned on me that she was black.

There were plenty of old kinfolks on Granny's side of the family, too, to define my sense of aging. Granny's sister, known in our family as Aunt Sister, was twenty years older than Granny and the oldest of a family of ten children of which Granny was the baby. Aunt Sister's husband, Uncle Henry—and Papa's uncle—died when I was a little girl. It was the first funeral I ever went to.

If my Granny was old, Aunt Sister was ancient, wearing her hair in a silver coil on top of her head. Once, she took it down and let me brush it for her, its silky, silver lengths unwinding down to her waist. She talked about when she was a girl, and it had been black then. I have seen pictures of her as a girl from the turn of the twentieth century with her hair piled up like a Gibson Girl. She looked a lot like Granny, except taller.

At some point, Aunt Sister lost her mind and had to go live in a home, her only son Hamilton being too occupied with his second wife to tend to his Momma. For long years, she lived in that dim, half-light of knowing, when, suddenly, she started writing people post cards. Her handwriting was a little shakier, but she knew who she was and where she was and wanted to know what was going on with her kith and kin.

I accompanied Granny to see her several times in those later years. Once we took old pictures for her to look at. When we first got there, Aunt Sis didn't recognize us, and it kind of hurt Granny's feelings. I reminded Granny that maybe it was hard for Aunt Sis to believe her baby sister was a white-haired old lady. After the pictures came out, Aunt Sis remembered everything, and they spent the afternoon laughing and reminiscing, no longer white-haired old ladies in an antiseptic-smelling hospital for the aged, but girls again with long, black hair, soft round cheeks, and dancing brown eyes.

When we left, Granny hugged her sister and there were tears in her eyes. My Granny never cried about anything, being that iron-willed breed of Southern woman, and it took me by surprise. We didn't say much on the way home, but it seemed that Granny was lost in that limbo in which baby sister remembered big sister like she used to be, tall, and strong and knowing it all.

She cried at Aunt Sis's funeral, breaking down when they played "Amazing Grace."

"They played that at Momma's funeral," she said.

The tears she had not let herself shed at that long ago loss finally flowed freely as the last guardian of her childhood memories was taken home, even if, by then, she, too, was an old lady.

Granny had another sister, but she was nothing like Aunt Sister. Named Ruby and anything but a jewel, Granny's middle sister was the meanest woman I ever knew. The announcement of an impending visit on one of her biweekly postcards was enough to throw Granny into a nervous fit. Ruby always signed her cards, "Love, R," in which Papa found no end of amusement and irony.

Aunt Ruby was a grass widow; her husband, brother to Aunt Sis's husband and another of Papa's uncles, had left her and the two children for a new life in Michigan. Ever keeping up appearances, Aunt Ruby was always flawlessly coiffed, sweetly scented, and impeccably dressed. Her home was also perfect, like a museum exhibit, hermetically sealed, in which nothing ever changed. It always smelled like lavender and bug spray, in contrast to Granny's house which always smelled like dinner.

Aunt Ruby would arrive in town on the Greyhound bus, and Granny would immediately get a headache. Ruby had a way of insulting you that you didn't realize you had been insulted until later.

"Put on some weight, now, haven't you?" she would remark in that lilting and mock pleasant voice.

She could slide that knife of meanness in between your ribs and eviscerate you, and you wouldn't have the sense to know it she did it so sweetly. Her end was more befitting her personality than her stylized life had been. She too ended her days in a nursing home. Confused in the dark of the night and old age, she got up to go to the bathroom. Unfortunately, she didn't make it and wet herself in transit. In her bafflement and unsteadiness, she slipped on the wet floor and bashed her head in on the toilet. They found her the next morning, cold and dead on the bathroom floor, reeking of urine.

My most intimate contact with the elderly was with my grandparents. They were in their fifties when I was born, but they always looked like old people to my child's eyes. They were never old in that stereotypical way though. Granny never resembled the blue-haired ladies in sensible shoes who stooped along behind their carts at the grocery store. She loved her high-heeled shoes and had a different pair for every outfit. Her hair, no longer the lustrous black of her youth, was iridescent silver. She worked at keeping her figure and walked every day.

Yet, the indignities of age will have their way. Her hands became a fascinating map of spots and wrinkles and blue veins, irresistible to us children, in contrast to our dimpled, smooth, brown ones. Dawson used to love to torment her about the sagging skin of her upper arm, shaking her hand in mock respect. Papa was equally dapper, despite the onset of the effects of the years. When his hands too showed signs of age, he bought himself a five-carat diamond ring as a consolation prize. Despite the havoc of age, they remained pretty vain, I guess.

It wasn't that they fought looking old. They didn't hang on to being young in the ways that people do now. Although Papa, every fearful of going bald, did have hair plug surgery. They wouldn't slow down. In their late sixties, they made a trip that circumnavigated the globe, visiting countries on every continent except Antarctica. Papa took seriously the childhood commission his sainted mother had given him that the world was his for the having, and he and Granny wanted to see of it as much as they could. They took later trips to the Holy Land and to Australia as they neared eighty. They prided themselves at being able to keep up with their younger traveling companions.

Back home, Momma and Aunt Norma always feared that we would get some overseas phone call that something terrible had happened, but I think there was also pride that neither Granny nor Papa was going gently into old age.

They did have to make allowances in time, however. It was most apparent on family occasions. We always had the biggest get-together around Thanksgiving. Not only did we have that holiday, but Papa's,

Granny's and Aunt Norma's birthdays as well. Our November dinner would be an extravaganza of food—turkey and dressing, venison and roast beef and potatoes, sweet potato casserole, Jello salads, fresh peas, and, most importantly, Granny's ice box yeast rolls.

We cousins had contests as to who could eat the most, with Aunt Ginger's youngest, Beatrice, holding the record at twenty-one. Lately, Della and I were thinking about that; if Beatrice had eaten that many, and all the other cousins had eaten anywhere near that many in competition, plus the adults had eaten their fill, how many of those rolls must Granny have made?

The culmination of the festive meal was not just pumpkin pies, but coconut-orange cake, a family recipe that is the best thing you have ever put in your mouth. I have that recipe, along with the recipe of icebox rolls, in Granny's own handwriting. The cards have yellowed with age, but they are precious to me as the original Declaration of Independence as historic relics. As we ate the birthday cake, and celebrated our thanksgiving at being a family and being alive, we listened to the tape of last year's dinner—a recording Granny always surreptitiously made during dinner. We laughed at the youthfulness of our voices, the inanity of the conversation, and teased Granny for being able to pull off the recording each year without us knowing it.

Yet, as the family grew to include spouses of grandchildren and then great-grandchildren, Granny struggled to keep up with the workload of cooking for such a throng. We all pitched in, but we noticed that it took her longer and longer to get over the event. So, we did what most families do; we discontinued the large family events for smaller individual family dinners, which Granny and Papa took turns attending.

This change in our family routine was, after all, only logical, but I think we lost a lot more than we gained. Yes, Granny and Papa got to be guests of honor, but they lost the pride of being hosts of the feast. That shift not only fragmented our ever-enlarging family, but took away some of the gravitas that age is supposed to bestow. We may have kept Granny from cooking herself to death, but it may have also been a statement of her eclipsed centrality or even a declaration of their loss of power over their own lives. It meant that she was growing old—and we all know where that ends.

With Sam's phone call, more than ever, my first impulse was to push my parents to sell that now overwhelming house and yard and whisk them off to a new life with me, with Sam and Dawson only several hours away. But, for all the comfort that might bring me, it would say to my parents that their lives, plans, dreams, and routines are essentially concluded, and instead of being the sun around which we all orbit, they are now demoted to satellites in our busy lives. No matter how sweet all being together again might be, even Thanksgiving dinner might taste a little sour if that was the sacrifice they would have to make to have it.

We children may have our visions of what would be ideal, but regardless of age, the old still dream dreams. Daddy still had plans for what to do with the workshop, adding this convenience or that gizmo. They were still fighting to conquer their yard, keeping the vines out of the azaleas and the brush kept cut away from the fence.

Momma and Daddy still sing the sun in its course, ignoring the implication that sunsets have meaning. Even in the face of illness, Momma was still very much herself, emboldened even by a diagnosis that identified her suffering more specifically than just the generic and damning conclusion of aging. Now she had something to fight, and fighting was what being alive is all about.

Kinfolk were not the only old people in my life who characterized what maturity would look like. One of my best friends in my teen years was Mr. Guthrie. He was in his early nineties when I met him—and blind. I met him as a part of a community outreach service project for school. What was supposed to be a single visit, however, turned into a weekly ritual for him and me.

I don't know how it started. I guess I asked him, after we chatted a moment, how he imagined people to look like after he talked to them. He said that he never really thought about it specifically. I responded that I would always be curious what people looked like and if their faces matched their voices. His clever wit piqued, he asked me if my voice matched my face. I responded that I didn't know, that he would have to tell me. At that, I took one of his hands and put it to my cheek.

The Yankee school teacher may have been taken aback, but he never said so. Instead, he pinched my nose gently, and said, "I see, meine Kleine, that we need to give you something to do." He said that he had just gotten the latest installment of *Scientific American* and would I mind reading him some of it. So, I sat beside him on the sofa and read away the afternoon.

Over the next years, we read Margaret Mead, John Dewey, and Plato as well as monthly editions of *Scientific American* and *Smithsonian*. He was a Princeton graduate and had been a high school chemistry teacher.

Now a wizened grasshopper of an old gentleman, he still had a keen mind and a teacher's heart. Long ago, he had come to town and married a local girl, taking her back up north with him. They had had several children, one of whom was a world class organist who played all over the world. He and Mrs. Guthrie returned to her girlhood home in their later years.

Although he had been blind for a long time, it never seemed to stop him from wanting to live and learn. Young readers like me fed his mind and heart, and he, in turn, nurtured our visions of the future. Even when a busy college schedule got in the way of me reading to him on a regular basis, we talked on the telephone regularly.

I went to his hundredth birthday party, and took his hand, saying "Happy Birthday." Immediately, he recognized his *meine Kleine*. After that, he got more and more frail, and soon died, having achieved the milestone he must have set for himself. His son played an organ concert at his memorial service, and I turned the pages, thinking of those long-ago pages turned in reading for his father.

Every Thursday I was at Mr. Guthrie's house, but on a rare and occasional Saturday, Momma and I got to visit Eugenie Browning. She was like a character out of a novel, exotic and rare. On our Saturday visits, she would greet us at the door in a long, luxurious velvet dressing gown, her long white hair tied up in a matching silk ribbon. We would take tea and listen to the radio broadcast of the Metropolitan Opera with her.

She had been born in Minnesota to a wealthy family, although she would never have described it that way. Momma and I deduced their status since she had orthodontia in the late 1800's—a time when our family thought indoor plumbing was innovative. She had married a young, up and coming executive at Swift Meat Company, and they emigrated to a privileged life in Buenos Aires. She had servants for everything and never learned how to do the simplest things that most of us take for granted –like cooking, driving, or ironing.

It was a fine life until the Perons came into power, and Americans had to flee for their lives, leaving everything behind but what they could carry. She and Mr. Browning were in their fifties by that time, and Swift gave him a generous retirement package on which they settled in my home town. No package, however, could equal the luxury in which they had lived in the Argentine.

So, at fifty, Eugenie Browning set about to learn all those things she did not know how to do—to drive, to cook, to iron, to pay bills, to manage a yard, and to be a competent, modern woman. Instead of being sorry for herself and mourning for that which was lost, she was thankful for the opportunity to learn new things, no matter how mundane it seemed to most people. She looked on it as an adventure just as she had viewed living abroad.

In time, her husband became infirm through a series of strokes, and he died on Christmas Day. Yet, Mrs. Browning, with her typical aplomb, shushed any expressions of sorrow or pity.

"Dudley and I had opened our presents the night before," she said. Even the setback of loss didn't dampen her spirits, and she was grateful for the blessings she had been bequeathed by life.

As a widow, she continued traveling and living her life as deeply as she could. When walking in her neighborhood seemed too fraught with the dangers of crime or an unexpected fall, she built an indoor lap pool. "A lady needs her exercise," she would say.

During our Saturday visits, she would tell us about her adventures, laugh at the small disgraces of aging, and pass on the wisdom of a lifetime with humor and humility. Her skin, especially her hands, having always been protected from the sun, lacked the age spots Granny's had. They were like alabaster, which she credited with her nightly regimen of heavy-duty moisturizing followed by gloves she slept in.

She combated the inevitable wrinkles on her brow by lifting her eyebrows slightly, giving her an expression of fascination at whatever was being discussed. It was not an affected aspect, I don't think, but more a lifestyle choice. Long ago, she must have decided that life was a gift for which one ought to be grateful, even when the offering seemed anything but a happy one.

Once I asked her about happiness.

"Happiness is highly over-rated," she returned. "Instead, I prefer to focus on enjoyment, on well-being, and on living deeply." That wisdom was a bequest it took me many years to understand.

After deciding that she had not experienced a seaside vacation since her girlhood, Mrs. Browning rented a condominium on a remote barrier island, accessible only by ferry. She invited our family to be her guest at the beach if we could then bring her home.

Curious to see Mrs. Browning at the seashore and always eager for a beach adventure, off we went, ferrying over. I don't really recall the trip there, nor do the details of the visit stand out. Much more memorable was our departure and return home. At the appointed time, we collected

Mrs. Browning's luggage and boarded the ferry with all the other island visitors heading for home.

First, there was the incongruity of Mrs. Browning among all the browned and unwashed. There she sat in her silk print, long-sleeved dress—she didn't like old arms—with her white-gloved hands folded in her lap. Sitting erectly on her place on the bench seat, she watched the other occupants of the ferry with interest, smiling enigmatically at the more naked of our fellow passengers.

Suddenly, as it does on the water, a storm blew up. Although the channel was shallow, the violent pitch of the flat-floored ferry became most distressing. We were all instructed to don life vests and to secure any loose luggage or gear. The crew dropped anchor. Mrs. Browning held Samantha's hand and tried to draw her into conversation to distract the wide-eyed, frightened child from the crisis at hand.

Just as quickly as it had come in, the storm blew out, and we were soon back on land. Mrs. Browning declared her coast vacation a rare adventure as we drove her home. A day of darkness and gloom, clouds and somberness, under her upraised eyebrows and ever-expectant hopes, was transformed into wonder.

Once I got off the phone with Sam, I had to research Parkinson's Disease to learn what it meant for Momma. It had been in the news a good bit and its symptoms had become high profile with its celebrity victims, but I needed to know what sort of prognosis it would bring. The more I read, the more alternatingly appeased and agitated I began to feel. It is not life threatening, but its ultimate state is all but deadly—you can't move, you can't swallow, you can't speak. In some people, their symptoms are mild and their life expectancy completely unaffected. In others, dementia and early death are the prospects.

I felt nauseated the more I read envisioning my Momma in such a state. That's why she hadn't told us, I was sure. She had enough Granny in her to be repulsed by others' pity. Pity was for weak people. On the other hand, she also wouldn't want to have to comfort someone like her sister Ginger for what was her crisis. I wanted to call Momma, but hesitated, not wanting to inflict my fears on her.

It is one thing to come to terms with the fact that we are all going to grow old—if we are lucky—and to die. The hard thing about Momma's news was having to know what form that end could take. That somehow seemed too much to have to bear, like something forbidden in ancient stories. Having passed the summer solstice of my own life, I look forward to the coming years with the knowledge that the days will eventually grow shorter and shorter. Yet, the idea of Momma's disease introduced a new dimension of uncertainty to the certainty of aging.

Sitting on the porch in the waning day is one of my favorite things to do—listening to the sounds of a life as the light fades. It is then when I think about what sort of old lady I will be, but it rarely includes pictures of illness. Jeremiah and I are still full of plans, busy with children still to raise, but every now and then, we notice our conversation descends into a litany of ailments. Although we laugh at his mother whose description of people and places from home are punctuated with "he's dead now," we too know that folks our age are dying, as our high school reunion bulletins now have a whole page dedicated to "In memoriam."

We torment the children with visions of what our old age will be like. In one scenario, we will purchase large touring-class motorcycles, don biker regalia, and set off to see America. The boys snort and Anna-Aileene's eyes roll at the implausibility, which makes it all the more attractive.

In another fantasy, we will purchase a huge motor home like some traveling music group and spend the year making the rounds to our children's homes, pulling up and hooking our big orange extension cord or a water hose to their houses. The kids don't want to give us any encouragement because they harbor a fear that we just might do it. Now, whatever form our old age takes, we know that uncertainty and struggle will be in irrevocable part of it.

Before we got the news of her illness, Momma wrote me about my Aunt Ginger. She and several widow friends do a lot of traveling together. Aunt Ginger's widowhood and later years, freed from care of children, spouses, and then Papa, has been a liberating time for her. She has blossomed and found a fascination with historical research, traveling to courthouses all over the southeast to unearth records of long-dead family.

Her latest trip, however, ended up being a disaster. On a cross-country train trek from Seattle to Niagara Falls, a terrible virus afflicted the tour group. The worst case had been Aunt Ginger's friend and traveling companion, who became so ill she had to be evacuated via helicopter from a Canadian hospital to our hospital back home.

Lately, Aunt Ginger and this friend were supposed to go to our family's mountain lodge for a quiet retreat. When Ginger got to her friend's house to begin the trip, she was greeted instead by an ambulance taking her friend to the hospital. In bringing her suitcases downstairs, her friend had mis-stepped and broken her leg so badly it required surgery.

Momma wrote, "I have decided that the most dangerous steps are the bottom two. You tend to quit looking at the steps as you begin looking into the room you are about to enter . . . It is frightening to realize how dangerous two steps can be."

Once I talked to Momma, I felt consoled. The medication had already restored her speaking voice to its former strength, so her words had a mother's authoritative comfort. She was taking her medication, reading about diet and exercise, and ready to put up a fight. Now that her ailments had a name, she was ready to rally against it, not willing to give up being very much alive, with all its inherent risk and uncertainty.

Influenced by stories of old or today's television serials, we would prefer tidy and predictable conclusions with meaningful and beautiful heroic endings. Instead, we continue to be treated to messy opportunities to live, love, and learn—or as my brother says, die and forget it all—fragmentary lessons in humanity which we must piece together without knowing the pattern and find or make sense where and if we can.

Momma always says, "You won't get out of this life alive," usually when talking about the extreme measures folks go to to avoid aging and decrepitude. Hamlet came to realize that readiness is all, but ready for what? Death is inevitable, but, if any of the old people I have known are indicators, no matter how old we are, we are never ready for it.

Papa, whose body was old but whose spirit was new, always looked for something to be glad about in his later days—the smell of bacon cooking, a beautiful sunrise, a visit from his family. It is almost as if, like Icarus, we are drawn to the sun, to fly as intoxicatingly high as we can, until we crash on that distant shore. We hang on for the next adventure, the next birthday, the next magazine, or the next morning. In our decrepitude, we cling to beauty of each drawn breath.

Some, like Papa, go out like meteors. Others, like Granny are torn away from us. Others dream dreams until they dream their last one, slipping into that undiscovered country. Momma's diagnosis has lent a frightening reality to aging, a wake-up call that my parents *will* actually die, like their parents before them, and that I will take their place in line. In digesting the news of Momma's condition, I realized that I too had been ignoring the bottom of the staircase.

In my curiosity about all things old, I have always loved old cemeteries. Momma used to take us to the old city cemetery to search for the graves of Prince and Princess Murat, French nobility and distant relatives of George Washington, and who had fled the French Revolution. It was like looking for the Holy Grail.

For me, then, cemeteries are not ghoulish houses of horror but friendly places where history and the present can coexist, where lives being lived can appreciate lives being remembered. Wherever we go, I like to pause if we find an old graveyard. There you can chronicle a community—when an epidemic or hard winter took a host of children, how many generations a family had been there, or who married whom.

Some of the epitaphs are amusing, like the Confederate soldier "cruelly slaughtered by Yankees," or Papa's best friend's stone which declares, "This is the worst thing that ever happened to me." Daddy is always taunting Momma that he wants a giant, black marble obelisk that would be visible from the road. Momma, depending on her mood, will either smile benignly, knowing full well she would do no such thing, or fuss at him for being such a show-off.

The stones some folks set, either by their design or by their grieving families, say an awful lot. Toys or seashells or rocks are often left as little offerings to the departed. Then the gravestone becomes not a monument to that final destination but about the journey, or at least, as the poet Gray elegized, that even ordinary lives can be well-lived.

Some people may think my interest in cemeteries is gruesome and that old things are just that, old. They want the newest and best—a new car every two years, the latest iPod, the most recent edition in the series. New is good—it is adventure; it is living. But old is life too.

One of the amazing things about having all those photos hanging on the wall is the opportunity to see ourselves in our predecessors. Samantha looks just like Aunt Ruby, a renowned beauty in her time, but she has worked hard to tame her own peppery temperament so as not to end up like Aunt Ruby. Although Edward is built just like Daddy, there is something in his face that recalls Great-Grandaddy. He even stands like him, with his hands clasped behind his back. If you hold Anna-Aileene's picture up to one of Momma at the same age, you would think it was the same person, except for the change in hairstyle.

By seeing the past alive in the present, I can keep that bottom step in mind and put whatever current calamity I am absorbed with in context—like having opened our presents before we lose the giver. I sent Momma a book that details the dietary needs of Parkinson's patients. She quickly read large portions of it and began to assimilate its information as a new way of living.

My family eats our meals on Granny's dining table, the setting of those Thanksgiving celebrations of long ago. For a long time, if I opened the china cabinet door, I could smell her house—collards, ham, hoe cake, and moth balls. Sitting at the old table, remembering the old stories and looking at those old photos, I can savor the richness of the harvest of our humanity and be thankful for the banquet of living, even when the dinner served up—or the form it may take—is not what I expected.

People Can Surprise You

MY HUSBAND THINKS I watch too many crime dramas on television. He doesn't say that *exactly*, but I can tell he wonders how a tender mother of four can watch so much human depravity for entertainment.

He claims the most amazing thing about my questionable television taste is that I can go to sleep to such murder and mayhem. He watches along with me some times, but his mock enthusiasm for back-to-back reruns on the cable channel reveals his true feelings.

The very title of the most popular series and its many spin-offs *is* pretty ridiculous, inviting viewers to nurture a false sense of security in our chaotic world. *Law and Order*: The title is even more ironic when the very theme of many of the program's episodes is that justice is frequently not only blind but deaf.

Today's police shows are much darker than they were in my childhood. I grew up watching the microcosmic struggle between good and evil in weekly, hourly installments on *Perry Mason, Dragnet, Adam-12, Hawaii Five-O, Ironsides,* and later *Matlock* and *Murder, She Wrote*. I don't stop with just fictionalized series; I love to watch documentaries on axe murderers and serial killers—Jack, the Ripper, Lizzie Borden, and Ted Bundy.

Crime, especially murder, I must confess, is intellectually captivating: the mystery of the human psyche gone wrong, the scientific processes that police must use to gather and find meaning in the evidence, the matching of wits of attorneys and prosecutors; I was hooked from the time I read my first Agatha Christie mystery. The drama of the murder and the catching and convicting of the culprit seem a cathartic way to reinforce my hope that although bad things happen, ultimately, right prevails.

Shamefacedly, perhaps it is my own way of rubbernecking on the highway of life's mishaps while still congratulating myself for not holding up traffic.

I realize this curiosity of mine is totally inconsistent with my personality since I cannot watch actual violent acts on television—much less real life—without wincing and hiding my eyes. Until I was a teenager, I could not watch the infamous flying monkey scene in the annual spring replay of *The Wizard of Oz* in which the Scarecrow is rent to shreds. I have never seen either *The Exorcist* or *Silence of the Lambs* or sat through the first scene of *Jaws*, although I read all three novels.

Pregnant with my first child, I fainted in a movie theater once when the action of the "action adventure" feature was too intense with heads flying and blood spurting. I experienced chest pains during *Jurassic Park* when the T-Rex tried to eat the children out of the car like so many canned Vienna sausages at a picnic.

My husband likes boxing, but I cannot sit still when he has it on the television. He loves *America's Funniest Home Videos* and all those other blooper programs, but I find the anticipated possibility for spinal cord injury or head trauma to be too intense for humor. Those are real people, after all.

One May afternoon, the drama of murder and death met people real to me and brought real life home. A dear friend of our family, suffering from the residual effects of cancer treatment, stopped at a local shopping center that had an easily accessible bathroom in order to take care of business because he couldn't quite make it all the way home. He had taken the indignities of aging and treatment in stride and had located bathrooms all over town, should the need for one arise inconveniently. My daddy had done the same thing, making sure that a sudden need would not become a lingering embarrassment to his male pride.

Harrison Augustus Turnbull, Jr. stopped that spring afternoon, as he had done before, but this time he did not get back on his way home, feeling relieved and efficient. Instead, he emerged from the public restroom, stumbling, bleeding, dying. Calling for help to passersby going into a nearby shop, he pled for his life, according to workers catching a quick smoke out in the parking lot.

Gasping and bloody, Harry faltered into a nearby store, full of lunchtime shoppers, and fell into the small crowd of patrons. Bleeding from a dozen stab wounds to the face, neck and chest, he died in the arms of a stranger. The store owner said later that thought he recognized Harry, but that was only after Harry's obituary appeared in the paper.

When people die, it seems to be human nature for survivors to think back and amass in one big mental pile all their memories of the one lost. It is as if we must pull together all those things that are undying—our memories—in order to protect ourselves from the impermanence of life. Then, we can fool ourselves, at least temporarily, that that person is not *really* gone.

Some of my memories of Harry are entirely vicarious. Momma and Harry go all the way back to elementary school—the same school my brother and sister and I would attend. Pinewood Memorial Elementary was built as a WPA project, but it was abandoned for a different location in the seventies by the time my sister came along. The lovely old brick Gothic building was torn down, and an angular new office building was built in its place.

Momma skipped second grade—another long story—and in that jump made two lifelong friends: Eleanor and Harry. Eleanor's grandfather had designed both the elementary school and the high school as part of our town's Depression era recovery program. Harry was the "fat boy" in the class, a rich business man's son, and much too smart in a time in which being smart was not what won popularity among one's elementary school peers.

He was a show-off in his way, playing the piano by ear and doing crossword puzzles in pen, but he was bullied on the playground. Then, those dusty scuffles were considered a normal part of growing up. Today, we have police on campus and children leave in handcuffs, and bullies create psychological pathologies manifesting untold misery and murder.

In puppyish, boyish devotion, Harry carried Eleanor's books from school on the trips home for lunch or for the evening as the trio wound their way around the pond and down the street. Harry beamed adoringly as he listened for the millionth time that the pond had been named for Eleanor. Mother's female pride was prickled at this small fabrication, a fabrication that bestowed on Eleanor a grandeur, if imaginary, that made Momma feel plain by comparison. It must have been the same way my cousins used to feel when I boasted that black-eyed Susans were named after me because my Daddy told me so.

Momma lived on the other side of the pond from the school, while Eleanor and Harry lived a little further on in Versailles Gardens, our town's first incarnation of what we now call a gated community, its allusion to European splendor adding to its mystique as did the large, brick and wrought iron gate that marked its entrance. That sort of thing did not seem to make as much difference then as it does now, Momma says. In her memory, rich and poor had more in common in the generation born in the Depression than they do today.

Harry's daddy was a stock broker and realtor, and Eleanor's daddy was an architect and artist with an independent income. Our papa was a tailor. Now, Papa had once fitted Thomas Alva Edison and Henry Ford in his youthful, itinerate days. He owned Palace Men's Shop as well as a chain of ladies' shops all over the state, but he had never advanced beyond the third grade in the primitive, south Georgia, turn-of-the-century one-room school house.

It never seemed to matter to him; indeed, it was a point of pride that he had been born dead and sent home for an idiot, according to his account. Men like him, some armed with little formal education, learned to read Shakespeare and Kipling themselves, worked hard to earn the name of the Greatest Generation, and rode the post-war wave of upward mobility. Papa's daughters went to college, and he would make millions in store profits reinvested in real estate and contemplate running for governor.

Not that there were not distinctions due to social strata and income back then. Fenley Walker Harris was a boy in Momma's class, but he had been held back several times. He was taller and bigger than the other children, and he wore overalls to school. Fenley Walker Harris—we always thought of him by his whole name—lived in our generational memory as notorious for kicking the ball during fierce, free-play, kickball battles all the way out of the schoolyard and down the road, into the pond. He stood out for his height and his worn but well-pressed clothes, more suitable for farming than school. But even he had his standing among his peers as designated kicker and as protector of little fat boys who played the piano by ear.

He would grow up to be a successful plumber, despite his humble beginnings. Later, the pond would change, too, and be made into a park with sidewalks and picnic tables where our town's annual Fourth of July fireworks and festivities would be held. Now, even that festivity has been outgrown, and the pond, even more lately, dried up in a mystery some attribute to the drought that gripped the Southeast.

But then, there was only a dusty path and a glistening pond, a backdrop for children's journeys to and from school as they chattered about blackouts and whether they would have birthday cake due to the sugar rationing, compared cartoons of grinning Tojo, and pretended to be Tarzan, Jane and Cheetah after having seen the latest Johnny Weissmuller movie at the Saturday matinee.

Moving up to high school changed things besides the path home. Momma and Harry were on the school newspaper together. Our town boomed in the post-war years of the fifties: the teacher's college became a university, and we finally got a real hospital—the one I, my siblings, and my children would be born in. Despite all this progress, prosperity perpetuated a naiveté—or some call it ignorance—that was not just special to our town.

Girls, dressed in saddle oxfords and poodle skirts with starched crinolines beneath, donned red lipstick and went to the movies, holding the sweaty hands of boys whom they would not kiss until after the third date. That was the rule—one of the many rules that governed everything. You did not wear white shoes after Labor Day or before Easter. Places farther north extended the white shoe moratorium to Memorial Day, but, in the Deep South, heat came sooner as did our white shoes.

Nice girls did not have pierced ears and did not hang out on the corner of Talbot's Drug Store with the *hotties* with their slicked-back hair and tight t-shirts worn shockingly as outerwear instead of underwear. It was a time of outward stability and seething undercurrents. Rock and roll's overt sexuality questioned traditional rules of decorum and repression. Many in the establishment viewed the Civil Rights Movement with terror, seeing it as elbowing its way into a status quo meant for whites only. I don't know how much of that beat Momma heard at the time; she listened to Mario Lanza, not Elvis.

Momma and Harry went their separate ways for college. Momma stayed in town and went to the local college where she met Daddy. Harry went to a military prep school and then off to the Ivy League. Their paths merged again back at Versailles Gardens, whose community clubhouse was home of our local Junior Woman's Club. There Momma met Harry's wife, Vivian. Harry had returned to town with his Yankee wife to join his father's firm and sell real estate.

At this point my memories of Harry are my own, but my early memories of the Turnbulls are vague and dreamlike around the edges as so many childhood recollections are. Maybe they aren't real memories at all, instead only recollections created by pictures in old photo albums. My memories of baby Sonny's (short for Harrison Augustus Turnbull III), Harry and Vivian's only child, christening and of whom Momma is the godmother—are selective. Mother would have been pregnant with my brother at the time, although *that* entire event went without my notice, being a three-year-old. A photo shows me in a new, red dress and new Mary Jane shoes—both of which I do remember. The reception at the Country Club is my only tangible memory of the event, especially the fireplace, the opening of which was as tall as my daddy.

In dream-time fashion, my next memory involves the elder Turnbulls. We were invited to go swimming at their pool—a real luxury and contrast to our usual visits to the Elks' Pool. Weeks before our swim, I had suffered burns on my feet that had only just healed. I don't remember what I was thinking to get into such a mess. Not quite five, I was still young enough to enjoy making mud pies on a summer day and young enough to not quite understand cause and effect realistically.

Daddy had been burning yard trash in his effort to tame the wilderness that was our yard. In a child's leap of illogic, I decided that ashes would make a proper icing for my mud pies—like make-believe confectioner's sugar. It had, after all, rained in the days after the fire. Being summer time, I was barefoot, and I walked, like some Indian spiritualist, confidently into the center of the burned pile where the ashes were whitest.

Unfortunately, the center of the pile was still hot, and my feet were badly burned. After the blisters had gone, the new skin was too tender for the rough surface of the pool's floor, and the soles of my feet were soon a bloody mess. Harrison Augustus Turnbull, Sr. would later drop dead by that pool as he enjoyed his evening martini.

What I remember most about Harry was when my parents and their young couple friends socialized together. Shared childhood memories and the earnestness of young parenthood forged friendships and provided companionship among them, although the Turnbulls also ran with another—and faster and richer—crowd. My keenest memories of Harry of that time are at the informal dinner parties Momma and Daddy would host.

Checkered table cloths and candles in Mateus bottles were the décor then. As the beer and the Wild Turkey would flow, Harry's piano pieces got louder and faster—he could play the circus march standing backwards at the piano—and his limericks would get raunchier. We children would sneak to the head of the stairs and lie on our tummies to peer through the banister railing at the grown-ups acting so differently than we normally perceived them.

I have a mental snapshot of Harry, lying stretched out on the couch, stocking feet resting—in adult disdain of rules—on the arm rest, drink balanced on his stomach, giving forth his seemingly endless supply of inappropriate poetry. This was in stark contrast to the snapshot of my Daddy, taken at one of these get-togethers and pasted now in one of Momma's photo albums, fast asleep on the floor, his drink miraculously balanced on his stomach. Someone, Vivian most likely, had taken it and sent it to him in the mail, with "Life of the Party" written across the bottom of the photo, as a joke.

My childish incredulity at seeing my parents and other adults as real people replete with senses of humor and even as perpetrators of hijinks was usually stretched to its utmost when the Turnbulls were around. Harry apparently hadn't changed much since his elementary school days. He was still brilliant and he still liked to show off—as he did playing the piano backwards. He was the person you could always count on to know the answer when you couldn't remember a piece of trivia—who acted in what movie or what the words were to an obscure or long-forgotten song. The price you had to pay for scratching that intellectual itch was Harry gloating that *he* knew it and you didn't. Both Harry and Vivian were staunch and extroverted know-it-alls.

Mother, with her own way of playing the game, delighted in catching them at it by purposely mispronouncing a word and waiting for one or the other to correct her. The trap set and the bait taken, Momma would laugh at the one laid low in her reverse upsmanship.

But Daddy and another of their friends, Ernie, played plenty of pointed pranks much more monumental than Momma's subtle brinksmanship. When Harry made his first hole in one, Daddy crafted him a four-foot-tall "1" out of wood, painted it a glittering gold, and carved a hole in it, presenting it to him with mock pomp like an Academy Award. The "1" hung in Harry's office for years.

We had spent that weekend with the Turnbulls at their river house. Somehow in the merriment of the moment, Daddy put his back out, and spent the weekend "walking like a crab," as Vivian described it. On the ride home, my baby brother and I, sweaty and whiny, sat in the front seat of our '57 Chevy with Momma, and Daddy lay flat on his back in the back seat.

Daddy got out of the car when we got home, but he got stuck later than night on their bedroom floor. Momma had to call the fire department to rescue him. We children watched from behind the doorjamb of the bedroom—we were admonished to not get in the way—as the burly firemen used a board to lift our prone Daddy off the floor and on to the bed.

Fire departments don't do things like that anymore, I have learned. Those days of rescuing kittens out of trees are gone, I was informed by the nasal-voiced dispatch operator whom I called to get help fishing out a squirrel that had somehow gotten into Momma's house and fallen into the downstairs toilet—and which she had only just discovered at a most unpropitious moment. Since we had no experience in fishing for squirrels, the squirrel went unrescued, and we left him to drown, disposing of him the next day.

I guess it is perfectly understandable in today's crowded and dangerous world that emergency professionals spend their valuable efforts on human victims of circumstance—but Momma was upset about it for days and has never felt the same about squirrels since.

Then there was the time after the Turnbulls had been influential in founding and opening our town's first art gallery, called simply *La Musee*. No one in town pronounced it correctly, but Vivian always did, since her major in college had been French literature. Our little gallery showcased local talent as well as traveling exhibits from larger and more noteworthy galleries. Vivian herself was quite an accomplished watercolorist, and her illustrations were included in nature books. The Turnbulls frequently had art hanging in their home on loan from the gallery in those early days.

Later, after Harry was rich in his own right, they purchased paintings and sculptures outright. They had several beautiful bronzes, one of which capped a fountain as a climax for their driveway entrance. Daddy fell in love with one of the paintings in their personal collection, a painting made by a young black artist who later went blind. In colors as warm as an Alabama summer, it depicts a girl standing outside a fence, looking at a house confined within. I always wondered if Daddy identified with the girl, on the outside looking in, and if that may be how he somehow still felt around people like the Turnbulls.

Daddy grew up on the wrong side of the tracks, and someone like Vivian who took a sketch pad instead of a camera on their yearly trips abroad must have seemed like she came from Mars. Yet, when that painting no longer complemented their décor, the Turnbulls sold it to Daddy for a dollar—and it hangs proudly my living room to this day. I guess everyone had a turn being outsiders at some point, so the symbol of alienation evolved into a loving reminder of friends of youth.

Yet in those early days when adversity and their own failings and failures had not yet softened their compassion towards one another, Vivian's perfect French accent and Harry's smirking reminders of the latest minutiae he had miraculously recalled when no one else could were all the challenge Daddy needed.

One night, while the Turnbulls were out of town, Daddy and Ernie, his partner in crime, let themselves into the Turnbulls' house and hung their own "art" all over the walls of the living room. Over the works on loan from the museum and their own Andrew Wyeth paintings hung kitsch-art pictures of purple mushrooms with Alice in Wonderland polka dots, maudlin kittens with big eyes, and Warhol-style Budweiser cans done in the finest schoolhouse tempera.

Having seen the men loading all these pictures into Ernie's station wagon—pictures which, now that I think about it, must have taken them all afternoon to paint—we children were sworn to secrecy. My parents' stifled giggles went on for days as they imagined the Turnbulls, who had come in late in the night and had not detected the prank, explaining the new décor to Sonny that next morning.

Even though Harry was a native Southerner, Vivian always made a point of remembering that Daddy was a native Alabamian and that Ernie's family owned nearby tobacco fields, beginnings that somehow by their geography rendered them inferior to some folks' minds. In the warfare of friendship, I guess things had to be balanced out and the witty outwitted; so, they played their practical jokes.

The last prank I remember was perpetrated while the Turnbulls were building their dream house. Their palatial home sat on an expansive acreage that had once been a territorial governor's farmland. The house was bigger than an elementary school, spreading out in what seemed like acres of rooms: countless bedrooms and bathrooms, library, playroom, kitchen, pantries, formal dining, family dining, art studio, billiard room, and a screened pool porch grandly called a *lanai*.

The most splendid room, however, was the living room. The focal point of the room was a freestanding marble fireplace, but the most amazing part of the all-white room was that it housed two identical Steinway baby grand pianos, standing end to end. That way, Vivian and Harry could give recitals—or have them given—in their home. It was amazing to me that anyone could live in a house with a room big enough to hold two pianos, not to mention enough space to seat scores in a benefit featuring pianists Ferrante and Teicher.

But, at the time of Daddy's prank, the house was only a foundation and stud walls. He and Ernie snuck out in the nighttime and erected a huge sign, which read "Another Fine Home by Jim Walters," in scale with the grandeur of the house-to-be. As a child, I had no idea what it meant, not knowing about modular, "pre-fab," packaged homes sold by Jim Walters, advertised in magazines and in our Sunday comics section. I can only imagine Vivian's indignation at this swipe at her home that would boast marble tile, gold fixtures, and Spode sinks.

Part of me wonders now if jealousy inspired these pranks, but mostly, I think it was men's versions of boyish pranks. My brother would manifest the same form of wit in high school when he and some of his friends left a sign on the island in the middle of the old pond offering social commentary on some "visiting" sculpture that had been placed there and other places in town. The local paper offered a front-page picture of the sign—a huge wooden sign erected by "Vandals for a Better Tomorrow"—which read simply, "Art?"

Whether what prompted Daddy's tricks and Harry's conspicuous consumption was friendly, male competition or something less admirable, time had its own way with all the friends. Vivian died a decade before Harry, after a thirty-year battle with colon cancer. When Vivian finally succumbed after the third recurrence would not remit, Harry had remarried quickly and unwisely to a woman who lacked Vivian's intellect, style, beauty, or talent. He boasted that he married Marianne because she didn't remember World War II.

All of us thought he had lost his mind, and our suspicions were confirmed when Marianne threw out all of Vivian's beautiful French bone china because it was "chipped." After she renovated all traces of Vivian out of the Turnbull mansion, it seemed that the Turnbull money had run out, too. They ended up having to sell the place in order to live. Bad went to worse for them when Harry's own firm encouraged him to retire, the firm his grandfather had started. He was reduced to looking for a job at age sixty although his obituary would kindly report it as "in business for himself" and being "semi-retired."

Marianne, who had previously lived in a cement block duplex with window air conditioner units, thought Harry had a lot more money than he did—or maybe he had a lot more money before he met Marianne, as most of us believed. She acted like it was a comedown to have to buy a home on the golf course of the nicest subdivision in town. Neither

Marianne, spending more money than he had, nor the alcohol that became his habit to consume assuaged Harry's sense of loss it seems.

On that spring day, when Harry's path brought him to that restroom, crossing that of a sociopathic drifter, it was not the loss of a wallet full of cash but of a gold ring that Vivian had given him that Harry balked at parting with. Police speculated that Harry's reluctance in giving up the ring was what set his assailant off. Whatever it was, Harry was dead nonetheless.

It was a spring day and hydrangeas were in bloom. The weather was mild, with summer's heat and humidity only a future promise. There was a wafting breeze that carried on it a hint of the coast's salty air and the laughing voices of children from a nearby elementary school. Before Harry emerged bleeding from the restroom, an unkempt, unshaven stranger in a green camouflage jacket and with a knife stuffed in his belt barreled past a young woman who was taking a smoking break from her job at one of the nearby shops.

She made eye contact with the rough man with shaggy, dirty hair and a big knife in his belt—both an unaccustomed sight in this upscale shopping center. Later, when she tearfully testified at the trial, she noted that she would never forget the face of the man who ran into her but who mercifully spared her unlike the man in the bathroom. Police used her description to create a sketch which was quickly circulated by the news media. The school down the street—where Harry's own grandchildren were innocently learning—was placed on lockdown as law enforcement canvassed the area with dogs, seeking the fleeing suspect.

One of my brother's college friends described our home town as a nice place to live but you wouldn't want to visit there. Although it boasted a university, our town was still a small town in mentality as well as actuality. You couldn't go to either of the malls without running into someone you know. People still speak on the sidewalk as they pass. Traffic is terrible because there are only two main highways that intersect downtown.

Yet, even with its small-town comfort, our town was no stranger to grisly murder long before Harry's death. When I was five, a family was slaughtered in their own home on a Saturday afternoon. They were discovered by the sole survivor, a daughter who returned from babysitting for neighbors during the Saturday afternoon football game. Uncle Ewell had presided over the trial, and it was one he had a hard time living with, since two of the dead were girls his own daughters' ages.

We experienced our first city wide curfew when trick or treat—it was Hallowe'en—had to be done before dark for fear that the killer would add more victims to his tally. The murder was never solved, but it was believed by many that the pastor of a local church was a prime suspect.

When I was in college, an infamous serial killer slaughtered several girls in the sorority house across the street from my dorm. A decade later, he was electrocuted, and people celebrated. More recently, a woman was kidnapped from the mall parking lot, only to have her charred, tortured body found the next day, tied between two trees with her own jumper cables.

We children had also grown up with grisly, gothic tales of Southern small-town violence. Papa had come to the rescue of a woman whose husband was chasing her with a butcher knife down the street in front of the men's shop. The man had cut her throat, and Papa told us she had to hold her head on with her hands. She died of her wounds in Papa's arms.

Daddy, growing up in an even smaller, southern Alabama town than we lived in then recounted many sordid sagas from his youth driving a wrecker—an early version of rescue in those days. A fireman had been decapitated by flying slate roof tiles, dislodged by the heat of a fire; another man was cut in two when he was fishing from a bridge and a car didn't see him. Daddy himself accidentally shot his friend Pot-eye's big toenail off with a b-b gun.

There were also songs of murder to accompany real life. Daddy sang to us of "Poor Little Marion Parker," allegedly a local girl lured away from school by a friendly stranger, and who was found later, chopped to bits. Then there was Great-grandma Wilfred's admonition to avoid black men with paper bags because they usually carried pieces of little white girls they had cut up. My great grandmother's fears were a part of racist imagination of her time, but Marion Parker did turn out to be a real girl. She wasn't killed in Alabama, however, but in California somewhere, and the story had become real to Daddy through the radio.

But this murder, Harry's murder, touched a nerve. Harry had, after all, been a somebody—and he was our somebody. The local paper ran several pieces about how Harry's death had shattered the local peace in a larger way than just a single, senseless act of violence. We had experienced those after all. Some saw it as growing pains as our town transformed into a city, a place where the friction of strangers was bound to elicit violent responses on occasion.

But, for us, it wasn't about shifting socio-economics or urban blight, it was personal. It was our friend who was slaughtered by a knife-wielding stranger at mid-day. The fugitive was apprehended a few days later, either by good police work or by serendipity, depending on whom you talked to. Apparently, he had left a trail of death as he made his way to our town, killing a man to steal his truck. That missing truck was what brought the police's attention to a motel near the interstate, a few blocks from the murder scene. There, they cornered the man with his knife, and the two cases became one. The man was apprehended and charged with felony murder.

Mourning does not end when the funeral is over. It also doesn't begin just with death. Vivian's death had changed Harry. Marianne's throwing out Vivian's china, chips and all, was just a small part of the loss. Sonny inherited the river house after Vivian died—and a few of her paintings and one of her pianos—but a lot of what was Vivian's was lost in Marianne's remodel of Harry, including Harry himself.

What hadn't gone through Marianne's hands was lost in Harry's loss of himself. Folks gossiped about his early retirement and his drinking. Since Momma is Sonny's godmother, Momma and Daddy were frequently included in holiday festivities at Sonny's house after Vivian died. Momma saw her role as being a surrogate grandmother to Vivian's grandchildren who never got to meet their vivid and lively grandmother.

Vivian would have loved the children. All four—which we imagined was Sonny's reaction to being an only child—bore her stamp in one way or another. Two were named after Vivian, and they all either had her freckles or her large eyes or her artistic talent.

One of my last memories of Vivian is of her visit to me when Edward was born. She came to see me in the little bungalow we lived in. It was Papa's—and where Momma was born and where Momma and Daddy lived when I was born. We had worked hard renovating it, but it was a far cry from the Turnbulls' estate. Yet, Vivian had softened over the years and in her struggles with cancer. She held my baby tenderly, remarking about his beautiful eyes, his perfect toes. She rocked him to sleep, complimenting me on the platform rockers Aunt Ruby had given me which I had recovered. It was a small moment in which nothing mattered in the world but the sweet and even breathing of a sleeping baby.

Vivian's funeral had been held graveside. She had wanted to be cremated, but neither Sonny nor Harry could bear the idea. Harry ordered a double tombstone with his name carved into the stone with hers, only the dates of his death missing. We were pretty horrified at the idea, but it was a strong indicator of Harry's mood at the time.

Harry's funeral was at the Methodist Church even though he wasn't a Methodist. Marianne was, and it was her last act of remodeling. Harry was an Episcopalian as was his father and grandfather before him. He didn't attend much, although Sonny did after his mother died. I guess Harry was less of a snob than he seemed in some ways. The church's bulletin always contained a weekly admonition to "remember the church in your will." Harry promised that he would, including the phrase, "Hey! I'll never forget you" in his will. I wondered, when he died, if he really did do that. I wouldn't have put it past him.

I had moved away by the time Harry was murdered, so I did not go to his funeral. Momma recounted how Sonny gave the eulogy, a heart-rending soliloquy to his father, celebrating that which was great about him and trying to forgive that which wasn't. He was his daddy, and he loved and missed him, and anything else was simply prolog. His words were as much for himself as for the assembled mourners.

Harry's death served as a wake-up call that life is short and mistakes can be irrevocable. It was every parent's silent prayer: he did not want his own children, now small and impressionable, stung by any mistakes he would make as he had been by his father's.

Yet, we are all touched irrevocably by our parents and our grandparents, from their eye color to their tastes and talents, by their triumphs and their tragedies. Sonny's children understood more of what was going on and were left disoriented and afraid. Sonny's oldest child Gus, with his grandfather's name and face as well and whose birth I had witnessed, developed irrational fears—thunder, loud noises, bugs. He could not bear to be parted from his mother. Eventually, Gus returned to a child's routine, even if he lacked a child's blissful ignorance of the dangers of the world.

Sonny's oldest daughter Bug seemed fine until the trial. Then she developed anxiety attacks and suffered crying jags. No wonder. A year and a half's worth of healing was re-aggravated by reliving the gory details of Harry's death as the newspaper and local news carried tidbits of the trial daily. The children were shipped off to their momma's folks up north—Sonny too had married a Yankee wife—to avoid the bludgeoning a public trial can give to your peace of mind, but Sonny remained.

Sonny was a judge. He had majored in business and worked in his daddy's firm for a while. When that didn't work Sonny laid carpet for a while in an effort to break the family mold. Eventually, however, he went to law school. He had Vivian's independence, people said, and social conscience. But there he was, in a courtroom as victim.

Since Harry's murder had been perpetrated in the course of a felony—robbery—the prosecution asked for capital murder. The defense did not have a very good hand to play. Forensic evidence was damning: the murderer's bloody fingerprints in the bathroom and Harry's blood on his clothing and his knife. Eye witness testimony put him at the scene at the time.

Then the public defender started trying her case. Her defense strategy was self-defense—that the murder had been instigated by Harry's aggressive behavior and triggered by the defendant's long history of abuse. Mother's indignation was palpable over the phone when she called to tell me.

Aggressive—Harry was anything but that. He could be a smartass and he could be a know-it-all, but he would not have been "physically aggressive." After all, as the fat boy in elementary school, he hid behind wit and Fenley Walker Harris. Whatever faults Harry had, Momma couldn't stand the idea of a defense that would intimate that Harry in some way deserved his end, that his behavior mitigated the desecration of being stabbed a dozen times in a public restroom.

That's when she decided to testify. Momma called Sonny and then the prosecutor. She reminded them that she had known Harry since third grade, had known him through high school, had been godmother to his son and grand-daughter, and had been there when his first wife died. She knew Harry and could testify with fervent faith to his nature and to his latter-day physical ailments.

I wondered at my mother, always so critical of Harry in those later years, suddenly coming to his rescue—or at least the rescue of his character. But maybe it wasn't he she was rescuing, but something in herself. She was powerless when her childhood friend was murdered. She was powerless to help her godchildren cope with the senselessness of loss.

Now, at least she could do something, if only a small thing, to help redeem her friend and fight for his innocence in his own end. Mother was grilled three times—that was her word for it—once for discovery, once for the judge, and finally in front of the jury. She made the judge laugh when she demurred from a straight answer when asked how old she was. Harry would have approved of the irony of laughter at his murder trial.

Whether it was the evidence, Momma's testimony, or the ludicrousness of a 66-year-old man with cancer and a bad back picking a fight with an armed vagrant in a public restroom at mid-day, the jury returned with a guilty verdict within a half hour of their retiring to the jury room. Everyone felt pleased and thought that things could now be set right. The killer could be killed. Society could have its closure, whatever that means.

But that is when things got really interesting. Sonny surprised everyone when he testified in the penalty phase of the trial, and, in defiance of the culture of vengeance and everyone's expectations, asked that the jury not award the death penalty to the man who murdered his father. Despite the unspeakable cruelty of the murderer's action, an impassioned Sonny implored the jury to let it all be over. If the man were given life without parole, the family could move on, could begin to heal. If he were given the death penalty, they would have to relive the horror every time an appeal was mounted, ripping open old wounds and creating new ones.

In our state, appeals usually stretch out for a decade or more. It was time to bury Harry, once and for all. According to the eleven o'clock news broadcast, he looked right at the jury members with those eyes so much like his mother's, and said unwaveringly but in a low, quiet voice—made smaller by the enormity of where he was and the circumstances under which he was speaking—and challenged the jury to let go of the need for vengeance which diminishes us all.

No one would disagree that Harry did not deserve that grisly end; Sonny introduced the idea that neither did his murderer.

Sonny also claimed a victim's right to speak to the assailant from the witness stand at sentencing. He testified that he had tried to hate his father's murderer but that instead he had only pity for him. Showing a strength and courage none of us knew he had, Sonny told the man that he wasn't forgiving him necessarily for the man's sake, but for his own.

In that moment, Sonny seemed to come to the point he could forgive himself and his father for all those things we regret and resent in a lifetime but which seem trivial in the face of death. A writer in the paper extolled his astounding message after the trial, calling his statements and actions better than any Sunday sermon. What it was was an incident of life imitating art. A *Law and Order* episode portrays the mother of a victim of a thrill killing forgiving his killer; like murder, it seemed all the more amazing in real life.

Shortly after the killing, Sonny wrote a column for the paper, expressing public gratitude for the community's support and pleading with the community to not live in fear, to continue to frequent the shopping center where the murder happened, and to let the Turnbulls be a part of the community's healing. His public stand to find community in tragedy, to find goodness in bad things, to stand for life in the face of death, even for the undeserving, somehow lent some meaning—even if after the fact—to the whole event.

Harry's senseless denouement gored what I knew of life and order on a very personal level, but the public words and private strength of his son, the rallying of a community, Momma's testimony for friend from the third grade somehow cleansed my understanding of it, wiping up a spattered sense of security from off that public bathroom floor, urging me to replace a vision of carnage with a memory of love and life.

Bad things don't make sense, but maybe they aren't supposed to. Whatever sense we make of it comes in what it does to us afterward, sometimes loudly and biblically from a voice out of the whirlwind or, more often, softly, in defiance of a culture of vengeance. People are murdered in real life. Real people and real life usually don't wrap things up as tidily as they do on television, everything solved in an hour, because real people can surprise you, even your friends from childhood or your own Momma.

Reunion

"If I weren't dreading this so much," Jeremiah said as we accelerated down the interstate through the mountains, "this would be the highlight of my summer."

Jeremiah's seemingly contradictory feelings centered on the reunion with his three best friends from college toward whom we were speeding that late Sunday afternoon. The last time they had all been together was ten years ago.

This week's reunion, despite the delay of years, was urgent; Obie's cancer had recurred for a third time and he was not responding successfully to treatment. Fearing that, if they missed this opportunity, the next time they would come together would be at Obie's funeral, busy schedules were rearranged around Obie's chemotherapy timetable so that we could all meet at his farm in the hills of east Tennessee.

I could tell that Jeremiah felt a mix of longing and dread in anticipation of this gathering as he was alternatively pensive and garrulous with forced high spirits to distract us both from things neither of us wanted to think about.

I had my own reason to feel trepidation at this meeting. Although we meet with one of the trio yearly, I would be meeting for the first time two of Jeremiah's closest friends. Being the second wife, I always wonder what feelings I will confront in others who knew Jeremiah before we married and who were friends with his first wife. Jeremiah assured me that men are different from women in this regard, and that they would like me fine. They would accept whomever he had chosen on that basis alone.

Besides, Obie had been married at least five times that they knew of, and they had accepted all of his brides as they came and went. I didn't know if that was comforting or not. I guess I nursed a secret hope that they would like me for me, but acceptance would be a start.

Jeremiah and I fit together so well, it seemed logical that those who liked him would like me. But, those friends from your youth love you not necessarily because you have all that much in common any more but because you shared a special time and special experiences that bond you forever. Shared dreams, disenchantments, ideas and laughter transcend divergent career paths or how many women you married.

Then there is always that small awkwardness when people ask, "So how is it that you and Jeremiah met?" To be so traditional—even old fashioned—I began my romance with Jeremiah in a most unconventional way for someone like me.

Long ago, most people met at church or school or through friends. In my youth, the singles bar was all the rage for meeting Mr. or Mrs. Right. The downside and dangers of that venue of love served as the subject of a chilling psychological thriller novel then movie, *Looking for Mr. Goodbar*, and suddenly that location and that lifestyle lost a lot of its allure.

The gym or the grocery store became the next setting for the search for affection in a more health-conscious world. Not that many psychopathic killers hang out in the produce section, it seems to me. Then came the internet. Chat rooms were like the singles' bars of the previous generation, except suitors didn't have to change out of their pajamas or buy anyone a drink.

Yet that social vehicle also brought risk as predators could be virtually invited into your living room. When I tell people that Jeremiah and I met on the internet, their eyebrows raise, expecting something salacious. Instead, I disappoint them—or amuse them, depending on how well they know me—with the fact that we met via a John Milton list serve message board.

As if that isn't eccentric enough, we initiated our first communication talking about two of Milton's poems frequently eclipsed by *Paradise Lost*, "L'Allegro" and "Il Penseroso." But, what did anyone expect of two people who read the dictionary for entertainment?

Our courtship was equally unconventional for someone like me. I lived in Alabama, and he lived in Philadelphia. Most of our early communication, once we got past our natural caution and talking about literature, was through the written word. Even through the seeming modern miracle of instant messaging, this sort of contact always struck me as a throwback to earlier days.

Granny kept a treasured stack of yellowed Western Union telegrams, tied in a pink ribbon, in her bureau drawer. These missives were Papa's earnest pleas to Granny to wait for him. They had been sweethearts since they first caught sight of each other across a table at a childhood birthday party.

Papa's wanderlust, however, left Granny vulnerable to the attentions of one Royal Bradford, the school superintendent who lived in the only painted house in town. Granny enticed Papa with the news that Royal had proposed, but she didn't know what she should do. Papa, trapped in the Everglades with a month before the ferry returned, fired off telegram after telegram. His words won her heart, and they married later that year.

The vehicle of email and even telephone conversations permitted Jeremiah and me to discover each other's hearts and minds first. Not only did we share a love of literature but also of music, philosophy, and Andy Griffith. Our youth, separated by miles, had been spent listening to the same music—from Old Time Gospel to classical to rock n' roll. We both had Grannies who baked blackberry pies, and we watched Lawrence Welk with our Papas. We had the same bent sense of humor, old fashioned values, and rebellious spirit. It was love.

We met, face to face, and the strong feelings planted in words were harvested in flesh. I loved his blue eyes, wild, curly hair and hands big enough to palm my head like a basketball. He found my brown eyes captivating and my tiny hands amazing. I cooked with abandon, just like his Granny. His gait reminded me of Papa.

There was always that sense that we were reuniting rather than just meeting. I suppose you could get Jungian about it, or even Freudian, but the truth was, despite being middle aged parents, we fell in love with the same foolishness of youth. We courted long distance over the many miles of interstate, meeting half-way in out-of-the-way locations, cramming a lifetime of living into weekend increments, and putting a lot of miles on our cars.

Partly in jest, I asked Jeremiah to marry me pretty early on. He, more serious than not, had said yes, but middle-aged love, unlike young love, is complicated. We had children and homes and jobs. It was going to be a matter of getting all the other parts of our lives to cooperate with love. Since teachers are more portable than theologians, we decided I would look for a job where he was. I mounted my search like a field general with plans, contingencies, and fallback maneuvers, but Jeremiah maintained the fear that, despite our good fortune, that all of it could fall through at any minute—or that I would lose my nerve and decide I couldn't give up leaving home.

For me, there was only the small matter of telling my children—whom I had kept apprised of my desire to move—and my parents—whom I pretty much kept in the dark. The hardest part about divorcing, moving, and remarrying was the parental disapproval; but, as I have learned, both as a child and as a parent, parents don't always know everything.

Obie had married a divorcee with seven children. Apparently, they were church friends, and they had gradually grown in love and trust. He had helped her through the serious illness of one of her children, and she stuck with him when his cancer returned. Together they bought an old farmhouse on a hill, refurbished it to meet the needs of growing children, and filled it with love and music.

Now, under Naomi's influence, Obie had changed some. He was reportedly a conservative, a Republican, and maybe even a bit of a fundamentalist. Jeremiah recounted Daniel's description of this new wife as someone who home-schooled her children and didn't believe in having a television. I had to admit that this depiction seemed a bit strange, but I didn't want to be guilty of being judgmental of a man's new wife, being one myself. Besides, Obie was always changing, Jeremiah said.

Obie was one of those people who was a force of nature, who came at life with all his guns blazing, according to his friends. He had lived a mercurial life, a hard life really, as if he were looking for something. Jeremiah laid the blame on Obie's father, Obadiah, Sr. When Obie was a freshman in college, his father had divorced his mother, and remarried. The new wife quickly had a son whom his father named Obadiah, Jr., just like our Obie.

The rift that this seeming replacement caused cut deep into Obie, taking his already untamed tendencies to riotousness. Obie's work at school suffered, and he dropped out of school for a while. He came back, off and on, to pursue his English and religion majors, but, at some point, his daddy called him back home to help him with the family business.

Obie's internal war with himself moved outside to open combat with his father. After five years at school and no degree, Obie relented and went home. He did finally get a degree—and a wife—along the way. That first marriage didn't last through Obie's outrageous escapades and drinking bouts.

More wives followed—among them a ceramic artist, a country-western singer, and a woman with two children. When he was first diagnosed with cancer, he left it all and went on a trip across America in a motor home all by himself, looking for something to fill that hole inside him.

Riding down the interstate toward our reunion and hearing about Obie's recent remarriage reminded me of our move at about that same time ten years before—except the car was now mostly empty. Barely letting the dust settle from the end of the school year, we had supervised the movers loading the thousands of pounds of books and furniture into the moving van as we loaded up my van with children and pets.

Momma and Daddy had fled to the mountains before moving day. They couldn't stand the reality of it, I guess. Then and only then did Jeremiah start to relax. I guess he worried that leaving my parents would just be too much and I would back out. Once I had made up my mind that marrying Jeremiah was what I wanted and needed to do, little, if anything, could have held me back.

The trip up is another story, but once the children and I were all moved in and Jeremiah's boys had moved their furniture and belongings accumulated at Jeremiah's apartment, Jeremiah and I had to decide about how and when to marry. Cohabitation was out of the question; we had teenagers, and we didn't believe that making what had been our private relationship into a public statement was appropriate if we wanted our blended family to indeed be a family.

One option was to date a while and accustom the children a bit more slowly to each other and to us. The cost of maintaining two households, however, seemed an extravagant expenditure for propriety. Besides, to our mind, the best way to get used to something is to get used to it—that is, to live with it. So, Jeremiah and I decided to marry sooner rather than later.

The when decided, then there became the matter of how. Ideally, we would have sealed our nuptials with loving parents and siblings at hand. But we were in Philadelphia, Jeremiah's folks were in east Tennessee, and mine were in south Alabama. We had only a matter of weeks before my children had to return to Alabama for visitation with their father. It came down to the question of whose feelings would we hurt by choosing one family's needs over another's; so, we decided to be fair and to hurt everyone's, so to speak. There was no way to coordinate everyone to anybody's liking, so we decided to harmonize only those who most intimately mattered: the children.

Jeremiah called the county clerk and made the appointment with a justice of the peace for us to elope, scarcely more than a week after we had gotten settled. The idea of eloping with four children in tow is a comical vision, I know. In my reverie of remembering, I wondered how Obie and Naomi managed it. My great-Grandaddy had done it. Left a widower with five children, he quickly married a spinster lady young and strong enough to tend his brood and see to him.

Miz Willa had fit the bill, and the knot was tied. For a honeymoon, Grandaddy took her—and the five children—to Panacea, Florida to see the sulphur springs there. The idea of any bride taking her step-children along on the honeymoon had seemed daunting enough to my child's imagination, but to have Panacea as a destination! Panacea has the rare and wild primeval beauty of the Florida wiregrass country, but it is basically a hole in the ground with little else to recommend it.

Now, coming from a place like Sparksville, Georgia, Panacea may have seemed really exotic for the new family, for all I know. To us children two generations later, Panacea was a place to hold your nose through as we traveled from home to the coast. I can picture Papa as a boy along with his three brothers and a sister, sweating, fidgeting and itching in their dark and heavy dress clothes, swatting the bugs that swarmed around their pomaded hair. Papa would run away in a few short months when Miz Willa proved to be a stern replacement for his dead mother.

The morning of our wedding day dawned, and Jeremiah came and got me early that morning so we could go to the courthouse to apply for our marriage license. In this new day and age, you don't have to have blood tests like you did for our first marriages, so it was only a matter of filling out the forms, demonstrating the proper documentation of identity, and securing the essential piece of paper. We arrived at the courthouse characteristically early, so we enjoyed watching the assemblage of people who were also there to do what we were there to do.

First, there was the young woman who was making arrangements to have a justice of the peace go to the jail because her young groom was in lock-up. There was some consternation about those arrangements, understandably.

She kept exclaiming, "But he's just across the street. How hard can it be?" Obviously, the path to true love was even rockier than I had ever envisioned.

If the young jailbird couple had not been enough to try the patience of the kind-faced but slightly bovine clerk, the next pair certainly took difficulty to the next level. The couple was mismatched to begin with. She was of late middle age, even possibly nearing sixty, but he was a wizened husk of a little man, stooped over his cane, and shuffling off to find a seat. The comical incongruence of the twosome tickled Jeremiah and me, allegedly patiently waiting our turn. That was only the start of it, however.

Apparently, the lady didn't have appropriate identification or there was some confusion about her identity. The first problem was that the names on her birth certificate and her driver license didn't match. She then produced other documentation of her personhood, including a government i.d. Apparently, she wanted to obtain her marriage license in the name on her driver license and not the name on her birth certificate. She explained that she did not go by the name she had been given at birth, and that all her other evidentiary documents had her preferred appellation on them.

The clerk tried in varying ways to explain that her legal name, short of having a court document verifying a legal name change, was the name that appeared on her birth certificate, and that only under her legal name would she be allowed to marry.

The exchange got increasingly heated as the woman produced more and more scraps of paper with evidence of the name she preferred, but the lady behind the counter was unwavering.

"If it's good enough for the federal government—alluding to her government i.d. badge—why isn't it good enough for you?" the applicant shrieked.

Sighing wearily but displaying no emotion, the clerk recounted for the fifth time that in order to get married in this county, you had to do so under your legal name, and, for the blustering, huffing and puffing woman opposed to her, that was the name on the birth certificate.

While this exchange was taking place, the elderly gentleman starting coughing and wheezing, and Jeremiah and I feared he would die before the matter of his bride-to-be's identity was resolved. Ultimately, the clerk's implacable and stone-faced demeanor won out over the screeching woman with the identity crisis. With her paperwork in hand, the disgruntled and renamed woman almost left her geriatric groom behind in her dudgeon.

Jeremiah and I stepped cautiously up to the counter. With the complication presented by our predecessors, we feared the clerk would be in a less than kindly humor. We meekly presented our birth certificates, our divorce decrees, and our marriage license application, complete with the correct and legal names entered therein. By this time, both Jeremiah and I were just about to burst with contained laughter, and our bemused state must have shown, because the beleaguered clerk smiled warmly, relief all over her face.

"Now this is what I am talking about," she said, more to herself than to us.

Our transaction took only a matter of minutes, and we were ready to return home, since it had now been over an hour since we had left home. As we descended the stairs to the main lobby of the courthouse, we were assailed by men in dark suits and with Bibles in hand. I guess they were itinerant ministers or something, because they quizzed us if we needed someone to marry us.

Jeremiah replied in a voice deep and final, meant to scare off the pack of parsons, "No, we are marrying each other, thank you," and, taking me by the hand, strode purposefully out the door. Later we had a big laugh about how, if we ever got down and out, we could set up a booth at the courthouse. Not only was Jeremiah an Old Testament theologian, he was an ordained minister. We giggled all the way to the car, thinking about how he could marry them while I could provide flowers and a keepsake—a one-stop wedding shop.

Upon our return home to the kids, the afternoon passed uneventfully, although there was less of it available since our foray to the courthouse had taken so long. Anna-Aileene was concerned about what to wear, envisioning being a flower girl or at least some important and official personage at the ceremony to come. We finally decided on the white lace dress she had worn for Easter.

I wore red. In the middle ages, brides wore their best dress; it wasn't until Victorian times that white became *de rigueur*. Since scarlet and purple dyes were the most difficult to make, clothes in those colors were very expensive and usually reserved for aristocracy and royalty. My red dress was my statement—of a connection to a new history and of freedom from white wedding expectations. I had had a white wedding, and although the wedding was lovely, the marriage was not.

Jeremiah and I decided we wanted a marriage and not a wedding. In the same manner, instead of a diamond ring, we bought a new bedroom suite on which to start our new life together. We did purchase matching wedding bands and had them engraved in Hebrew, "My beloved is mine and I am his," from the Song of Songs.

When the appointed time came, we loaded into the van and set off for the apartment of the justice of the peace who would perform our ceremony. We arrived early—as we always do for everything—and found the Justice out in the yard walking her dog, a small and trembling variety of terrier. Now, I was all for making a statement through our clothing about not being so tied to superficial conventions, but the lady justice was wearing a set of lavender lounge pajamas, the sort so many elderly ladies wear in the Gulf Coast, the blousy top and shorts being cool and comfortable. It seemed oddly out of place at this time and place, however.

As we got closer to her and her dog, her appearance offered even more visual comedy. Her hair was styled in a teased and poofed style of a previous generation, with a big bow as well, in what we in the Deep South fondly call *big hair*. The most remarkable of all was her make-up, particularly her false eyelashes which gave her the look of some animatronic robot. All I could picture in my head was Trixie Bear at the Country Bear Jamboree in Disney World, an enormously large lady bear, fashioned after Lulu on *Hee-Haw*, who is lowered from the ceiling on her trapeze, bow in hair, elongated eyelashes batting coquettishly if mechanically.

I was very careful not to look at Jeremiah as we left the yard so as not to get tickled; the dog having done his business, we ascended the external stairs in an odd parade up to the lady's apartment.

Once we entered her apartment, I was overcome by two sensory impressions. First, the décor of the place could only be described as early 1970's bachelor pad, with heavy, square and darkly stained furniture with brown and gold plaid upholstery. The room itself was dark, the pinch-pleated, harvest gold draperies having been drawn against the afternoon sun. The drapes, however, were slipping sloppily off their runners, and little slivers of daylight pierced the strange darkness of the room.

At the far end of the room we entered, there stood large, long, looming bar of the same dark wood—a free-standing piece of furniture like something out of an Old West Saloon—replete with worn, gold, Naugahyde padding in lieu of a foot rail and beveled mirror with an engraved and painted Budweiser insignia. This decorative style seemed totally at odds with the appearance of the lady who lived there. With her lavender ruffled lounge wear, false eyelashes, and hair bow, I would have expected pastels and calicos and lots of toy ducks or pigs with bonnets on them.

My second impression, which quickly overwhelmed the first, was the odor of dog urine. The children's eyes went wide, and Jeremiah and I both shot them that parental, "Don't say a word" look.

Our justice in lavender beckoned us into the darkened depths of the room, and we followed, staying close together, the children all but running up Jeremiah's and my heels. She disappeared into the bowels of the apartment for a moment to put her dog into a back room. Upon being segregated from us, the canine started yapping in that high-pitched, incessant, terrier sort of way.

As we had huddled together near the door awaiting her return, she again motioned to us into the room and to arrange ourselves in front of her coffee table altar in the traditional wedding posture, with her facing us, the bridal couple, and with two children on each side. Interestingly, the children arranged themselves not by biology but by age, with Wilson and Edward on one side and Anna-Aileene and James on the other.

That would pretty much be how they assembled themselves from then on, with occasional variances due to temperament. Wilson and Anna-Aileene are driven, tidy, and can lapse into self-absorption. Edward and James are creative, slovenly, and sensitive to those around them. But, at that moment, the ties of age were stronger, as the younger Anna-Aileene and James held hands while Wilson and Edward stood awkwardly, hands in pockets.

The justice had produced a white notebook from which she read the ceremony. As she read the traditional words, she looked back and forth at Jeremiah and then at me, slowly raising and lifting those false eyelashes, evoking even more intensely my previous image of the animatronic Trixie Bear. Although Jeremiah and I were facing one another and held each other's hands, we could barely make eye contact. I watched the corner of his mouth twitch under his moustache in that characteristic way he does—just before he bursts out laughing.

In addition to Justice Trixie Bear's intoning of the marriage rite, we were treated to an uninterrupted chorus of dog yapping. The barking dog, the terrible smell, the eyelashes and the Wild West bar were almost too much for me. In what may have been mistaken for modesty, I looked at the floor as I said my vows. I wished for the ritual to hurry and be over so that I wouldn't choke on the laughter that kept trying to bubble its way up my throat.

Thankfully, we finally said our last "I do," and were prompted to seal the deal with the requisite kiss. Anna-Aileene's eyes danced; at last, there would be some semblance of romance in this odd reenactment of a wedding! The boys' eyes rolled, fearing we would get mushy on them. Our chaste peck relieved their anxiety, although Anna-Aileene looked mildly disappointed.

We couldn't get out of there fast enough, but the closed door of her apartment did not offer the discretion we knew the kids needed to give vent to all the impressions of the bizarre occasion they had just witnessed. We shushed the children's explosive questions as we quickly descended the stairs to the freedom of the yard and parking lot and then the safety of the van.

Once there, Jeremiah and I exhaled in laughter and relief. The kids shot rapid-fire questions and comments at us about the smell, her clothes, and the dog, all the while laughing uproariously. The boys saw the comedy of the moment, but Anna-Aileene was mostly indignant. How can you have a wedding, even an elopement, with a dog howling in the background? she wanted to know.

After the ceremony, we had planned a family dinner to celebrate, making reservations at a Mexican restaurant since we all loved Mexican food. I recalled the pictures of Momma and Daddy's elaborate reception. Since they married in December, her attendants were all dressed in tea length red velvet. In the photos, the young couple stands against the ornate backdrop of an imported trellis and archway festooned with holly and poinsettias. The setting for the theater of the receiving line was equally baroque.

In one picture, Daddy is feeding Momma the accustomed bite of wedding cake. Momma remembers that Daddy mortified Granny by playfully remarking just after that moment, having seen the time on his wrist watch, "Oh darn! We're missing *Gunsmoke*."

Our post-nuptial feast would be thankfully less complicated, if a bit eccentric. We drove across town, giving the children plenty of time to get all their giggles and exclamations out. Since it was only five in the afternoon, we were the first customers at the restaurant, itself garlanded with crepe paper, silk flowers, piñatas, and Dos Equis advertisements. The mariachi Muzak soundtrack welcomed us cheerfully into the brightly trimmed room, a tremendous and welcome contrast to Justice Trixie Bear's den.

We were escorted into the restaurant with a good deal of pomp by several staff members after Anna-Aileene announced that her parents had just gotten married. Since they didn't have any other customers at the time, we were seated in a small private room, appropriate in Anna-Aileene's mind to the momentousness of the event. There, we feasted on the spicy fare, our mirth warmed by the food and made louder by having to shout over the Muzak. We toasted our new family, the children with their Dr. Peppers and Jeremiah and I with our margaritas. Ice cream pleased the little ones and finished our banquet.

Jeremiah and I shepherded our full flock out of the restaurant to head back home. The summer sun had yet to set, and the warmth of the day had not abated. The children chafed in their dress clothes, and we hurried home to comfort and play clothes. Once home, our brood separated to their own pursuits, video games and movies. It wasn't long before the older two were rooting in the refrigerator for something to eat—to fill that bottomless pit otherwise known as the adolescent male stomach.

Jeremiah and I, also changed into more comfortable garb, stood in the kitchen and watched and listened. What we heard was the cacophony of a happy family. Ours was only hours old, but we thought we were off to a good start.

My reminiscence was brought to an end as we turned off the interstate on to the back roads that would take us at the tiny town in eastern Tennessee and the appointed hotel where we would meet Daniel and Luke. Daniel was an Old Testament professor like Jeremiah, serious and quiet but with a wicked sense of humor and a love of the music of Harry Chapin.

Luke was a historian specializing in the church in Latin America. He had fought with the Sandinistas in the eighties and was known for his often-affected naiveté. All three of them, Jeremiah, Daniel and Luke, had gone to college thinking they would be ministers. Daniel and his wife and Luke had arrived earlier in the day, having less distance to travel, and they were there to meet us in the lobby when we got there.

Hugs and introductions were exchanged accordingly, and jokes and manly digs soon followed. I was welcomed like long lost kinfolk, and my fears at being the new wife abated. Slowly, the years seemed to melt away under the torrent of laughter, and the three men were no longer middle-aged, balding, graying and with spreading waistlines. They were young again, young like our Wilson and Edward.

Obie and Naomi came to the hotel, too, and more hugs and loving jibes were exchanged. Obie looked much better than Jeremiah expected. The only apparent ravages of his disease seemed to be his cue-ball bald head, about which his friends teased him mercilessly. Naomi fell right in with Susannah, Daniel's wife, and me, as we watched our men folk laugh and grow young again.

They whiled away the evening catching up on who was where and memories of past practical jokes while we women talked about our children and Obie's disease. The feat of toilet papering a famous chandelier and the outwitting of the notorious Pinkerton security guard were relived with great gusto and Jim Beam.

At one point, the fellows decided to call Freeman, one of their number with whom all but Luke had lost touch. First, Luke called Freeman, now a stand-up comic and part-time minister in New York City, but he only reached the answering machine. Believing Freeman was screening the call, Luke called into the machine, yelling for Freeman to pick up the phone.

After loudly admonishing him to answer again and again, Luke, as if to convince the seemingly elusive Freeman to pick up, informed the machine that Obie, Daniel, and Jeremiah were there too. Then abruptly after these impassioned pleas to be heard, Luke announced nonchalantly, "Okay, bye, "and hung up.

This exact same routine was repeated verbatim by Obie, Daniel and Jeremiah, in turn, provoking side-splitting, rolling-on-the-floor guffaws. Naomi and I shook our heads and smiled; boys will be boys. In about fifteen minutes, who should call Luke but Freeman, laughing so hard he could barely breathe. They passed Luke's cell phone around, and each man caught up with Freeman, with gales of giggles resurrected each time the phone reached a new speaker. Apparently, some things never change.

When we looked at our watches again, it was well after two in the morning. Luke said he couldn't believe it; he always is in bed by 9:45 at the latest, he proclaimed with a wink. Knowing we would spend the next day together and that people our age need their sleep, we reluctantly parted, hugging and laughing some more. Jeremiah and I dropped into bed like felled trees. We slept hard, thanks to the twelve-hour drive and the relief that Obie didn't look or act like he was dying.

Awakening in the morning, our age became more apparent and we wondered if anyone had gotten the license plate of the truck that had metaphorically run us over. Strong coffee seemed to brace us all, and we piled in Daniel's car to go out to Obie's. We traveled mountain back roads, going back in time as we rounded the curves in the road. Gum Springs had once been a small community which boasted a train depot, post office and a general store, and a couple of churches. Now, it was little more than a Post Office zip code designation.

Obie's house sat proudly on the hillside overlooking what had been the train stop, the front porch still festooned with patriotic bunting from the Fourth of July and his fiftieth birthday celebration. I laughed to myself that it made perfect sense, even as little as I knew of him, for Obie to have been born on the day we celebrate with fireworks. Obie, Naomi, the host of children, and the baying dog poured out of the house onto the porch to greet us as we drove up.

This morning, we hugged and kissed like family, remarking how well or how little we had slept, teasing about being old. The older kids came forward confidently to shake hands and be introduced; the younger ones lingered back a bit, but obviously curious about these people whom their Daddy had described to them in the past years. Obie was their Daddy for all intents and purposes; Naomi's first husband had left when the youngest was a few months old and was later killed in a work site explosion.

I felt a bond with Naomi, both of us blessed in our second marriages with men who loved our children like their own. We settled on the porch in rocking chairs with glasses of iced tea and watched the day go by, the sun playing in and out of the clouds, leaving dappled shadows on the mountains, and the conversation meandering on about anything and everything.

There was a garden below the house; its rows neat and filled with the promise of plenty. The children pointed out what they had planted and we discussed the virtues of seedless over seeded watermelons along with the virtue of one translation of the Bible over another.

Later, Obie got some of the children to get out their instruments and play for us, and we were treated to old time music from the hills with guitar, mandolin and fiddle. We tapped our feet and hummed along, caught in the spell of family and fun. I couldn't help thinking about our children and how we had grown together as a family—as Obie's had.

I remembered back to that night after our funny wedding ceremony. Standing in the kitchen, we had looked at each other and laughed at the antics of the children, ordinary things that ordinary happy children do. Laughter was one of those things that we had rediscovered in ourselves and each other. For all the significance of the day, the moment seemed blessedly ordinary. We had smiled more broadly and embraced.

After the upheaval and uncertainty of divorces and single parenting and long-distance romance and moving, we felt a relief as if we had come through some arduous survival course and emerged alive. Ordinary was okay with us, and, trite expression notwithstanding, there *is* no place like home. The comedy of the day was spice enough.

For me, that day brought a comfortable redefinition of home. Up to then, home was tied to place—where my mother had been born, where I had been born, where my children had been born, and where my grandparents were buried. On that day, home became, cliché or not, where my heart was, there with Jeremiah and our children.

From the first time I laid eyes on Jeremiah, he had seemed like an old friend, ironically whom I had only just met. The comfort of familiarity and the delight of discovery had marked our courtship from the beginning. Now, here we were—old, married people. There was a solace in those words.

As I tapped my foot to the fiddle tunes in the present, I felt the rhythm of that first evening those years ago beating a steady tempo throughout the ensuing years. Jeremiah and I found our own cadence and became pretty much a tag team. He is good at staying up late to wait for teenagers coming in by curfew, and I am primed in the early morning when getting someone off somewhere on time is essential.

I would keep the pantry organized and inventoried, and Jeremiah would do the marketing, finding bargains to keep our three hungry boys—not to mention the hungry girl—fed. Although we both love to cook, by the end of long work days, we are frequently tired. But I would play sous-chef and he would cook or vice versa, and somehow it got done.

Family meals were an important way in which we melded our two families, sharing favorite meals and learning to like new ones. My kids learned to love Granny's Goulash from Jeremiah's Momma, and Jeremiah's boys learned to love shepherd's pie, but everyone loved homemade fried chicken and gravy. Our meal times were quickly the best part of our days, much like that first Mexican feast was.

The kids would come in late from band practice, wanting to know first when dinner was and then what we were having. At one point I began to think that was my new name as step-mother would be "What's-for-dinner," as that was how I was usually greeted. Then the barrage of chatter and explosions of laughter would begin.

Our dinner conversations reminded me so comfortably of those I had enjoyed at a child as we too had to keep the unabridged dictionary near the table. The kids learned to share the evening chores and became an efficient and cooperative unit. It became a source of pride for Jeremiah that our kids could pack the car for a trip in under fifteen minutes.

In the early days of our marriage, people, I guess having read or experienced horror stories of step-children and step-parents, would ask me solicitously if our children got along. I always responded honestly—and gratefully—that they got along like real brothers and sisters; they got along until they didn't.

Dinner brought us together in a special way at Obie's too. Bless her heart –as if she didn't have enough on her, Naomi prepared quite a feast for all of us: pulled pork barbeque, homemade pickles, fresh-churned ice cream. We stood in a circle, holding hands, and Obie offered the grace. I could feel Jeremiah breathing harder beside me; I didn't even have to look to know he was filled with emotion. This moment was what Obie had been looking for his entire life—the blessing of home, family, and friends, and the chance to be the Daddy his father never was. In fact, it is what we are all looking for, whether we know it or not.

No sooner was the blessing said when the children, especially the older boys, after politely offering to let the grown-ups go first—they had been raised with old-fashioned manners—swarmed the food. The talk lessened while we concentrated on our food, with occasional grunts of approval from the men and requests for the pickle recipe from the women.

After we ate, Obie proudly took me on a tour of the house, noting where they had rebuilt and remade, and refinished—his great-grand-mother's spool bed, the elegant master bath, the daughter's room. As the day had progressed, Mary, the only girl of the seven children, had warmed to me, and now followed me and Obie on the tour. She wanted me to see her dolls, her books, and her new dress. She was about nine, the age Anna-Aileene had been when Jeremiah and I married. Mary was definitely a Daddy's girl now, and Obie was as proud of her as he could be as he touted the latest book she had read and piano piece she had learned. Obie had taken a broken family and a run-down house and fixed them—and in turn repaired himself.

Jeremiah and I are really good at fixing things, both having spent a good part of our childhoods at someone's elbow, watching. I was always Daddy's Little Helper, accompanying him on his ritual Saturday errands, repairing the lawnmower, refinishing a special find from the flea market.

Jeremiah and I soon found that old pattern was renewed in our new life together.

We refinished Grandma Swann's rocking chair and Granny's dining room suite. He would ply the stripping compound to eat the years of old finish away, and I would scrape the goop off. I would sand and he would apply the finish. We came to an easy accord about how to restore these family treasures: repair them to sturdiness and restore their finish, but leave some of the character they had picked up along the way. When it came time to finish the arm chair of Granny's dining room suite, we decided not to replace the part of the armrest that had broken off when Papa had one of his tantrums. I felt like it would serve as a gentle reminder of not only who we were, but what we might not want to be.

Both Jeremiah and I like old things—what would you expect out of an Old Testament professor and an English teacher? And so, at some point we bought a vintage Ford truck. The 1964 wonder wasn't quite the 1957 model of his dreams, but its engine made that wonderful rumble that engines made in bygone days when gas was a dime a gallon. We have had many adventures with that truck. Freudianly evocative if you ask me, I have spent many a Saturday morning at Jeremiah's elbow, handing him one tool or another or gapping spark plugs while he cleaned the distributor caps.

The truck, christened New Henry after his Granddaddy's Old Henry of Jeremiah's childhood, despite our loving care, would break down quixotically. The truck drama would usually play out as Jeremiah had taken off on some Saturday errand, leaving with a list of things to do. In a short while, however, I would get a call—usually from some place like the dump—that he was stranded and that I needed to come either give him a push for a rolling start or bring some tool he needed to fix whatever was broken. So, after finding the tool or rope or chain that I needed to save the day, I would race off for another truck escapade. Then, usually on the side of the road, we would open New Henry's hood and dive into fixing whatever was wrong.

There have only been a couple of times we couldn't fix New Henry, the worst being when the wheel fell off. Jeremiah had taken the truck in for its yearly inspection, and the mechanics almost inspected it to death. Jeremiah was about a mile from the shop and had picked up some speed when he felt the back end fall sickeningly downward and heard a horrific, screeching, metal-on-pavement sound.

Then out of the corner of his eye, a disconcerted Jeremiah saw his wheel fly across the road into someone's yard. After responding to that phone call and seeing New Henry's sorry state, I was thankful for the old days of heavy steel frames and chassis that kept Jeremiah in one piece that day.

The sun seems to set earlier in the mountains, and it was soon time to take our leave of Obie and his family. As we walked, hand in hand, to the car, Jeremiah got choked up again, this time grieving that Obie, after having found what he wanted and needed, would now have such a short time to enjoy it. I reminded him that, first, at least he had found it; so many people never do. I also prompted him that none of us knows how long we have. Obie, although looking at a hard fight with this third recurrence of his cancer, had a lot to live for. Sometimes, that made the difference.

Eventually, the cancer would win, but Obie would have triumphed in the good he would leave in his wake in the world. Jeremiah sighed but agreed. I think he was feeling the regret and vulnerability those of us who come to our loves later in life. Ultimately, you have to decide that the path you took was the path that got you where you needed to be, despite its difficulties. It was always a matter of being grateful that you had actually found who and what you needed—like Obie had.

In the decades since our funny wedding day, Jeremiah and I have raised our four children, with the two older ones finishing college, Anna-Aileene getting ready to start—and James learning to drive. The mundane milestones of childrearing and householding have been treasured moments for us, as they have cemented our family and validated our love that could provide the safe haven home for our children to grow.

People are always asking who belongs to whom biologically in our family, and Jeremiah and I smile. Like people who have lived together a long time who start to look alike, our children have come to favor each other, crossing genetic lines. I have heard Jeremiah's words coming out of my children's mouths, and I have noticed his boys adopting my ways.

Each morning as I awaken with Jeremiah snoring beside me—I usually wake before he does because he hates mornings so—I start my day with a humble gratitude at the gift of being able to redefine tradition and family and adhere to it at the same time. It should be of little surprise that one of the things that cemented my decision to marry Jeremiah in those early days was a poem—not by Milton, but by Edgar Lee Masters.

The poem, part of his *Spoon River Anthology*, is an epitaph in which the speaker rues never having taken any risks in his life, fearing the madness that wrong decisions could bring. In the poem, the speaker admonishes the reader to lift our sails and "catch the winds of destiny, wherever they take the boat." Our course towards each other may have been stormy and serendipitous, but the destination of our togetherness is sanity and substance.

Our union was in actuality a reunion, a reconciliation of who we really are with who we need to be. Meanwhile, our identical volumes of *The Complete Works of John Milton* sit side-by-side on the bookshelf, testimony to our love of literature and our appreciation for the chance that brought us together and the love that kept us there.

In a recent telephone conversation, Momma told me that she and our friend Earlene had been extolling Jeremiah's virtues, when Earlene declared to Momma that she prays for Jeremiah every day and gives daily thanks on behalf of us all that I found him. Momma said that she didn't quite know what to say to Earlene, but I knew exactly what to say: Amen. It is the same Amen we had all heartily joined in saying grace at Obie's, thankful that blessings don't always come when and how you expect them, but they do come.

Homemaking

I HAD WRITTEN THE letter with a great deal of trepidation. Momma's illness had progressed to a point that she needed more care than Daddy could give her. Both parents were suffering from declining health and abilities. The home help people they had hired needed more supervision and better instructions than Daddy could give—and that was hard to manage from a thousand miles away. When yet another call came in the middle of a faculty meeting that Daddy was being rushed to the hospital with chest pains, and I made yet another mad dash home, it was becoming clear that things couldn't stay the same. Then HRS visited and filed a report that Daddy wasn't really competent to care for Momma on his own.

How could we do it? How do you tell your parents that they aren't competent to carry on their daily life, especially if they don't have the capacity to realize it for themselves? How do you ask them to leave the home that Daddy built? How will I feel when our four have to ask the same questions? It made me queasy.

But I wrote the letter because a telephone call wouldn't do. They needed to see the words and look at them again and again and think about what they meant. I asked my parents to move in with us.

After I mailed it, I emailed a copy to Samantha and Dawson, telling them that, in case Momma and Daddy never spoke to me again, they would know why. In the letter, I had tried to lay out a reasoned but compassionate argument for them to seek their care with me. Our fears that illness could separate them in different facilities was a primary concern. Their unwillingness to go into assisted living was another. I didn't expect that they would ever speak to me again.

Three days went by. Late in the evening, the phone rang, and it was Momma.

"We got your letter," she said carefully.

"Yes," I answered, equally cautious. "What did you think?"

At that point, I decided to do what we always do in tense moments in our family: introduce humor. "So, I sent the letter to Dawson and Sam after I mailed to you in case you got mad and never spoke to me again."

I could hear Momma chuckling. "We aren't mad. Not at all. We have talked about it all day, and we have questions."

Jeremiah and I had broached this question back when we were courting and knew it was getting serious. He both kept bringing up things that were potential deal-breakers so that, if I had to walk away, it would be quick. In those early days, Jeremiah had said that he expected to have his parents live with us when they were elderly. Unperturbed, I replied that we would need a big house because my parents would be living with us too. I remember that he smiled, grateful and relieved.

I thought about my Granny. They lived in the little yellow house that was all of 900 square feet with three daughters and her mother for three months out of the year. I guess people had less need for personal space, and they certainly had less stuff. Granny had packed big Victorian revival furniture in that small space, as well as all sorts of other visiting relatives. When I lived in the same house, which was on everyone's way to everywhere, I always had an extra person at the table. Granny, on a visit to see baby Edward on her way to the grocery store, had asked me, "Now if I am ever an old widow lady, you are going to let me live with you, aren't you?"

"Of course, Granny. You can always live with me," I responded smiling. It became a game we played. Where she would sleep. What we could cook. Little did I know then that we would never get to do that, that she would be gone in a few short years; but decades later, here I was moving my parents up to live with us.

Orchestrating a move is a nightmare. I would rather have sharp sticks stuck in my eyes and my fingernails torn out by the roots than move. Yet, I had already moved twice in the intervening fifteen years. My move to the suburbs of Philadelphia was executed with military precision. Boxes had color-coded dots for the room they were to be taken to. Lists were made and distributed to the mover as well as the children so everyone knew what went where. My parents couldn't bear that I was moving, so they went to the mountains. Sonny came to lock up the house for the realtor as we left. Four children eager to get their new rooms set up made unpacking easy.

Our next move was about a mile down the road when we bought a house. Jeremiah did it bit by bit during that cold January, using New Henry. Momma and Daddy's move would have to be organized long distance. I was not hopeful.

The next step was to find the right house. Our current house which we had spent years upgrading and customizing would not work. Too many stairs. The new house had to have first and second floor master bedrooms. It needed many bedrooms to entertain not just our four children and their spouses but my siblings and their families are well. Most empty nesters downsize. We had to upsize.

The only thing worse than moving is selling your house. Despite the fact that our house was well –advertised with pictures and description, tastefully decorated with traditional neutrals, the stupid comments kept coming. "I was looking for an open floor plan," said one. Why did you come see a center hall colonial then, I thought to myself. "I can't see kids in this house," said another. I thought back to the flute section sleepover with fifteen girls sleeping side-by-side in the big room. "Where would you put a grand piano?" asked yet another. Right where I did, I thought. I despaired for the human race if people were really this stupid.

Meanwhile, we started looking for a new home. Jeremiah and I would do a "drive-by" of any listing I found on the internet before we broached it with our realtor. No sense in wasting everyone's time. This house was beautiful but too remote. The other house was beautifully appointed but had a dreadful view. Another had an open floor plan. There would be nowhere to escape each other except the bedroom. Finally, we found it.

We knew it was the one the minute we rolled up the long winding gravel drive that reminded me of the road to the Lodge. Jeremiah all but burst into tears when he saw the yard and house. It was like his Granny's and our current house and all the houses we loved—and that was just the outside. We called the realtor, telling her we would be in terrible trouble if the inside was like the outside. She met us at the door, "You are in terrible trouble."

Needless to say, in the months between sending the letter and deciding on a move date, there was a great deal of chaos. Initially, we thought we could take our time, sell our house, buy a house, move in and get settled, and then move the parents. Nothing ever goes the way you think. The housing market tanked. Our initially enormous equity shriveled as we lowered the price again and again, only to get more and more dumb comments. Our realtor was mystified. Momma was not doing well. They needed to move soon.

Taking a leap of faith, we decided to buy Heart's Ease without our house having sold. We set the move date for Momma and Daddy. All the backing and forthing and negotiating completed, we closed on the house on December 20. The day before, Jeremiah and I had hired a crew of his students and mine to pack the rental truck. That night, we slept in a hotel near the lawyer's office where the closing would take place. Up early with time to kill, we walked aimlessly around the nearby mall.

While Jeremiah was in the bathroom, a woman came up to me, over-laden with bags. I asked if I could help her. No, she said, she was just going to go home. She had hoped she could buy her son a hat with his favorite team's logo, but she didn't have enough money. The bags were all her belongings. It dawned on me that she was homeless. I asked her to take me to the store. There I bought the hat for her son. I had a home. Hell, I had two homes.

Our same crew of students met us at the new house that afternoon and we made quick work of our well-organized horde. At that time, I regretted being an academic—and being married to one. We are both bookaholics, and boxes of books are heavy.

That night and the next day, we unpacked the kitchen, and set up a pallet in our room. Setting up the Sleep Number bed would have to wait. I prepared an airbed for Momma and Daddy in their room. Since we would be back on Christmas Day, I put out the stockings, filled them with goodies, and set up a small fake tree with lights pre-wired. Move or not, we had to have a Christmas. Jeremiah and I agreed on no presents; we were giving each other a house.

Jeremiah had to preach the next day, so we left after lunch, getting halfway by nightfall. We were exhausted and slept like the dead. That is, unless we had to roll over. The next day, we got moving early. No sense in wasting time in Nowhere, South Carolina.

We arrived to find Momma, Daddy and the house in an advanced state of chaos and decay. She looked very thin and fragile. Daddy had taken to boxing up the books, his bunny collection, and his tools. Boxes created a labyrinth in their already crowded living room. A hired student from the community college, their caregiver, and family friends had tried to help in the sorting process.

Momma had been fretful about her inability to go through things to determine what needed to go and what needed to be thrown out. I told her to bring everything and we would sort it out once it was here. Little did I know.

We spent the night of the 23rd at the family home. Momma and Daddy had taken up residence in Dawson's downstairs bedroom, so Jeremiah and I slept in their room upstairs. Daddy had precociously had the phone and cable cut off. Even though we were in my childhood home, we felt cut off.

I had thought it would be hard to take them out of the home Daddy had so lovingly built and that we had had so many happy days in. I had been fearful to leave it forever, knowing that Daddy wanted to sell it and that they would never see it again, except in pictures. With the dreadful mess it was in, however, and with the state of decay and neglect that had come from their decline, it was easy. I felt the elation of an escapee from Alcatraz.

Christmas Eve morning dawned with bright promise that we all feel on that day. I had packed Momma and Daddy's suitcase with two weeks' worth of clothes, their toiletries and a few treasures, although the movers would be bringing their things at the end of the week. Momma had a beautiful Cybis statuette of a fairy sitting on a turtle. It used to sit in a leaded glass box on the mantle. I asked if that ought to come with us too. Daddy said no, the movers would do it. They would do it, alright.

Then there was the question of what to do with the guns. I don't like guns, although like the good Southern girl I was, I had learned to clean and fire a range of weapons. Papa had hunted, and Uncle Ewell had been a crack shot, but I didn't see a need for guns in my life and, like others, was alarmed at the plague of gun violence.

We reasoned that it was wiser to bring the guns with us in the car and not leave them to the temptation of anonymous movers. I wrapped them up in towels and put them in a fabric grocery bag so that their identity wouldn't be clear to a casual observer. I don't know why, but I felt like I was doing something wrong.

Momma was anxious, but let us be in charge. She asked the same questions over and over again, mostly about her cat. We had made plans to get the cat boxed the day we arrived, before we took down a suitcase. Savvy, Puzzle the Cat knew that suitcases meant going to the vet for boarding, so she would immediately go missing. Jeremiah had work gloves and his long sleeve coat on. Even so, she managed to scratch him as he stuffed her in the cat box. We loaded our car and Daddy's and we were off.

Although I was worried about Daddy driving, I knew they needed to feel in charge of this decision. That meant leaving town under their own steam. Momma and Daddy were in Daddy's car, and Jeremiah and I were in ours, although we had the cat. After a while, Daddy got tired, so I drove his car with Momma and he rode with Jeremiah. Once again, we were in South Carolina.

It was an odd thing to be in a strange place for Christmas Eve. We had a good dinner. Momma and I sung "Silent Night." I thought about the traditional story of Jesus' birth, about Mary and Joseph being in a strange place. But I had my Momma safe and sound, and we were going home. Despite my weariness, it took a while to fall asleep. Strange sounds and smells, the cat intermittently yowling, Momma and Daddy snoring in the adjoining room kept me awake.

I remembered being a child and not being able to go to sleep on Christmas Eve. Dawson and I were infamous for waking up our parents at 4 am to see if Santa had come. Christmas Eve was a big deal in our family. Momma and Daddy always hosted an Open House.

Days ahead, Momma, and later I, would bake and prepare cakes and cookies, dips and savories. Of course, we had to have eggnog. It wasn't store-bought stuff out of a carton. It was whipping cream and raw eggs and Wild Turkey whipped into a creamy, dreamy punch bowl of Christmas cheer. No wonder the smell of whiskey always reminds me of Christmas.

Later, once we had joined St. Luke's, midnight services were added to our Christmas rituals. When Jeremiah and I married, we added a tacky lights tour of the suburbs to our yearly customs. We would go to an earlier church service, then pile in the van to ride around town looking at the lengths to which some folks decorate their yards. We made up awards, and laughed at ourselves and our own lack of yard décor. We would end up at home with a big pot of chili, commemorating our wedding feast.

Now, part of my ritual is to bring out the ornaments and to remember where they came from or who made them. Momma belonged to a group of women called the Homemaker's Club. We teased about it, but I eventually joined after Edward was born and I was a stay home mom. Making ornaments always took precedence over most other programs each month. Then there was the yearly ornament exchange. Quilted or cross-stitched, painted or bejeweled, they were old friends we got to visit with once a year.

Even before the "Homewrecker's"—Daddy's name for it—Club, Momma had had a penchant for Christmas creativity. Since my birthday was two weeks before Christmas, many birthday party favors had been Christmas ornaments. Fat Santas, green elves, and gold cherubs joined our ornament family in those years. But that wasn't all. There was the Lunar Module that Momma coated with glitter and the spools joined together with string and decorated with ric-rac and glitter. The more glitter the better.

Christmas Day that year got underway in that strange hotel room, but Momma's eager face made it all alright. We breakfasted and left, after stuffing the uncooperative cat back in her box because Momma couldn't bear for her to be cooped up all night. Jeremiah was only mildly wounded from her biting and scratching. After patching him up, we wished each other Merry Christmas, but we all felt a little sheepish and out of kilter.

Six hours later, we were rolling down the gravel drive Jeremiah and I had come to love to the house that would be Home. The kids were there and ready to greet us. Hugs and kisses and Merry Christmas were exchanged. I had bought two pans of Stouffer's lasagna, a couple of bottles of wine, and a cheesecake and put them in the freezer. Our new neighbors had sent goodies as well. James had been charged with getting several bags of salad greens. It would be a humble Christmas, but we were together.

After dinner, we went into the living room to open presents. We had unrolled the rug and put our furniture in place. Those who didn't have a chair sat on boxes. The stockings were unloaded, and gifts were opened. The children had all gone in together on a huge hanging railway clock. Jeremiah misted up as he and I looked at each other over the shredded wrapping. Time together—our greatest gift.

Perhaps it was the small and slightly scraggly artificial tree, or perhaps Christmas is just a time for remembering. Momma reminisced about their first Christmas in the little yellow house. They had been married ten days. Aunt Mary had brought a small pre-decorated artificial tree and left bags of canned goods under it. Daddy gave Momma a silk blouse, embroidered with her monogram. A year later, I was there, and Granny had a picture of Momma holding me, wearing that blouse.

The next few days after Christmas were spent getting things set up and settled. Phone, internet, cable all turned out to be much more complicated than they should have been. We had to have a landline before we could have internet. The satellite company wanted us to have internet before they installed the dish. Nothing seemed to be going according to the careful plans I had made. I was tired of being nice to people on the telephone, and I had to employ my schoolteacher voice more than once.

I should have known that the toils of installations were to be preface for the horrors of the arrival of Momma and Daddy's stuff. They had lived in that house for 52 years, and Momma, an amateur historian, believed in saving every artifact to document our life and times. We knew it would be a lot of stuff, but there is knowing, and there is *knowing*.

The truck was scheduled to arrive by noon on the 28th. Sonny, faithful in all ways, had been there to open the door for the packers the day before and that morning for the movers. It was raining on us, but it was supposed to clear off. Noon came and went, but we got a call that 3 pm was their new ETA. They had hired two guys from Craig's list who had gotten there at the original time. It was awkward. Momma was anxious. Jeremiah and I began to feel existentially tired—and we hadn't even seen the truck.

The next call we got was from the truck driver. He was in a semi tractor-trailer, and there would be no driving up the gravel road and drive way. He was threatening to unload all the stuff in the parking lot of the elementary school on the corner and leave. He had a schedule. I flew into a rage.

Calling the owner of the moving company, I started blasting, not mincing words or stemming my use of profanity. He wanted to make the excuse that salespeople don't always communicate with drivers, but since I had only ever talked to HIM, that explanation was a lie. Caught, he had to backtrack, and come up with a plan. Meanwhile, Jeremiah took off to find a U-Haul rental place that was open on a Sunday. Only armed with internet on my smart phone with spotty coverage, I researched the nearest one, and called Jeremiah between tirades to the movers.

Finally, at 4 pm, the first load from the truck came up the driveway. Meanwhile, Anna-Aileene had rounded up high school friends, home for the holidays, so we had more hands on deck. I had bought more food and more wine to feed the workers and the volunteers. I had a detailed plan as to where things should go, but at some point, after the furniture was in, it became a matter of finding a dry place to stuff the boxes.

The mother-in-law suite with its bedroom, sitting room and kitchen became the repository everything that we didn't know what it was went. It was quickly floor to ceiling—with ten-foot ceilings. We toiled on in a light mist until midnight, when the driver again started making noises about leaving, even though he had been sleeping his truck cab since their arrival. Daddy, whom I had tried to keep fed and comfortably out of the way under the guise of taking care of Momma, started muttering that he wanted to know where his gun was.

The mover representative, tired from the journey and the unloading and chafing from his colleague's threats to leave, decided he would back our shuttle truck up to the barn where the last load of boxes would have to go. Like so many disastrous moments, it unfolded in what felt like slow motion. When Jeremiah and I saw what he was going to do, we started running and yelling. He had pulled into the grass to be able to back up, and before he heard us, he was up to his axles in mud. There was no backing up.

So, all hands fell in to unload the last truckful, trudging up the hill in the rain to the barn. Anna-Aileene and another friend toiled over unwrapping the furniture from the shrink wrap to free the packing blankets that had to be returned to the mover. So, while we were up to our ankles in mud, Anna-Aileene was knee-deep in shrink wrap.

The two young men who had been there since noon, random hires from Craig's List, were exhausted. Daddy gave them each $100 because they had gone above and beyond what they had been led to believe they were hired to do. One of them would help us several times later that spring in moving things from downstairs to upstairs. I ended up giving him the world's largest coffee table that Samantha had passed on to me when it wouldn't fit in her house upon returning from Israel. Young enough to be thrilled with free furniture no matter what, he left with it precariously propped in his trunk.

By 2 am, Jeremiah and I collapsed on the pallets and mattress we were using for beds. Edward, James and Anna-Aileene were beat. We all promised to sleep in and to take it easier the next day. The days that followed were like a scavenger hunt, looking for boxes with china, with clothes, with important papers.

Like an archaeologist might discern from unearthed evidence, we discerned there were two packers. One was so conscientious that he even wrapped the Tupperware in bubble wrap and included bagged, dirty cat litter. The other we nicknamed "Meathook" since it felt like he had just raked whatever was there into an open box.

Meathook must have packed the Cybis fairy. In that box I found, unwrapped, the leaded glass box home of the fairy who had bounced around inside unprotected, along with Daddy's microscope and other odds and ends. Sick at heart, I pulled the treasure box out from the detritus, only to see that one of its rear feet was shattered. It was one moment that I was glad I was not a person to panic, because every nerve in me was screaming. Calmly, I located the super glue, Momma's magnifying glass, tweezers, and a quiet place. It took me several hours to reassemble the dozens of pieces.

In the end, I was able to reassemble it so that all but a tiny place on the bottom of the foot was whole again. Looking at it in its box, no one would ever know. At that point, I took the box to Momma.

"Look what I found," I crowed.

"I have been worrying about that," she admitted. Then I told her the truth. She took it out and examined it, giving me a grateful and knowing look. "And what about my jewelry," she asked. "Should we file an insurance claim?"

"Let me keep looking in the boxes," I replied, fearing that the jewelry which had gone missing months before the move was, along with the white washcloths and teaspoons they had accused the helpers of stealing, most likely accidentally thrown in the garbage can.

One miraculous Saturday, going through a box of what seemed like the world's oldest Tupperware that I remembered had been housed in the cabinet atop the refrigerator, there they were—rubies, diamonds, emeralds, pearls. All of Momma's jewelry, hidden in a safe place and forgotten, was there. I shrieked and ran through the house and plopped it all in her lap.

"It's all here," I crowed.

"It's a miracle," she said.

What was really miraculous was that only the Cybis fairy and a few dishes were broken in the move and the months of moving boxes from one place to another. Less of a miracle and more attributable to hard work, we had unpacked all the boxes by Easter. Of course, that had required building floor-to-ceiling bookshelves to house all of not just Jeremiah's and my books, but Momma and Daddy's too. In those months, we painted, remodeled, and arranged to make the new house our home. Mark started a garden, and we ate vegetables fresh from the ground. Our ground.

When I was a little girl—and even into adulthood—my concept of home was geographical. The Deep South. Daddy and Momma's house. Granny and Papa's house. I was rooted to a place in nearly the same way I was attached to my family. I went to the same high school as Momma. I went to the same college as my parents. I lived in the same dorm Momma had. As a married woman, I lived in the house Momma was born in, the little yellow house.

Leaving to remarry and make a new life, I had to redefine what home was. Instead of a location, home was internalized; it was a feeling. It is the feeling you get watching your four children play Risk and laugh into the night at the kitchen table with the smell of popcorn filling the house. It is the feeling you get when you and your husband finish painting a room, but you haven't even had to say a word or discuss what to do because you know instinctively how to work together. It is the feeling you get looking at your grown children and their spouses gathered around the table at Thanksgiving, grateful to be together and eat good food.

It is the feeling you get when you tuck your Momma in bed at night, and she smiles up at you and says, "Today was a good day. I love you."

www.ingramcontent.com/pod-product-compliance
Lightning Source LLC
Chambersburg PA
CBHW072131160426
43197CB00012B/2062